A Lenten Journey
with Jesus Christ *and*
Blessed Elizabeth
of the Trinity

An Invitation of Grace,

a Prayer of Hope,

and a Gift of Peace.

A Lenten Journey
with Jesus Christ *and*
Blessed Elizabeth of the Trinity

Daily Gospel Readings

with

Selections from the Writings

of

Blessed Elizabeth of the Trinity

REFLECTIONS AND PRAYERS
BY
SR. VILMA SEELAUS, O.C.D.

WITH ADDITIONAL INTRODUCTORY MATERIAL BY
PETER J. MONGEAU

Christus Publishing, LLC
WELLESLEY, MA
www.ChristusPublishing.com

Christus Publishing, LLC
Wellesley, Massachusetts
www.ChristusPublishing.com

Copyright © 2011 by Christus Publishing, LLC

All rights reserved. No part of this book may be reproduced or utilized in any form or by any means, electronic or mechanical, including photocopying, recording, or by any information storage and retrieval system, without permission in writing from the publisher.

Vilma Seelaus, O.C.D., is a nun of the Carmelite Monastery in Barrington, Rhode Island, where she has served as prioress and formation directress. A member of the Carmelite Forum, she is known for her insightful lectures at their annual meetings. As an author, her interest is to offer a contemporary understanding of the presence of God in human life. Audio tapes and CDs on spirituality have been published by Alba House and she has contributed articles to spiritual journals such as *Spiritual Life, Carmelite Digest, The Way, Review for Religious* and others. Her book, *Distractions in Prayer: Blessing or Curse, Teresa of Avila's Teaching in the Interior Castle* has been translated into Korean.

Peter J. Mongeau is the Founder and Publisher of Christus Publishing, LLC.

Publisher's Cataloging-in-Publication Data
Seelaus, Vilma.
  A Lenten journey with Jesus Christ and Blessed Elizabeth of the Trinity : daily Gospel readings with selections from the writings of Blessed Elizabeth of the Trinity : reflections and prayers / by Vilma Seelaus ; with additional introductory material by Peter J. Mongeau.

  p. ; cm.

  ISBN: 978-1-936855-02-5

  1. Lent--Prayers and devotions. 2. Elizabeth of the Trinity, Sister, 1880-1906. 3. Elizabeth of the Trinity, Sister, 1880-1906--Prayers and devotions. 4. Catholic Church--Prayers and devotions. 5. Carmelites--Prayers and devotions. 6. Prayer books. I. Mongeau, Peter J. II. Title.

BX2170.L4 S44 2011
242/.34   2011943222

Printed and bound in the United State of America

10 9 8 7 6 5 4 3 2 1

Text design and layout by Peri Swan
This book was typeset in Garamond Premier Pro with Snell Roundhand as a display typeface

CONTENTS

Acknowledgments ✦ 1

Dedication ✦ 2

An Invitation from Blessed Elizabeth of the Trinity ✦ 3

Blessed Elizabeth of the Trinity: A Short Biography ✦ 7

The Order of Discalced Carmelites: A Brief History ✦ 10

Blessed Elizabeth of the Trinity on Prayer: Our Life in Christ within the Indwelling Trinity ✦ 14

Lectio Divina and the Practice of Prayerful Reading ✦ 18

On the Daily Gospel Readings ✦ 22

Ash Wednesday and the Days after Ash Wednesday ✦ 25

First Week of Lent ✦ 35

Second Week of Lent ✦ 59

Third Week of Lent ✦ 87

Fourth Week of Lent ✦ 115

Fifth Week of Lent ✦ 145

Holy Week ✦ 177

Paschal Triduum ✦ 217

Easter Sunday ✦ 239

Epilogue ✦ 243

APPENDIX A:
Calendar of Lent 2012–2021 & Lectionary Cycle ✦ 245

APPENDIX B:
Selections from the Writings of
Blessed Elizabeth of the Trinity ✦ 250

Suggestions for Further Reading ✦ 252

Internet Resources ✦ 254

About the Author ✦ 255

ACKNOWLEDGMENTS

The Gospel passages are taken from the *Lectionary for Mass for Use in the Dioceses of the United States of America, second typical edition* © 2001, 1998, 1997, 1986, 1970. Confraternity of Christian Doctrine, Inc., Washington, DC. Used with permission. All rights reserved. No portion of this text may be reproduced by any means without permission in writing from the copyright owner.

Reflections and prayers copyright © 2011 Christus Publishing, LLC.

DEDICATION

To all who seek to live the sacred art of mindfulness.

AN INVITATION FROM BLESSED ELIZABETH OF THE TRINITY

Lent, a very special time in the Church's liturgical year, has its origins in Love—God's love for us expressed in the life, sufferings, death, and resurrection of God's Beloved, Jesus Christ—and in *God's passionate desire that we open ourselves to receive Love* and give it expression in our lives. When Lent's focus remains on externals, on what we will *do* during this sacred season, the depth of divine intimacy to which Christ invites us might escape out attention. The life and writings of Blessed Elizabeth of the Trinity are offered here to draw us beyond externals to the realization of our deepest human potential, union with God through love.

The writings of Blessed Elizabeth have special significance for our postmodern world. Consumed as many are by consumerism and surrounded by fears of terrorism, suffering from various forms of nature's upheavals, from our unstable economy, and from so much else, unfortunately, attendance at church has diminished. At the same time, interest in spirituality has gained in popularity.

Books such as Eckhart Tolle's *The Power of Now: A Guide to Spiritual Enlightenment,* Thich Nhat Hanh's *The Miracle of Mindfulness,* and other titles of this nature, indicate that hunger for spiritual realities is not lacking in our confused, secular age. The gift that Blessed Elisabeth brings to today's spiritual quest is to root it within the Gospel of Jesus Christ and to focus our attention on the reality of God's indwelling Presence. Toward the end of her short life, even in the midst of intense suffering, her heart overflowed with desire that others come to know the depth of God's love for them. She writes: "In the light of eternity God makes me understand many things, and I come to tell you as though it were coming from Him" (Letter 324). Again she writes: "Ah, I wish I could tell everyone what sources of strength, of peace and of happiness they would find if they would only consent to live in this intimacy" (Letter 302). "I wish I could make myself heard by everyone in order to tell them of the vanity, of the nothingness of what passes, unless it is done for God" (Letter 340). In various letters, her desires that others experience this great mystery of God's indwelling Presence are called such things as, "her program of life," "her secret," her "testament." She would encourage her dear ones to ask her help after her death since: "she will love even more in Heaven!" Different from some other saints, she saw her mission to be hidden, wholly interior. Eleven days before her death she expressed it in the following words:

"I think that in heaven my mission will be to draw souls by helping them go out of themselves to cling to God by a wholly simple and loving movement, and to keep them in this great silence within that will allow God to communicate himself to them and transform them into Himself" (Letter 335).

How can we experience this inner silence, this sacred space within that awaits realization in the heart of each one of us? Through our Lenten journey with Jesus Christ and Blessed Elizabeth, her writings in conversation with the Gospel of the day will help us open ourselves to God's self-communication.

Contemporary mindfulness practices can be helpful, but Elizabeth takes us beyond what we ourselves can do into what be might call, *the sacred art* of mindfulness that is deeply rooted in the Christian, biblical understanding of God's Trinitarian indwelling Presence. Blessed Elizabeth helps us to realize that in our very essence we are connected to God, that as Scripture puts it, we are created in the divine image and likeness. She helps us to experience its meaning in our everyday lives.

As the Bishop of Dijon noted in his foreword to the first edition of her works, Elizabeth's language, personal, simple and affectionate, assumes in places a somewhat solemn style that does not at all correspond to her personality. Her premature death at age twenty-six did not allow her time to discover fully her personal style and vocabulary. For this reason, in the direct quotes from her writings, we will recognize her own manner of punctuation. The profound depth of her message however, takes us beyond any human limitations of expression and opens the heart to a deeper life in Christ.

Short as her life was, Elizabeth absorbed not only the profound teachings of Scripture regarding God's indwelling presence, but also the mystical dimension of the teachings of the Carmelite mystic and poet, St. John of the Cross, as well as of Ruysbroeck, the great Flemish mystic, whose words she frequently makes her own.

While the writings of Blessed Elizabeth are rich with theological content and flow easily with mystical insight we can never forget that her experience was always based on faith. She understood well from her mentor in Carmel, John of the Cross, that "faith is the only proximate and proportionate means for union with God." She knew that nothing that we can think or feel or experience captures the great and holy mystery we name *God*. God is Elizabeth's heaven on earth but *"heaven in faith, heaven in darkness."* What she so luminously writes is always written against the background of faith. On the twelfth day of her Last Retreat she expresses her great faith in God:

And if I fall at every moment, in a wholly confident faith, He will help me up. I know that He will forgive me, that He will cancel out everything with a jealous care, and even more, He will "despoil" me, He will "free" me from all my miseries, from everything that is an obstacle to the divine action.[1]

---

1. *Elizabeth of the Trinity: The Complete Works,* vol.1, trans. Aletheia Kane (Washington, DC: ICS Publications, 1984),156.

In a spirit of confident faith we too can have the daring trust that God's love for us is not contingent on our being perfect before God. Instead, it is by reaching out in faith to God whose love incites our desire to ourselves live in a more God-like manner that we grow increasingly pleasing to God. As day by day, during this Lenten Season, with reflective hearts we read the Gospel and the writings of Blessed Elizabeth, with her, we will come to a deeper realization of the awesome mystery of God's indwelling Presence. By the advice she offers to family and friends in her letters, and by her retreat reflections, she will guide us into the *sacred art* of mindfulness so that in time, awareness of God's Trinitarian indwelling Presence might become a familiar reality.

BLESSED ELIZABETH OF THE TRINITY: A SHORT BIOGRAPHY

Elizabeth Catez was born July 18, 1880 at the military camp of Vor in France where her father, Captain Joseph Catez was stationed before being sent to Dijon some months later. As is true of anyone striving for holiness, Elizabeth was no ready-made saint. Along with being intelligent, musically gifted, with a lively personality, in her early years she was known in her family for her fiery temperament. According to her sister, as a child Elizabeth, "was very lively, even quick-tempered; she went into rages that were quite terrible; she was a real little devil." Her mother called her, "a big chatterbox."

By modern standards, her schooling was minimal. Around the age of seven she received private lessons in French and the following year her mother enrolled her in the Conservatory in Dijon. Later her mother also engaged a private tutor for Elizabeth and her sister. At that time her "rages" were such that her teacher threatened to send her as a boarder to a nearby Good Shepherd house of correction, and as a threat, even prepared her little bag. Her teachers would say of her: "That child has a will of iron, she is determined to have what she wants."

The priest who prepared her for her first communion and knew her well told an intimate friend of her mother: "With her temperament, Elizabeth Catez will be either a saint or a demon." In 1887, shortly after the death of her beloved grandfather, after several heart attacks her own father died in her arms. This left Elizabeth at the young age of seven, with a keen sense of the fragility of life. Around the same time, Elizabeth was also being graced with a subtle sense of God's indwelling Spirit moving her toward what she called "a complete awakening to the things of God." The experience was intensified at the time of her first confession and again on the day of her first Communion. To the amazement of these who knew her, a change took place. Elizabeth began to make observable efforts to control her fiery nature and to be more in control of her feelings. Again, it was after communion one day that in the depth of her heart she heard the word, "Carmel." She understood this as an interior call to belong exclusively to Christ and from this point on her one desire was for Carmel's life of prayer.

In spite of her inner longings, she joyously took part in the social life of her circle where her delicate sensitivity towards beauty and friendship easily found expression. She also became active in her parish, teaching catechism and doing whatever she was asked. However in the midst of her many activities: parish life, tennis, luncheons, dinner parties, travel, etc., along with musical success at the conservatory where she was a prize-winning pupil, Elizabeth's heart was in Carmel. In one of her early visits to the Carmel of Dijon, the prioress had spoken to Elizabeth about her name as meaning "house of God." Awareness of this reality led her gradually to develop an increasing spirit of interiority and attentiveness to God. Already at eighteen, while she could give herself fully to the present moment and the concrete situation cost what it may, through it all, it was observable among her wide circle of friends that she radiated the presence of God.

After years of disapproval, her mother finally consented to Elizabeth following her religious vocation. In her twenty-first year, on August 2, 1901 Elizabeth entered the Carmel of Dijon in France.

In Carmel, Elizabeth's habit of interior recollection was immediately apparent as was her quest for continuous prayer and singing praise to the Indwelling Trinity. Her outgoing and energetic spirit also found expression in self-giving in community and also in the many letters she wrote to family and friends as well as in her retreat notes, poems and spiritual treatises, all of remarkable depth. The editors of the *Complete Works* estimate that nearly *two thirds* of Elizabeth's writings have never been published.

Her overflowing, communicative and very affectionate heart left her much loved by community, family, and friends. Elizabeth's idea of holiness was simply to remain at the Source, the Indwelling Trinity, and to live by love. Her seeming passionate need for friendship served as a natural foundation for her intimacy with God. The natural and supernatural worked together in Elizabeth.

In 1903, two years after entering Carmel, Elizabeth was diagnosed as suffering from Addison's disease. At the time, there was no known cure, and it was to be the cause of her death. After intense suffering she died on November 9, 1906, at age twenty-six. As was true of everything in her life, she wove the pain and increasing disability from the disease into her life with God so that she would write to her sister, quoting St. Paul, "In my own flesh, I fill up what is lacking in the passion of Christ for the sake of His body which is the Church" (Col. 1:24). Two weeks before she died Elizabeth wrote to Sr. Marie Odile, who was then in the Carmel of Paray-le-Monial,

Let us live by love so we may die of love and glorify the God Who is all Love (Letter 335).

Her mission continues in the hearts of each one of us as we ponder her words in the light of Christ, the Living Word, who speaks to us in the Gospels in this, our Lenten journey.

THE ORDER OF DISCALCED CARMELITES: A BRIEF HISTORY

The Carmelite Order receives its name from its place of origin: Mount Carmel in the Holy Land. We know nothing of the identity of the early Carmelites other than that they were Europeans who came to Palestine at the time of the Crusades. These laymen, with a few priests, settled as hermits in the caves of the mountain near what was known as the Spring of Elijah. The memory of this great prophet permeates Mount Carmel and the hermits saw themselves as living in his prophetic spirit. Early in their history a small chapel was built dedicated to Our Lady and the hermits became known as "the hermit brothers of the Blessed Virgin Mary of Mt. Carmel." At their request, somewhere between 1206 and 1214, Albert, Patriarch of Jerusalem gave the hermits a Formula Vitae, a formula of life. The only text still in existence is the one modified and approved by Pope Innocent 1V in 1247. From that date Albert's formula of life became a Rule recognized by the Church.

Due in part to the Saracen invasions in Palestine, the Order gradually expanded and foundations were made in France, Sicily, and later in England. Following the fall of Acre in 1291, the few remaining Carmelites were massacred ending the Carmelite presence on Mount Carmel until their return in 1631.[2]

As the hermits adjusted to life in Europe, they found themselves unique in that they could claim no recognizable founder. Integral to their survival became mythical tales of the Order's direct descent from the Prophet Elijah. Like Dominic for the Dominicans, and Francis for the Franciscans, Elijah was declared founder of the Carmelites. The well-known words of this great prophet Eli'jah: *The Lord God lives in whose sight I stand and With zeal have I been zealous for the Lord God of Hosts* shaped the hearts of these hermits as they adopted a mendicant style of life to meet the needs of their new environment.

During the thirteenth and fourteenth centuries, pious women, often directed by the Carmelites, lived as hermits. Others lived a form of community life known as a *beaterio* in the tradition of the Beguines taking the Carmelite Rule as their guide.[3]

When John Soreth became General of the Order in 1451 he worked toward affiliating these disparate groups of women with the Order. Carmel was thus further enriched, as women became an integral part of Carmel's long history.

The earliest recognized convents of women in the Carmelite Order were established in Florence, Italy, and Gueldre, Holland. This was the period of political, ideological, and ecclesial unrest that preceded the Protestant Reformation. For these and other historical reasons, a vast dissimilarity existed among the various groups of Carmelite convents in Europe. Many continued to live in the style of the Beguines whereas Soreth envisioned a group of cloistered nuns who would have prayerful contact with God as their chief preoccupation. One such monastery was that of the Monastery of the Incarnation in Avila, Spain where St.

---

2. For a more detailed history of the Carmelite Order, see Peter-Thomas Rohrbach, *Journey to Carith: The Story of the Carmelite Order* (Garden City, NY: Doubleday, 1966).

3. The Beguines were associations of women without vows who sought ways to express their Christian faith in a visible way. They had no official recognition and their status as women did not allow them to do apostolic work.

Teresa of Avila spent her early years as a Carmelite.

The general, John Soreth never traveled to Spain so the nature of Carmelite monasteries in that country varied from place to place. The Incarnation was one of eleven monasteries of nuns in Spain at the time. While austere and prayerful, the monastery allowed for frequent visitors and exits from the monastery with considerable disparity between the nuns from wealthy families and those from poor circumstances. The latter often suffered want due to overcrowded conditions and the monastery's inadequate financial resources.

Through her own struggles to respond to God's call to a more focused life of prayer, and in the face of much opposition, Teresa founded the first monastery of the Reformed Carmel known as the Discalced Carmelites on August 24, 1562.[4] In doing so Teresa introduced something new within the Church, placing emphasis on the apostolic and ecclesial dimension of prayer which envisioned the life of prayer as a service.[5] Teresa died on October 4, 1582 at age sixty-seven after founding fifteen monasteries of Discalced Nuns as well as initiating the reform among the Friars.[6]

In 1604, just twenty-two years after Teresa's death, six Nuns, including Anne of Jesus and Anne of St. Bartholomew who had been intimate friends of Teresa, traveled to France to establish the first monastery of the Reform in Paris. In September of 1605, Anne of Jesus founded the Carmel in Dijon.[7] After two years foundations were made in Brussels and then in the Spanish Netherlands.

---

4. For a details of Teresa's Reform, see *The Collected Works, Teresa of Avila: The Book of Her Life*, translated by Kieran Kavanaugh, O.C.D. and Otilio Rodriguez, O.C.D. (Washington, DC: ICS Publications, 1976), vol. 1, chapters 32–36. See also *Journey to Carith*, chapters 5–6.

5. See Collected Works, The Teresian Communities, vol. 3, 23ff.

6. The Gregorian Calendar was introduced that year so Teresa's feast is celebrated on October 15.

7. Blessed Elizabeth of the Trinity entered the Carmelite Monastery of Dijon on August 2, 1901. In 1979 the Carmelites of Dijon relocated to the village of Flavegnerot, 13 miles southwest of Dijon.

In 1790, a small group of Carmelites from Hoogstraten and English Antwerp founded the first Discalced Carmelite Monastery in the United States. Sixty-six subsequent foundations have been made. Of these, twenty trace their roots to Mexico where the nuns arrived in 1604 making the first foundation in the United States in 1915. Five Carmels trace their roots to France, the first foundation in the United States from France being made in 1927.[8]

As the two branches of the Order, known as the Friars and Nuns of the Ancient Observance and the Discalced Carmelite Friars and Nuns have expanded through the years in different continents, the spirit of Elijah and of Teresa continues to inform their Carmelite lives. The Living Flame of Divine Love that transformed the heart of Blessed Elizabeth of the Trinity continues to burn as both Friars and Nuns live out their commitment in today's world.

---

8. See *Carmel in the U.S. 1790-1990* (Eugene, OR: The Queen's Press, 1990).

BLESSED ELIZABETH ON PRAYER:
OUR LIFE IN CHRIST WITHIN THE INDWELLING TRINITY

As a child, on the eve of her first communion, Elizabeth had visited the Carmel in Dijon where the Mother Prioress explained to her the significance of her Hebrew name: *Elizabeth*, that is, the "House of God." Through the years a mysterious presence always accompanied her. On November 21, 1904, two years before her death, Blessed Elizabeth wrote the Prayer to the Trinity. The intense desires of her heart overflowed in words that expressed her many years of mindfulness of God's indwelling Presence. As a prayer to the Trinity, it gives expression to her unique relationship with God as Mystery, and as her beloved Christ crucified by love. The Spirit is a consuming Fire of Love and God as her Father, bends lovingly over her. Prayer for Elizabeth is a personal encounter with God.

BLESSED ELIZABETH'S PRAYER TO THE TRINITY

O my God, Trinity whom I adore, help me to forget myself entirely that I may be established in You as still and as peaceful as if my soul were already in eternity. May nothing trouble my peace or make me leave You, O my unchanging One, but may each minute carry me further into the depths of Your Mystery. Give peace to my soul; make it Your heaven, Your beloved dwelling and Your resting place. May I never leave You there alone but be wholly present, my faith wholly vigilant, wholly adoring, and wholly surrendered to Your creative Action.

O my beloved Christ, crucified by love, I wish to be a bride for Your Heart; I wish to cover You with glory; I wish to love You . . . even unto death! But I feel my weakness, and I ask You to "clothe me with yourself," to identify my soul with all the movements of Your Soul, to overwhelm me, to possess me, to substitute Yourself for me that my life may be but a radiance of Your Life. Come into me as Adorer, as Restorer, as Savior. O Eternal Word, Word of my God, I want to spend my life in listening to You, to become wholly teachable that I may learn all from You. Then, through all nights, all voids, all helplessness, I want to gaze on you always and remain in Your great light. O my beloved Star, so fascinate me that I may not withdraw from Your radiance.

O consuming Fire, Spirit of Love, "come upon me," and create in my soul a kind of incarnation of the Word: that I may be another humanity for Him in which He can renew His whole Mystery. And You, O Father, bend lovingly over Your poor little creature; "cover her with your shadow," seeing in her only the "beloved in whom You are well pleased."

O my Three, my all, my Beatitude, infinite Solitude, Immensity in which I lose my self, I surrender myself to you as Your prey. Bury Yourself in me that I may bury myself in You until I depart to contemplate in Your light the abyss of Your greatness. November 21, 1904[9]

---

9. *Elizabeth of the Trinity: The Complete Works*, vol. 1, trans. Aletheia Kane (Washington, DC: ICS Publications, 1984), 183

Two words from her prayer might be helpful to reflect upon—the word *still* and the word *wholly*. The word *still* suggests an inner disposition of heart, a contemplative attitude of loving, attentive mindfulness that can exist on a level deeper than the wanderings of the mind. It reminds us that while we have our part in prayer, ultimately prayer is something that God does in us in Christ. It is God loving us, and God desiring our response of love that moves us to pray. Blessed Elizabeth gives expression to the desires that God has placed in her heart. Her petitions reflect the deepest dimension of our person—our capacity for union with God through love and God's desire that this be realized. How difficult it is for us to be *still* even for a short time with our many contemporary means of instant communication to distract us with it diversions. Blessed Elizabeth would encourage us to occasionally take a quiet moment as the day allows, to remember God's indwelling Presence, and to offer a short prayer of gratitude for this awesome reality.

God is a very *personal* presence for Blessed Elizabeth. The depth of her relationship with God in Christ is very evident. Christ is Adorer, Restorer, her Savior, her beloved Star who fascinates her and in whose radiance she desires to live. She would spend her life in listening to Christ the Eternal Word of God. She prays that the Spirit of Love come upon her that she might be another human person in which Christ can renew His whole Mystery. Her letters and her retreat notes give continued expression to her love for Christ.

Christ desires to continue His human and divine life in each one of us. Through our Baptism we have been *incorporated* in Christ and in the Eucharist, Christ continues to transform us into Himself. St. Augustine reminds us that in receiving the Eucharist, it is *our mystery* that we receive; *we are the Body of Christ!* Blessed Elizabeth would be *wholly* present to Christ.

The word *wholly*, used five times in her prayer, is of special significance. Much in today's world can keep us half-hearted in our response to God. Hopefully, as we prayerfully enter into our Lenten journey with Jesus Christ and Blessed Elizabeth, the desire to be *wholly* responsive to God's love and to reflect this in our lives will grow in us. Then in our own "nights, voids and experiences of helplessness, in union with the suffering Christ," we will not lose heart. In confidence and trust, united with Christ, we will pray that our sufferings bear fruit for ourselves and for others in newness of life so that the mystery of Christ's Resurrection becomes for us a living reality in the joy of Easter, Christ's Risen life alive in us.

LECTIO DIVINA AND THE PRACTICE OF PRAYERFUL READING

The Gospels invite us to walk in the footsteps of Jesus Christ. The practice of *lectio* facilitates living in the presence of the One who guides us toward the full realization of our human potential. Jesus stirs into flame the heart's transcendent potential. Through the gifts of faith, hope and love, we deepen in our prayer relationship with Christ and we come to recognize His presence in the everydayness of life. The practice of *lectio* enables us to avoid the detours of which the saints alert us as daily we struggle with what has been called, "our perfectly imperfect nature."

The practice of *lectio* has its origins in the Hebrew Scriptures. Psalm 1, a wisdom psalm, introduces the Psalter by proclaiming that *the just person delights in the law of the Lord and meditates on God's law day and night.* In the early Church, *lectio divina,* then known *lectio sacra,* quickly found its place among the sacraments of the Church, the Liturgy of the Hours and Interior Prayer. Vatican II in the Dogmatic

Constitution on Divine Revelation, *Dei Verbum,* links as food and nutrition the Word of God with the Body of Christ received in the Eucharist. Prayerful meditative study of sacred Scripture therefore, is not only the soul of theology as it was for the early theologians of the Church; it is also the lifeline of every Christian through the ages.

In the ancient monastic tradition, meditation meant slow, prayerful reading of the Scriptures so as to hear with the heart as the mind ruminates over a word or phrase. Like a cow repeatedly chewing its cud, the monk was encouraged to "chew over" the word of God. In Latin, the word *meditatio* derives from the Sanskrit root *madh-a*, which means *wisdom*. Christ, the Wisdom of God in our human flesh, lives His Risen Life *in us* as we meditate, chew upon, and turn the Scriptures over and over in the mind until the words are internalized so as to form themselves in the heart. God's Word becomes our identity as it finds practical expression in daily living, in the choices we make, and in our behavior toward others.

The twelfth-century letter known as the "Ladder of Monks," written by Guido II, prior of the Grand Chartreuse, formalizes the process of *lectio*.[10] Drawing on the vast tradition of lectio already extant, Guido articulates four stages: *reading or hearing a text of Scripture; meditating, pondering the text; prayer flowing a response to the text; and finally, contemplation as quiet presence to God who speaks in the silence of the heart.* These stages are not intended to be sharply divided, but are integral to each other, like the ebb and flow of the tide as it washes over the sands of the beach and then recedes to its shoreline containment. As St. John of the Cross writes: *"seek in reading, and you will find in meditation; knock in prayer, and it will be opened to you in contemplation."*[11]

Mary, woman of faith, is our model for the practice of lectio. Mary *pondered in her heart* the unfolding events of the life of her Son. She conceived The Word in her womb not only as a physical reality, but she also gave birth to the Word in the womb of her heart as daily in faith she embraced the Father's will. As we ponder the Word in our heart,

---

10. Guido II, *The Ladder of Monks and Twelve Meditations,* trans. Colledge and Walsh (Kalamazoo, MI: Cistercian Publications, 1978).
11. From *Sayings of Light and Love, in St. John of the Cross: Collected Works,* trans. Kieran Kavanaugh (Washington, DC: ICS Publications, 1991), 97.

and as the word is daily born anew in us through prayer and meditation, through liturgical worship and faith-filled action, the Church will increasingly become a Contemplative Church and will birth Christ anew in our suffering world.

To practice *lectio*, find a time and place that enables a quiet presence to God. Choose a body position that supports prayerful presence to the Word of God. If possible, find a time in the day when distractions and interruptions are less likely to intrude. Otherwise we become discouraged and give up the practice. On the other hand, life cannot be controlled, so all is not lost if circumstances temporarily call us forth to other things. *Lectio* rests on openness to God and not on personal effort or on an ideal situation. We simply do the best we can with what is available to us.

To hear the voice of God speaking to you through the Scriptures it helps to begin *lectio* by listening to *yourself*, to the feelings in your body, to the thoughts running through the pathways of the mind. Try to name what your feelings indicate—a worry, a concern that needs for the moment to be placed in the hands of God—feelings of anticipation about something exciting to which you look forward, etc. Give your feelings a name: peaceful anticipation, anger, anxiety, tiredness, or whatever it may be. This enables us to become more present to the sacredness of the moment by placing our feelings and concerns in the hands of God. Then open the text of Scripture and slowly, prayerfully begin to read.

The Scriptures carry within themselves many layer of meaning found in their literary, historical, and theological perspectives. Reading the text considering these various points of view can enlighten our understanding and deepen the text's significance for our lives today. Through a *literary* approach, we view the text within the context of the book of which it is a part. For instance, Matthew's Gospel was written primarily for a Jewish Christian community while Luke writes primarily for Gentile converts. For this reason, each offers a specific theological message in their accounts of Jesus life, death, and resurrection.

The *historical* situation in which the text occurs also adds insight. For example: Jewish laws of the time forbade eating swine and even forbade being near them. In this context we can understand the shocking effect on the Jewish leaders when they hear Jesus tell the parable of the prodigal son reduced to being a swineherd who was lavishly welcomed home by his father.

Along with the literary and historical perspective of any text is its *theological* message. The words of Jesus were frequently heard by the religious leaders of his time as challenging their limited understanding of the God they worshiped. How did they respond and what does the text say to us about our relationship with God? Unfortunately, if we separate the text from its literary, historical, and theological context, we too easily fall into the dangers of misinterpreting its meaning or taking a fundamentalist approach. At the same time as we become increasingly familiar with the different layers of interpretation within the Scriptures, the Holy Spirit will quietly and unobtrusively guide our mind and heart to the text's deeper meaning for our lives today.

The Spirit will lead us from the meaning of the text itself to meditation as we might ask ourselves: how is God, through this text, speaking to me and to my life today? Then begin quietly to ponder the text, enter into conversation with it; become like Mary who pondered God's words in her heart. If a particular word or phrase strikes an inviting note give it a moment of silent attention. Attentive reading of the text and meditating on its meaning draws the heart into *prayer* that in time, begins to flow through the entire process of *lectio*.

For example, in the Gospel of the Wedding Feast, we might be drawn to pray to Mary asking her to hold before Christ the empty places in our heart for him to fill. Or we might pray that our feeble efforts to love and to serve be transformed into wine. As the Scriptures touch the heart's deepest desires, words of praise or of profound longing might then draw the soul into *contemplation*, into the silence of God. God may gradually lead the soul into the inner wine cellar deep within the heart—a dimension of ourselves which according to St. Teresa, is inaccessible to us except through God's invitation. Teresa writes:

> I understand this union to be the wine cellar where the Lord wishes to place us when He desires and, as he desires. But however great the effort we make to do so, we cannot enter.
>
> His majesty must place us there and enter Himself into the center of our soul.[12]

---

12. St. Teresa of Avila, *The Interior Castle, Collected Works,* trans. Kieran Kavanaugh and Otilio Rodriguez (Washington, DC: ICS Publications, 1980), 340.

ON THE DAILY GOSPEL READINGS

As noted, this book presents daily readings and prayers for every day of Lent, weekdays, and Sundays. The daily readings begin with a Gospel Reading, followed by a selection from Blessed Elizabeth of the Trinity's writings, a reflection, and a prayer.

The Gospel Readings are from the Roman Catholic *Lectionary for Mass for Use in the Dioceses of the United States of America*. The *Lectionary* for Mass contains the readings for Mass selected from the Bible.

If you were to attend daily Mass during Lent in the United States, you would hear the same Daily Gospel Readings included in this book. For example, the Ash Wednesday Gospel Reading, Matthew 6:1–6, 16–18, is the same Gospel Reading you would hear when you attend Mass to receive your ashes. In fact, on each day at all the Masses of the Latin-rite Roman Catholic Church throughout the world, the same readings are heard in Mass, read in the vernacular language or Latin.

There are two main components of the Lectionary: Sunday and Weekday readings. Sunday readings are arranged on a three-year cycle:

Year A, Year B, and Year C. The Gospel Readings for Year A are generally from the Gospel of St. Matthew, Year B are generally from the Gospel of St. Mark, and Year C are generally from the Gospel of St. Luke. St. John's Gospel is read on Sundays in Year A, B, and C during specific liturgical calendar periods.

The Weekday readings are on a two-year cycle: Year I and Year II. Year I are odd-numbered years and Year II are even- numbered years. The Weekday readings during Lent are the same for Year I and Year II although each day's reading is different. In the book, the Weekday Gospel Readings are also the Weekday Gospel Readings in the Lectionary.

For Sundays in this book, you have three different selections of readings and prayers. Each selection begins with a different Gospel Reading, the Gospel Reading from Year A, B, or C of the Lectionary.

Appendix A, the Calendar for Lent 2012–2021 & Lectionary Cycle, lists the specific dates for the next ten years for Ash Wednesday, the Sundays of Lent, and includes the Sunday Lectionary Cycle for the year. Please refer to the table to determine the current year's Sunday Lectionary Cycle: Year A, B, or C and select the appropriate Sunday reading for the present year.

This book in a small way invites you to pray each day with the Church and your fellow Christians in the world on your Lenten journey with Jesus Christ and Blessed Elizabeth of the Trinity.

Peter J. Mongeau

"He is always living, always at work in our soul; let us allow ourselves to be formed by Him; may He be the soul of our soul the Life of our life so that we may say with St. Paul: 'For me to live is Christ.'"

Blessed Elizabeth of the Trinity
Complete Works, vol. 2: Letter 145

ASH WEDNESDAY
and the Days after Ash Wednesday

Ash Wednesday

Gospel

Jesus said to his disciples:

"Take care not to perform righteous deeds in order that people may see them; otherwise, you will have no recompense from your heavenly Father. When you give alms, do not blow a trumpet before you, as the hypocrites do in the synagogues and in the streets to win the praise of others. Amen, I say to you, they have received their reward. But when you give alms, do not let your left hand know what your right is doing, so that your almsgiving may be secret. And your Father who sees in secret will repay you.

"When you pray, do not be like the hypocrites, who love to stand and pray in the synagogues and on street corners so that others may see them. Amen, I say to you, they have received their reward. But when you pray, go to your inner room, close the door, and pray to your Father in secret. And your Father who sees in secret will repay you.

"When you fast, do not look gloomy like the hypocrites. They neglect their appearance, so that they may appear to others to be fasting. Amen, I say to you, they have received their reward. But when you fast, anoint your head and wash your face, so that you may not appear to be fasting, except to your Father who is hidden. And your Father who sees what is hidden will repay you."

Matthew 6: 1-6, 16-18

BLESSED ELIZABETH OF THE TRINITY

About to "bury herself in the solitude of the desert," Blessed Elizabeth wrote to a priest friend of the community:

"Yes, Monsieur . . . have a good Lent, as you say there is much to expiate, much to ask for, and I think if we are to meet so many needs, we must become a continual prayer and love much. The power of a soul surrendered to love is so great."

Complete Works, vol. 2: Letter 225

REFLECTION

In the Gospel for today, as we begin our Lenten journey, Jesus uncovers for his followers the many levels of motivation that insinuate themselves into even the best of our actions. He invites us to be aware of what today we might call ego contamination—wanting our good deeds, the traditional practices of Lent: prayer, fasting and almsgiving, to be noticed and admired. But as we slowly and reflectively read this Gospel, a further invitation opens up before us. Notice how frequently Jesus directs our attention to the God whom Jesus lovingly calls "Father." If we are not to perform righteous deeds in order to be seen, it is because of our relationship with our "Father who sees in secret." The heart of this Gospel is an invitation to develop a deep and intimate relationship with God so that everything that we do will be done in love and not for selfish motives.

In the Jewish culture of Jesus' time, a deep bonding existed between a father and his son. Male children were identified as the son of the father. Simon Peter was known as Simon bar Jonah—that is, Simon, son of Jonah. Jesus could find no better human image than "father" to express the intimacy of his relationship with God and he invites us to enter into the love relationship with God that he enjoys. The Father who sees in secret wishes to repay us by drawing us into the intimacy that Jesus experienced. The Lenten practices of prayer, fasting and almsgiving are means of expressing our love for God.

Blessed Elizabeth desired to bury herself in the silence of Lent in order to become a continual prayer. She also desired to love much. Lent is about growing in love for God through prayer and through willingly, "doing for others in secret." The practices of Lent help to empty us of all that hinders the free flow of God's love into our hearts. Lent is a journey of love in imitation of Christ who so accepted the reality of our human condition, with its diminishments, misunderstandings, and injustices to the extent of surrendering to false accusations and a painful, degrading execution! The Cross stands as a witness to God's unconditional love for humankind and challenges us, as it did blessed Elizabeth, "to love much and to become a continual prayer."

What is my attitude toward the season of Lent? Am I willing to walk in the footsteps of Jesus these forty days with a generous, open heart? Does fasting remind me to pray for the nourishment that only Christ can provide? What prevents me, like blessed Elizabeth, to surrender to love?

PRAYER

Jesus, You addressed God as your "Father." Help me to change the things in my life, my attitudes, my way of relating to others, and especially my self-centeredness so that I too can pray with greater confidence to God as my "Father." Help me to believe in Your unconditional love for me. Help me to love the persons I find difficult to love so that like Elizabeth, this Lent will be a time "to love much" and I will begin to understand what it means for my life to become a continual prayer. I offer my prayer to the Father in your name, my ever living Lord. Amen.

THURSDAY AFTER ASH WEDNESDAY

GOSPEL

JESUS SAID TO HIS DISCIPLES:

"The Son of Man must suffer greatly and be rejected by the elders, the chief priests, and the scribes, and be killed and on the third day be raised."

Then he said to all, "If anyone wishes to come after me, he must deny himself and take up his cross daily and follow me. For whoever wishes to save his life will lose it, but whoever loses his life for my sake will save it. What profit is there for one to gain the whole world yet lose or forfeit himself?"

LUKE 9: 22-25

BLESSED ELIZABETH OF THE TRINITY

At the age of twenty Blessed Elizabeth wrote:

"My God, in union with Jesus crucified, I offer myself as a victim. I desire the cross as my strength and support, and wish to live with it, that it may be my treasure since Jesus chose it for my sake.... My Savior, I desire to return Thee love for love, blood for blood. Thou didst die for me, therefore I will daily endure fresh sufferings for Thee; every day shall bring me some fresh martyrdom because of my deep love for Thee."

The Praise of Glory, 47

REFLECTION

Blessed Elizabeth's passion for suffering was for her a fitting expression of her love. It reflected the attitude toward suffering common to her times. Trials were seen as an opportunity to expiate one's sins and those of the world, but above all as an opportunity to grow in love. Trials were also considered a proof of God's love. They were sent to special persons so God could reward them afterwards. Jesus was seen as the great example. By embracing the cross, He reconciled the world to His Father. In a less medically advanced era suffering was a fate to be endured. Elizabeth's desire for suffering was not motivated by hidden masochism but rather was animated by love, along the desire to overcome egoism through self-sacrificing love.

Out of love, Jesus surrendered to the condition of our human, finite fragility and to the disorder of sin that eventually led to His suffering and death on a cross. God's love for humankind, for each one of us, is at the heart of this mystery of our redemption. Pray for the grace that when the sufferings of life come your way that you may see them as windows of opportunity to mature in love and compassion for others in their sufferings and come to a deeper appreciation of Christ's love and care for you.

As you reflect on the words of Jesus in today's Gospel in the light of Blessed Elizabeth's ardent desire to suffer with Jesus, ask myself: What is my attitude toward the sufferings each day inevitable brings? Does even the slightest pain plunge me into feelings of self-pity as I reach for a bottle of pain relievers? Does preoccupation with myself in my difficult moments leave me uncaring and indifferent toward the needs of others?

PRAYER

Jesus, in spite of recoiling in the face of suffering and inevitable death, impelled by the force of love, you said in prayer, "Not my will but Thine be done." When life's sufferings overwhelm me help me to find peace in uniting myself with You. Give me the courage to take up the cross in the many forms it comes to me and to those I love. I hold before you the world's sufferings: physical pain, difficulty in relationships and between nations, struggles in family life, economic loss, world hunger, separation from loved ones through war, and the any other forms of human pain. United with you may your love draw me, with all who suffer, into quiet mindfulness of Your abiding presence, the source of strength and inner peace. In your name I pray. Amen.

Friday after Ash Wednesday

> # Gospel
>
> The disciples of John approached Jesus and said, "Why do we and the Pharisees fast much, but your disciples do not fast?" Jesus answered them, "Can the wedding guests mourn as long as the bridegroom is with them? The days will come when the bridegroom is taken away from them, and then they will fast."
>
> Matthew 9: 14-15

BLESSED ELIZABETH OF THE TRINITY

In a letter to a postulant, who had left the monastery because of ill health, Blessed Elizabeth writes:

"I think it is love which shortens our stay here below—in fact St. John of the Cross states it plainly. He wrote a wonderful chapter describing victims of love and the assaults it makes upon them. Our God is a consuming fire, if we always keep united to Him by a simple and loving gaze of love; if, like our adorable Master we can say at the end of each day: I do always the things that please Him, He will know how to consume us and we will fly like two little sparks to be lost in the great furnace where we shall burn joyfully for all eternity."

The Praise of Glory, 197

REFLECTION

Today's reading from the Gospel of Matthew and from Blessed Elizabeth again remind us that Lent is primarily about growing in the realization of God's passionate love for each one of us, and in the awareness of God's loving presence in Christ. Jesus speaks of himself as the bridegroom—the lover. During His time with them, the disciples of Jesus feasted on His presence and His words nourished and energized them. Jesus knew that after his Ascension into heaven, his disciples would have to fast from His physical nearness and from the inspiration of hearing His voice so their faith would need to be strengthened. As gradually they absorbed the reality that Jesus had indeed risen from the dead, Jesus reassured them: *Behold I am with you always even to the end of time.* These words became like a consuming fire that nourished their faith as they fasted from his physical presence. With Blessed Elizabeth, a simple and loving gaze of love now united them to Him.

Just as we consume the food we eat, Blessed Elizabeth assures us, God's love for each one of us is so great that God would consume us in the living flame of divine love. The fast of Lent, both from food and from all that keeps us from being a loving person, reminds us of our need for God just as hunger reminds us of our need for food.

Lent also invites us to let our fasting lead us to prayer—it reminds us that our deepest being is a *hunger for God*. As we fast from all that hinders love toward God and toward others, God's love enlarges our heart's capacity for love. Like Elizabeth, as God's love increasingly consumes us, we will fly like two little sparks to be lost in the great furnace where we shall burn joyfully for all eternity. God's fire is not about condemnation but about love.

Can I say at the end of each day that I do always things that please Him? Does fasting lead me to prayer? In difficult moments do I remember that Jesus promised to be with me always?

PRAYER

Ever-loving God, the mystics use the image of fire to describe their experience of your all-consuming love for them. I recognize my need for an ever-deeper faith in your love for me. Help me to fast from all that keeps the flow of your love in me from flowing through me to the many persons You place in my life. As I fast from food, keep me mindful of the many persons who are hungry for You, but who are also starving for lack of the necessary food to sustain human life. Alert me to the many ways in which greed and over-consumption cause me to be wanting in love and so less concerned for the needs of others. Relying on your strength I offer this prayer in the name of your beloved Son, Jesus Christ. Amen.

SATURDAY AFTER ASH WEDNESDAY

GOSPEL

Jesus saw a tax collector named Levi sitting at the customs post. He said to him, "Follow me." And leaving everything behind, he got up and followed him. Then Levi gave a great banquet for him in his house, and a large crowd of tax collectors and others were at table with them. The Pharisees and their scribes complained to his disciples, saying, "Why do you eat and drink with tax collectors and sinners?" Jesus said to them in reply, "Those who are healthy do not need a physician, but the sick do. I have not come to call the righteous to repentance but sinners."

LUKE 5: 27-32

BLESSED ELIZABETH OF THE TRINITY

As a child, Elizabeth was lively, fond of pleasure, and until age seven, subject to bursts of temper. A note by Blessed Elizabeth reveals the secret of her eventual victories. She writes:

"When a remark seems unjust to me, nature so rebels against it that my blood seems to boil in my veins.... Today I have had the joy of offering my Jesus several sacrifices connected with my besetting fault. How dear they cost me! It proves how weak I am, yet Jesus was with me; I heard His voice in the depth of my heart, and I was ready to bear anything for love of Him."

The Praise of Glory, 19

REFLECTION

By sharing a meal with the outcasts of His society Jesus demonstrates the universality of divine love. Jesus did not come to call the righteous because not one of us is righteous before God. We depend on God for our very existence. We all have need for God's mercy and for inner healing no matter how sincere our human effort to do good.

Blessed Elizabeth, along with the need to be in touch with the feelings of anger as they arose in her body, knew she also needed to be attentive to the voice of the Indwelling Spirit of Jesus. Aware that she was feeling anger, she could write, "my blood seemed to boil in my veins." She was sensitively attuned to her physical reality and could accurately name her emotions. She was also aware that God speaks to us through all that is human, especially through the emotional shifts we regularly experience. Everything is grace and within our feelings is the voice of the Spirit reminding us that our feelings should not determine how we behave or how we respond to others. Important as they are, they are not meant to have the last word. Elizabeth was sensitively attuned to the movements in her body but these did not dominate her responses. She knew her need for Christ's healing and guiding presence so that love for Christ would find expression in her relationships.

Am I aware of the importance of being in touch with my feelings? Do I tend to give my emotions thoughtless expression in a manner hurtful to others? If this happens do I have the sensitivity and courage to apologize?

PRAYER

Jesus, the example of your holy ones challenges me to be more attentive to the feelings in my body and the thoughts that roam the inner circle of my mind. My judgmental attitudes, my angry words, and uncaring actions need your healing mercy. I too am "sick and in need of a physician." I hear you telling the Pharisees that we all belong to the "communion of sinners" just as ultimately we hope to belong to "the communion of saints" in the life to come. Help me, like Elizabeth, to acknowledge my weakness and open myself to hear your voice in the depth of my hearts. In today's difficult moments, awaken in me the ready willingness to bear all things for love of you. In your name, Jesus I offer my prayer to you. Amen.

FIRST WEEK OF LENT

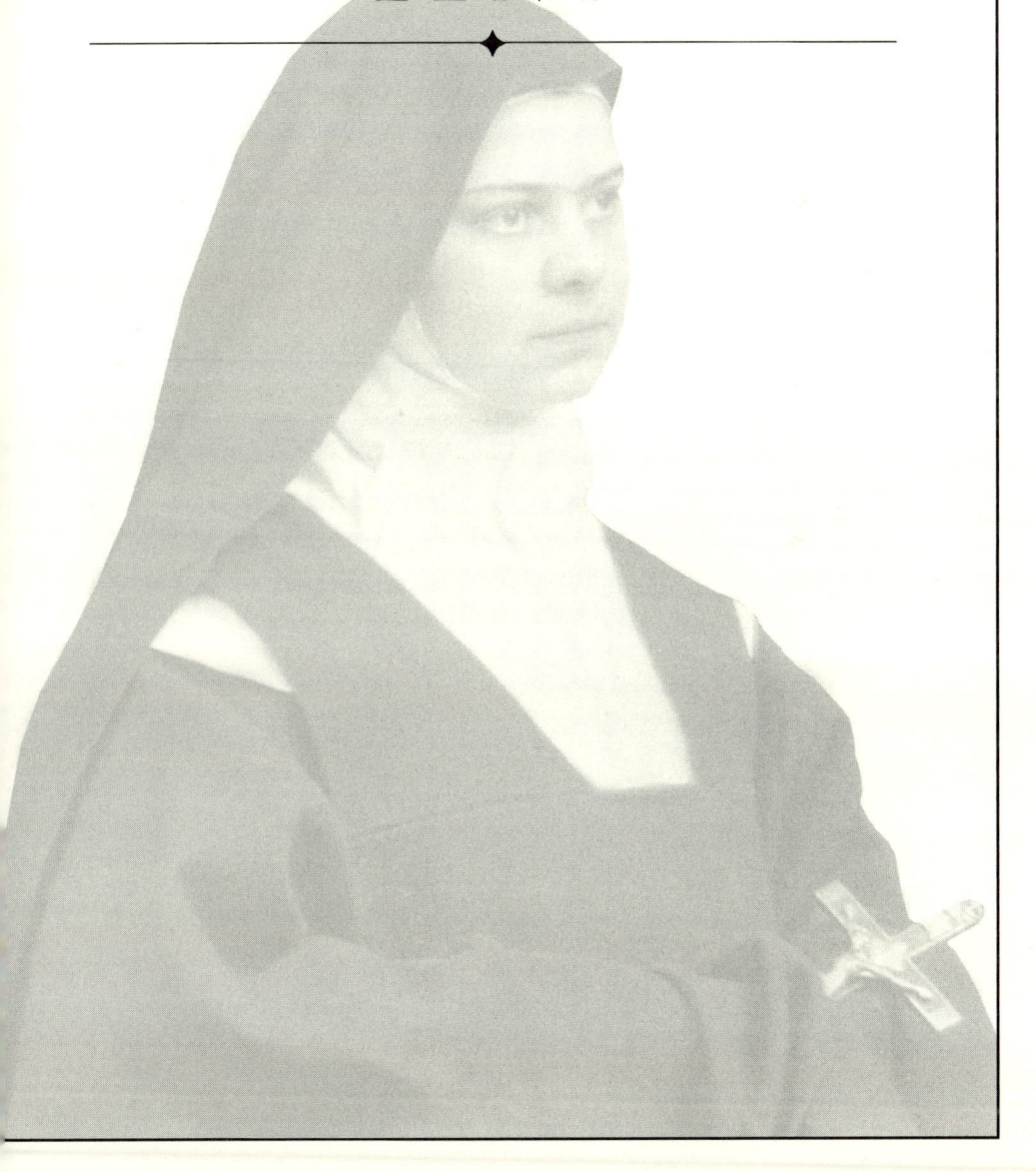

FIRST SUNDAY OF LENT — YEAR A

GOSPEL

At that time Jesus was led by the Spirit into the desert to be tempted by the devil. He fasted for forty days and forty nights, and afterwards he was hungry. The tempter approached and said to him, "If you are the Son of God, command that these stones become loaves of bread."

He said in reply, "It is written: / *One does not live on bread alone, / but on every word that comes forth from the mouth of God.*" / Then the devil took him to the holy city, and made him stand on the parapet of the temple, and said to him, "If you are the Son of God, throw yourself down. For it is written: / *He will command his angels concerning you / and with their hands they will support you, / lest you dash your foot against a stone.*" / Jesus answered him, "Again it is written, *You shall not put the Lord, your God, to the test.*" Then the devil took him up to a very high mountain, and showed him all the kingdoms of the world in their magnificence, and he said to him, "All these I shall give to you, if you will prostrate yourself and worship me." At this, Jesus said to him, "Get away, Satan! It is written: / *The Lord, your God, shall you worship / and him alone shall you serve.*" / Then the devil left him and, behold, angels came and ministered to him.

MATTHEW 4: 1-11

BLESSED ELIZABETH OF THE TRINITY

Having discovered her unique vocation, which was to be "a praise of glory," Elizabeth writes:

"*The praise of glory is a soul that dwells in God, with a pure, disinterred love which does not seek self in the sweetness of His love; a soul that loves Him above all His gifts, and would have loved Him as much had it received nothing, which wishes well to the object of its tenderness. But how can we wish well to God, except by accomplishing His will, since this will ordains all things for His greater glory? Such a soul should surrender itself fully, blindly to this will, so that it cannot possibly wish anything but what God wishes.*"

The Praise of Glory, 95

REFLECTION

Many lessons can be drawn from reflecting on this section of Matthew's Gospel—in particular—the importance of attentiveness to the Word of God so that its wisdom and insight come to mind in times of temptation and special need. The Word of God helps to mediate God's will to us so that like Elizabeth, we too can come to surrender ourselves fully to God's will. Jesus' response to the tempter is a message most important for our lives today. We do not live on bread alone. God's Word is the bread that sustains us in daily living and it guides us as we discern God's will, especially in important matters.

Satan offers Jesus all the power and glory of the universe. Our temptation might be to become attached to the good things of God's creation without reference to God. The writings of Elizabeth of the Trinity guide us in seeing all things in relation to God, including ourselves. We need frequently to remind ourselves that God's glory is the infusion of God's love into our universe and that we share in this mystery. Divine Love creates and sustains us in existence. Each person is called to be "a praise of glory." The mystery of our deepest self lies hidden in this reality.

If someone asked me to describe how I see myself, what would I say? Am I tempted to exalt in my successes in sports, in school, in business, in my profession, etc. and so consider myself better than others who might seem less successful? Do I tend to look down on others of a different race or culture and to consider them inferior to myself? Are these the temptations Satan uses to lure me into exalting myself over others?

PRAYER

Creating God of the Universe, through your loving presence you hold all things in existence. Your glory radiates from the grains of sand on the seashore to the vastness of the ever-expanding universe. It is you whom I desire to worship and serve. May all that I say and do be for your praise and glory. Gift me with humility of heart to see myself only within the radiance of Your love and to recognize that all is gift to be used for Your glory. I offer my prayer in the name of the Eternal Word through whom all things come to be. Amen.

First Sunday of Lent — Year B

GOSPEL

The Spirit drove Jesus out into the desert, and he remained in the desert for forty days, tempted by Satan. He was among wild beasts, and the angels ministered to him.

After John had been arrested, Jesus came to Galilee proclaiming the gospel of God: "This the time of fulfillment. The kingdom of God is at hand. Repent, and believe in the gospel."

Mark 1: 12-15

BLESSED ELIZABETH OF THE TRINITY

On the second day of her last retreat, Blessed Elizabeth wrote:

"A soul that debates with its self that is taken up with its feelings and pursues useless thoughts or desires, scatters it forces. For it is not wholly directed toward God. Its lyre does not vibrate in unison and when the Master plays it, He cannot draw from it divine harmonies, for it is still too human and discordant."

Complete Works, vol. 1: 142

REFLECTION

The Spirit *drove* Jesus into the desert. There are moments when the promptings of the indwelling Spirit are so urgent that we feel impelled to listen, even if we know it will mean suffering. In the spiritual journey the desert has always been symbolic of life's difficult times when prayer and life seems dry and barren and the heat of temptation bears heavily upon us. In such periods of desert dryness, we can find strength and courage in the realization that Jesus companions our journey. What is the kingdom of God if not Jesus' intimate indwelling presence?

Jesus' earthly journey ended not in death, but in his resurrection from the dead. That belief assures us that within all of life's desert moments is the potential for a deeper life in Christ. In nature, the autumn leaves fall to the ground and decompose to enrich the soil for further growth. Jesus is always present to enrich our lives and to help us find meaning in our struggles and so come to greater human and spiritual maturity through all that life has to offer.

Elizabeth of the Trinity reminds us that when the desert envelop us, not to becomes self-absorbed. Things like self-pity—feeling sorry for oneself or blaming others—deaden our ability to come forth from the desert with renewed energy to live Jesus message of care and compassion. Like Jesus we have the words of scripture to support us as we struggle with the inner demons that tempts us. It was only after the arrest of John the Baptist that Jesus began His own public ministry so as not be appear in competition with John. If we cultivate a listening heart, the Spirit of Jesus will guide us through our desert experiences— the times "when it seems all our leaves are falling to the ground"— and we will be enriched with greater sensitivity toward others in their struggles. Our "lyre will be in tune" and our life will echo in harmony with the kingdom of God proclaimed by Jesus.

Can I recognize movements toward self-pity in myself as it begins to take hold of me? What helps me at such times not to succumb to its darkening hold? Am I open to seeing the "hidden blessing" present even in my life's darkest moments?

PRAYER

Jesus, You willingly entered the desert of human life and shared with us deprivation, loneliness and the harshness of life in our world. Attune me to Your indwelling Spirit so that guided by You, with a listening heart, I will hear when the voice of temptation would draw me from living in harmony with You. Trusting in your strength I offer my prayer to you. Amen.

First Sunday of Lent — Year C

Gospel

Filled with the Holy Spirit, Jesus returned from the Jordan and was led by the Spirit into the desert for forty days, to be tempted by the devil. He ate nothing during those days, and when they were over he was hungry. The devil said to him, "If you are the Son of God, command this stone to become bread." Jesus answered him, "It is written, *One does not live on bread alone.*" Then he took him up and showed him all the kingdoms of the world in a single instant. The devil said to him, "I shall give to you all this power and glory; for it has been handed over to me, and I may give it to whomever I wish. All this will be yours, if you worship me." Jesus said to him in reply, "It is written: / *You shall worship the Lord, your God, and him alone shall you serve.*" / Then he led them to Jerusalem, made him stand on the parapet of the temple, and said to him, "If you are the Son of God, throw yourself down from here, for it is written: / *He will command his angels concerning you, to guard you,* / and: / *With their hands they will support you,* / *lest you dash your foot against a stone.*" / Jesus said to him in reply, "It also says, *You shall not put the Lord, your God, to the test.*" When the devil had finished every temptation, he departed from him for a time.

Luke 4: 1-13

BLESSED ELIZABETH OF THE TRINITY

On the thirteenth day of her last retreat Elizabeth wrote:
"The Apostle comes to my aid again to help me to fully realize this divine plan (to re-establish all things in Christ) and gives me a rule of life, 'Walk in Jesus Christ the Lord, rooted and built up in Him, and confirmed in faith as also you have learned, abounding in Him in thanksgiving.'

'Walk in Jesus Christ' appears to me to mean to go out of self, to lose sight of, to forget self, that we may enter more deeply into Him every moment—enter so profoundly as to be 'rooted' in Him, and that we may boldly challenge all events with the defiant cry, 'Who, then, shall separate us from the love of Christ?'"

The Praise of Glory, 251

REFLECTION

Luke's account of Jesus' temptation in the desert suggests that Jesus is here being tempted to deny His true identity as the Word of God become one with us in our human condition of hunger and thirst. He is also being tempted to exploit His divinity with marvelous signs, done not for the good of others but for His own aggrandizement.

Shortly before, at His baptism in the Jordan, Jesus heard the words from His Father, "You are my beloved upon you my favor rests." If Jesus had succumbed to the temptation to seek glory for Himself, which is a form of Satan worship, He would have been untrue to His identity in God as a Trinitarian unity of love. The incomprehensible mystery we call God, has been revealed to us in Christ in the familiar language of Father, Son and Holy Spirit. We are created in the divine image and likeness (Genesis 1:26–27). Christ now reflects to us our own deepest identity as one with the Indwelling Trinity. We are "rooted" in God's Trinitarian life. Each one of us is an image or "sketch" of God and this reality shapes our inner being and forms our deepest self.

Blessed Elizabeth lived in awareness of being rooted in Christ. She also recognized the temptation to make an idol of oneself through self-centeredness and prideful ego-inflation. Elizabeth's confident cry, "Who then shall separate us from the love of Christ" echoes Jesus' reply to the tempter: "You shall worship the Lord, your God, and him alone shall your serve." The world of advertising invites us to worship the god of consumerism.

Today many things tempt us to ignore the needs of others in pursuit of our own selfish interests. The Scriptures of Lent invite us to reflect deeply on the meaning of our life. We have been baptized *in Christ*. Our deepest self is etched in the likeness of Christ and each day offers us opportunities to resist the temptations of Satan so that the likeness of Christ might shine through us.

Is this how I see myself? Do my actions reflect my identity in Christ? Do I pray for the grace to be more deeply rooted in Christ especially in moments of temptation?

PRAYER

Lord Jesus, may your indwelling Spirit alert me today to temptations to self-centeredness and to the subtle ways in which I exalt myself above others. Root me in your divine life so that with my whole being I will "worship the Lord God and serve Him alone." May your Eucharistic Bread sustain me so that, rooted in You I may boldly challenge all events with the defiant cry, "Who will separate me from the love of Christ?" I offer my prayer to the Father in your name Lord Jesus, in whom I trust. Amen.

First Week of Lent — Monday

Gospel

Jesus said to his disciples:

"When the Son of Man comes in his glory, and all the angels with him, he will sit upon his glorious throne, and all the nations will be assembled before him. And he will separate them one from another, as a shepherd separates the sheep from the goats. He will place the sheep on his right and the goats on his left. Then the king will say to those on his right, 'Come, you who are blessed by my Father. Inherit the kingdom prepared for you from the foundation of the world. For I was hungry and you gave me food, I was thirsty and you gave me drink, a stranger and you welcomed me, naked and you clothed me, ill and you cared for me, in prison and you visited me.' Then the righteous will answer him and say, 'Lord, when did we see you hungry and feed you, or thirsty and give you drink? When did we see you a stranger and welcome you, or naked and clothe you? When did we see you ill or in prison, and visit you?' And the king will say to them in reply, 'Amen, I say to you, whatever you did for one of these least brothers of mine, you did for me.' Then he will say to those on his left, 'Depart from me, you accursed, into the eternal fire prepared for the Devil and his angels. For I was hungry and you gave me no food, I was thirsty and you gave me no drink, a stranger and you gave me no welcome, naked and you gave me no clothing, ill and in prison, and you did not care for me.' Then they will answer and say, 'Lord, when did we see you hungry or thirsty or a stranger or naked or ill or in prison, and not minister to your needs?' He will answer them, 'Amen, I say to you, what you did not do for one of these least ones, you did not do for me.' And these will go off to eternal punishment, but the righteous to eternal life."

Matthew 25: 31-46

BLESSED ELIZABETH OF THE TRINITY

Urging her to rise above her grief, Elizabeth writes to a friend:
"Is it not a comfort to think that He who is to be our judge dwells within us throughout our miseries to save us and to forgive our sins? St. Paul affirms positively that we are 'justified freely by His grace, . . . through faith in His blood.' [Rom. 3:24–25]. *How rich we are in the gifts of God, predestinate by divine adoption, and so heirs of the inheritance of His glory!"*

The Praise of Glory, 135

REFLECTION

Teachers usually do not give their student a copy of the exams beforehand, but this is precisely what Jesus, the Divine Teacher, does for us. He details the behaviors that enable us to "pass the test" when our time comes for our loving Creator to ask us to reflect on how we have imaged God before others. The test deals exclusively with human relationships. As the unveiled face of God is revealed to us, the awesome reality of ourselves as created in the divine image and likeness unfolds before our astonished gaze. We see not only God, but also into the depth of our innermost being. We see with stark clarity the un-God-like behaviors that have clouded the divine image before others. As we gaze into the heart of God as a communion of Trinitarian love, the ways in which we fail to love, our neglect of persons in their need, the quality of our relationship with others, is seen in all its shortcomings.

Blessed Elizabeth reminds us, "our judge dwells within us throughout our miseries to save us and to forgive our sins." While we sadden the heart of God by not being God-like in genuine love toward others, Jesus is ever present to encourage us to repentance and conversions of heart. The gaze of His merciful love sees not only our inadequacies, but also the neglects, hurts and abuses we may have suffered that we now unreflectively act out on others. As "predestinate by divine adoption and so heirs of the inheritance of His glory," we can pray for the grace to love with God's own love. Each day, "little by little" we do the best in our ability to express this love toward the persons God places in our life.

How often do I reflect on the events of my day to consider if I have passed the test that Jesus holds before me in this Gospel? If I have failed the test, do I take comfort, "to think that He who is to be *my* judge dwells within *me* throughout *my* miseries to save *me* and to forgive *my* sins?"

PRAYER

Merciful Jesus, your indwelling presence illumines the dark corners of my heart revealing the many ways in which I neglect you in others. At the same time, "You dwell within my miseries to save me." Grant that this realization might fill me with compassion and forgiveness toward those who may have neglected me in my need. Expand my wounded heart with desire to extend to others the merciful love I receive from you as I come to recognize you in serving them. I offer my prayer to you trusting in your merciful love. Amen.

FIRST WEEK OF LENT — TUESDAY

GOSPEL

JESUS SAID TO HIS DISCIPLES:

"In praying, do not babble like the pagans, who think that they will be heard because of their many words. Do not be like them. Your Father knows what you need before you ask him.

"This is how you are to pray:

Our Father who art in heaven,
    hallowed be thy name,
    thy Kingdom come,
thy will be done,
    on earth as it is in heaven.
Give us this day our daily bread;
and forgive us our trespasses,
    as we forgive those who trespass against us;
and lead us not into temptation,
    but deliver us from evil.

"If you forgive men their transgressions, your heavenly Father will forgive you. But if you do not forgive men, neither will your Father forgive your transgressions."

MATTHEW 6: 7-15

BLESSED ELIZABETH OF THE TRINITY

On the eight day of her second retreat, Elizabeth writes:

"'Our Father, who art in heaven.' We must seek Him, and above all, we must dwell in the little heaven He has made for Himself in the center our soul. Christ told the Samaritan woman that the Father seeks adorers "who shall adore Him in spirit and in truth" [John 4:23]. Let us be those fervent adorers and rejoice in His heart. Let us adore Him in spirit; that is, with the heart and thoughts bent on Him, our spirit filled with knowledge of Him imparted by the light of faith. Let us adore Him in truth by our actions, which make us true by our always doing what will please the Father, whose children we are. In short, 'let us adore in spirit and in truth.' Then we shall be children of God and shall learn by experience the truth of what Isaiah said: 'You shall be carried at the breasts, and upon the knees shall they caress you' [Isaiah 66:12]. In fact, God appears to occupy Himself solely with overwhelming the soul with caresses and marks of affection, like a mother who fondles her babe and feeds it with her milk. Let us listen to the Father's mysterious appeal: 'My son, (daughter) give me thy heart'" [Proverbs 23:26].

The Praise of Glory, 299–300

REFLECTION

This lengthy quote from Blessed Elizabeth takes us to the deeper meaning of this Gospel passage where Jesus teaches us how to pray. One's heart is the heaven where God dwells. To hallow God's name we need not "babble on" but simply keep the heart centered in God. The Lord's Prayer is a prayer of the heart and it finds expression in doing what we know pleases God, especially in forgiving others as God has forgiven us.

Christ is teaching us how to be God-like, how to live as God's children and be attentive to the will of God in the challenges of each day. As God forgives us, we are to forgive others. As Christ nourishes us through the gift of Himself, the living bread of the Eucharist, so are we to nourish others by our self-giving, caring and forgiving love. The Our Father is both a prayer and a way of life through which God caresses the soul with marks of affection like a mother who fondles her babe and feeds it with her milk. Frequently pray this prayer slowly, letting each word find a home in you. The Lord's Prayer wants to be so internalized that it will arise from our inner depth and begin to pray itself in us.

Am I able to penetrate beyond human concepts of "father" into the heart of God whose unconditional love enfolds me in being and draws me into intimacy? Have I ever slowly pondered each word of this prayer to lets it meaning penetrate my mind and heart?

PRAYER

Ever-loving God, as your very dear children you are all things to us: father, mother, friend, and beloved. You forgive our sins; you protect us from temptation and deliver us from the evils that keep us from being centered in your will. Keep me ever mindful that you dwell in "the little heaven you have made for yourself in the center of my soul." I offer my prayer to you, ever loving God, in the name of your beloved Son our Lord Jesus Christ. Amen.

First Week of Lent — Wednesday

GOSPEL

While still more people gathered in the crowd, Jesus said to them, "This generation is an evil generation; it seeks a sign, but no sign will be given it, except the sign of Jonah. Just as Jonah became a sign to the Ninevites, so will the Son of Man be to this generation. At the judgment the queen of the south will rise with the men of this generation and she will condemn them, because she came from the ends of the earth to hear the wisdom of Solomon, and there is something greater than Solomon here. At the judgment the men of Nineveh will arise with this generation and condemn it, because at the preaching of Jonah they repented, and there is something greater than Jonah here."

LUKE 11: 29-32

BLESSED ELIZABETH OF THE TRINITY

Elizabeth, having discovered her new name in St. Paul writes:

"The 'praise of glory' is a soul that dwells in God, with the pure, disinterested love which does not seek self in the sweetness of His love; a soul that loves Him above all His gifts, and would have loved Him as much had it received nothing, which wishes well the object of its tenderness. But how can we wish well to God, except by accomplishing His will, since this will ordains all things for His greater glory? Such a soul should surrender itself fully, blindly, to this will so that it cannot possibly wish anything but what God wishes."

The Praise of Glory, 95–96

REFLECTION

It seems that some of Jesus' followers were urging Jesus to display his miraculous powers, possibly to enhance their own position as followers of this great wonder-worker. They failed to penetrate the wisdom of his words, more profound than those of the great King Solomon. Jonah

49

resisted the will of God but after spending three days and three nights in the belly of the whale, his preaching brought the entire city to conversion. Jesus points to Jonah as foreshadowing his own death and resurrection. His followers failed to recognize that someone greater than both Solomon and Jonah was in their midst.

Blessed Elizabeth loved Christ not in order to receive signs of his love, "she would have loved him had she received nothing." Her one desire was to wish only what God desired of her. She did not seek sweetness in prayer, but simply desired to abide in God. Jesus, Holy Wisdom enfleshed in our midst, invites us to a faith like that of Blessed Elizabeth. We too are to surrender ourselves fully, blindly to God's will so as to wish only what God wishes and knows to be best for our transformation in Christ.

Do I put conditions on God, bargaining with God in the effort to have thing go my way instead of surrendering myself to God's will? Do I really believe that God's transforming love "ordains all things in me for God's greater glory," especially in life's difficult moments?

PRAYER

Jesus, when my life seems without evidence of your abiding presence, and all seems dark, give me the grace of a deepened faith that I indeed belong to you and that you are with me. The "sign" of your love at such times is your gift of fidelity by which I continue on in dark faith and in surrender, believing that you are with me. Save me from the demons of discouragement and keep me faithful to you so that like Blessed Elizabeth, I too may be a praise of your glory. I offer my prayer through you, Lord Jesus trusting that you will help me to let myself be loved by you. Amen.

First Week of Lent — Thursday

GOSPEL

JESUS SAID TO HIS DISCIPLES:

"Ask and it will be given to you; seek and you will find; knock and the door will be opened to you. For everyone who asks, receives; and the one who seeks, finds; and to the one who knocks, the door will be opened. Which one of you would hand his son a stone when he asked for a loaf of bread, or a snake when he asked for a fish? If you then, who are wicked, know how to give good gifts to your children, how much more will your heavenly Father give good things to those who ask him.

"Do to others whatever you would have them do to you. This is the law and the prophets."

MATTHEW 7: 7-12

BLESSED ELIZABETH OF THE TRINITY

From her bed in the infirmary Blessed Elizabeth writes to a dear friend:

"I am asking Our Lord Himself to be your Master, your Friend, your Confidant, your Strength; may He make your soul into a little heaven where He can rest with happiness, and remove from it anything that might offend His divine gaze. He loves brave and generous hearts, and he said to one of His saints: 'Your measure will be my measure.' So make Him a very large measure; He so desires to fill His little Louise. . . . And then remember that love must end in sacrifice."

Complete Works, vol. 2: Letter 291

REFLECTION

Why is it that Jesus' reassuring words, "ask and you shall receive, seek and you shall find," is not always our experience? We ask and it seems we do not receive or what we receive is not to our liking. We pray for the healing of a loved one and he or she dies leaving us bewildered and lonely. In such instances Blessed Elizabeth would encourage us to be open to the hidden blessing that in time will reveal itself if we remain open. As Christ gently drew his disciples to a deeper faith, Christ also draws us so that we too will trust in firmness of faith that our heavenly Father gives only good things to those who ask. With a brave and generous heart, we will try to act in such a way as not to offend the divine gaze as faithfully we do to others what we have them do to us so that the awesome gift of God's abiding presence might always be with us. Like Blessed Elizabeth, Christ, our Master, our Friend, our Confidant and our Strength would make our soul a little heaven where He can rest with happiness.

The words of Blessed Elizabeth to her friend, Louise, challenge us to reflect: is Christ truly my Friend, my Confident and my Strength? Do I have the eyes of faith to recognize the hidden ways in which my prayer may have been answered, different from my expectation? Do I treat others, as I would like them to treat me?

PRAYER

Gracious God and giver of all good gifts, in Christ Jesus, the greatest gift of all, you teach us to recognize all of life as your gift even when life entails sacrifice as it did for your beloved Son. Enlarge my heart to receive a full measure of your Love so that I may be a channel of loving kindness toward others as the overflow of your countless hidden blessings in me. I offer my prayer to you in Jesus name. Amen.

First Week of Lent — Friday

GOSPEL

Jesus said to his disciples:

"I tell you, unless your righteousness surpasses that of the scribes and Pharisees, you will not enter into the Kingdom of heaven.

"You have heard that it was said to your ancestors, *You shall not kill; and whoever kills will be liable to judgment.* But I say to you, whoever is angry with his brother will be liable to judgment, and whoever says to his brother, *Raqa,* will be answerable to the Sanhedrin, and whoever says, 'You fool,' will be liable to fiery Gehenna. Therefore, if you bring your gift to the altar, and there recall that your brother has anything against you, leave your gift there at the altar, go first and be reconciled with your brother, and then come and offer your gift. Settle with your opponent quickly while on the way to court. Otherwise your opponent will hand you over to the judge, and the judge will hand you over to the guard, and you will be thrown into prison. Amen, I say to you, you will not be released until you have paid the last penny."

Matthew 5: 20-26

BLESSED ELIZABETH OF THE TRINITY

To a Sister in her community Blessed Elizabeth writes:

"Do not feel sad or discouraged if your nature wars upon you or is the field of battle; I would even say, love your own misery, for it is the subject of God's mercy. When the sight of it saddens you or throws you back on self, the cause is self-love. In times of discouragement take refuge in the prayer of the Divine Master; He saw you and prayed for you on the cross. This prayer of His lives and is present eternally before His Father; it is that which will save you from your miseries. The more you realize your weakness, the more confident you should feel, for then you depend on Him alone."

The Praise of Glory, 189

REFLECTION

Jesus is pained that the scribes and Pharisees have yet to penetrate the meaning of God's Covenant love. They felt they were justified in sitting in judgment and condemning others because they forgot their own need for God's mercy and compassion. Feeling self-righteous, they condemned anyone who did not observe the endless precepts of the law. They also considered unclean persons who were ill or were foreigners and refused to associate with them. Jesus reverses such behavior and challenges the scribes and Pharisees, *just as He challenges us,* to be the first to reach out in a gesture of reconciliation, especially toward anyone who has anything *against us that* all persons might come to live together in peace and harmony. This is a gift worthy to be offered at God's altar.

Blessed Elizabeth reminds us that our very nature wars against us. The miseries of our self-love and our pride can keep us estranged from persons we love because neither is willing, with humility and courage, to reach out seeking forgiveness. Our weakness need not prevent us from a gesture of reconciliation since Christ is present, praying in us and desiring to save us from our weakness. Blessed Elizabeth reaffirms that the only worthy gift that we can bring to the altar is a heart free to love. Our true identity is in Christ who reveals the face of God as Trinitarian Relational Love. For God's love to truly be alive in us, we too must be in relational communion with others, as the Gospels will frequently remind us.

Do past hurts, or attachment to feelings of anger or resentment, keep me from reaching out seeking forgiveness? Do feelings of self-righteousness keep me in bondage, a prisoner of my human miseries?

PRAYER

Jesus, on the Cross you prayed to your Father to forgive those who treated you with injustice and severe cruelty. This prayer is eternally present before your Father. May it save me from my weakness and open my heart to love, to forgiveness, and to confidence so that with complete trust in your healing love I can offer the gift of myself on the altar of your love as a sacrifice pleasing to you. I offer this prayer to you, trusting in your merciful love. Amen.

First Week of Lent — Saturday

Gospel

Jesus said to his disciples:

"You have heard that it was said, *You shall love your neighbor and hate your enemy.* But I say to you, love your enemies, and pray for those who persecute you, that you may be children of your heavenly Father, for he makes his sun rise on the bad and the good, and causes rain to fall on the just and the unjust. For if you love those who love you, what recompense will you have? Do not the tax collectors do the same? And if you greet your brothers and sisters only, what is unusual about that? Do not the pagans do the same? So be perfect, just as your heavenly Father is perfect."

Matthew 5: 43-48

BLESSED ELIZABETH OF THE TRINITY

On the tenth day of her last retreat, Blessed Elizabeth wrote this reflection:

"'Be perfect as your heavenly Father is perfect.' When my Master makes me understand these words in the depth of my soul, it seems to me that He is asking me to live like the Father, 'in an eternal present,' 'with no before, no after' but wholly in the unity of my being in this 'eternal Now.' What is this present? This is what David tells me: 'They will adore Him always because of Himself' [Psalm 71:15]. *This is the eternal present in which Laudem Gloriae must be established."*

Complete Works, vol. 1: 152–53

REFLECTION

Created as we are in the divine image and likeness, Christ both challenges and empowers us to love as God loves so that God's indwelling Presence might have a visibility in our lives. God is Love and God's love does not discriminate among the good and the bad. The wideness of God's merciful love challenges us to be nonjudgmental toward others. We need not approve of sinful or inappropriate behaviors, but we cannot reject another in one's heart because of their sin. Certain circumstances, such as abusive actions, may necessitate physical distance, but the challenge to forgiveness is always in the heart calling us to love as God loves. If we often find it difficult to be cordial toward persons we dislike, but have not harmed us, how can we love those who hurt us by their words, or who do us physical of psychic harm?

Blessed Elizabeth offers us a path to follow in order to have a forgiving heart and therefore "be perfect as our heavenly Father is perfect." She invites us to live "mindfully." For her, this means the practice of striving, both to love, and to live in continued awareness of God's abiding presence. Each moment is a gift pregnant with eternity. Elizabeth calls it, The Eternal Now.

But how do we realize living mindfully in our often over-busy lives? A simple practice is to pause briefly to enter within—imagine yourself rock climbing down into a deep ravine where all is still and peaceful and where divine love invitingly draws you downward into your own deep center. This is a place beyond feelings of resentment, anger and the desire to retaliate. Here in the "eternal now" of God, in this center of peace, paradoxically, before us might arise images of past hurts: experiences of rejection by persons we love, the shame of sexual abuse, or of personal failures, etc.

Unfortunately, alongside the self as image of God, stand self-constructed images which tell us: "I am a bad person, I am not likeable, I can never succeed, etc." To be perfect as our heavenly Father is perfect means in this moment of the eternal now, to denounce these false, self constructed idols which control our lives, so that with Elizabeth, we will "adore Him always because of Himself," and grow to love ourselves and others with God's own love. As we learn to live in the "now of God" the perfection of God will flow through us with compassion and forgiving love.

Do I make efforts to be kind to persons I dislike and to make sincere efforts to come to a better understanding of them and their history of hurts, etc.? Do I pray for the grace of a compassionate heart? Have I ever entered into the deep cavern of my heart to face the false idols that too easily define my behaviors and constrict my ability to love?

PRAYER

Jesus, you are a true friend; you lead me into the truth of my own inadequacies and yet you never stop loving me. How can I reject others when you are so accepting of me even in my failures? Keep me centered in you and may your image and likeness in which I am created come to perfection in me. I pray in your name, Lord Jesus in whose friendship I rejoice. Amen.

SECOND WEEK OF LENT

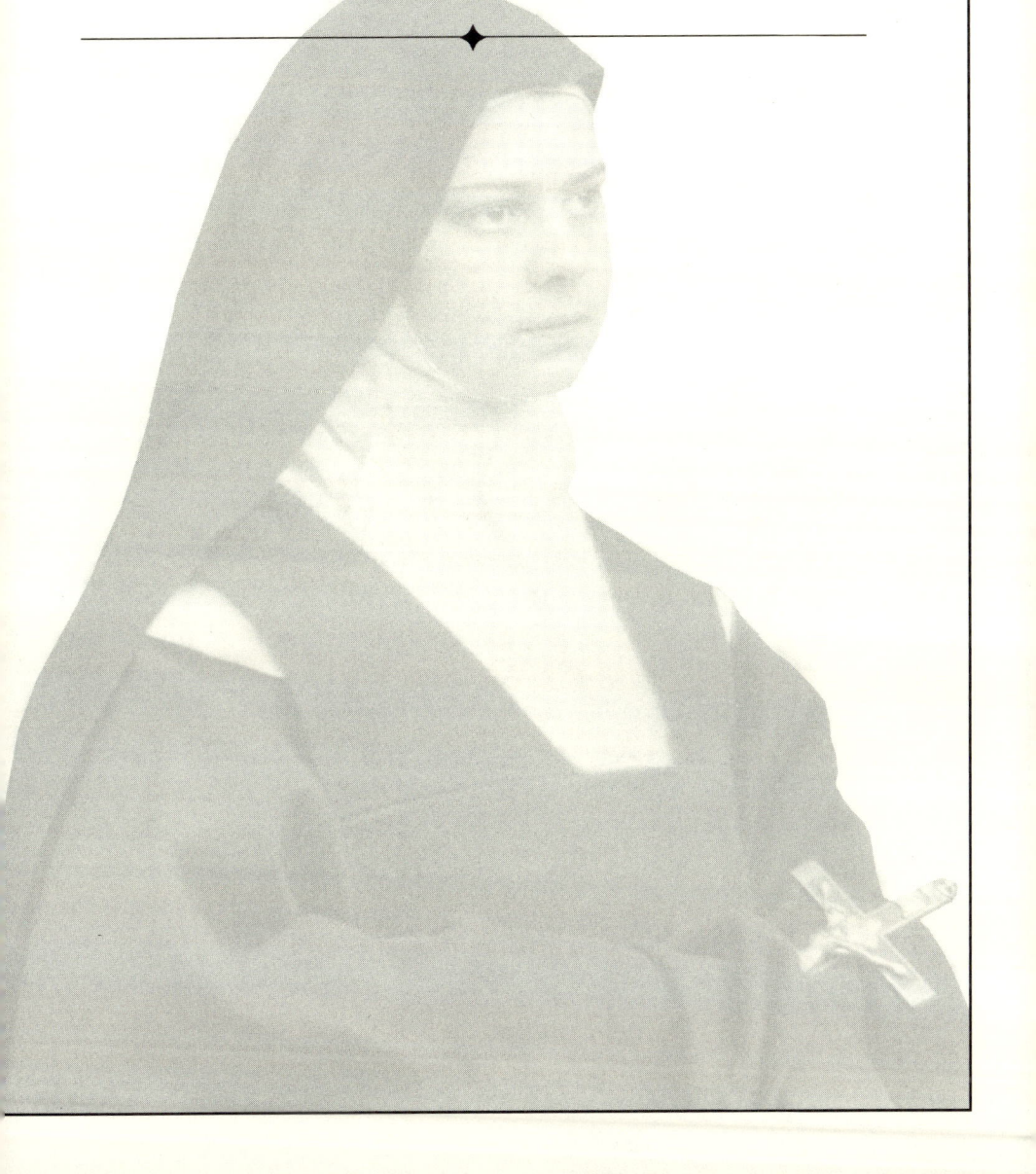

Second Sunday of Lent — Year A

Gospel

Jesus took Peter, James, and John his brother, and led them up a high mountain by themselves. And he was transfigured before them; his face shone like the sun and his clothes became white as light. And behold, Moses and Elijah appeared to them, conversing with him. Then Peter said to Jesus in reply, "Lord, it is good that we are here. If you wish, I will make three tents here, one for you, one for Moses, and one for Elijah." While he was still speaking, behold, a bright cloud cast a shadow over them, then from the cloud came a voice that said, "This is my beloved Son, with whom I am well pleased; listen to him." When the disciples heard this, they fell prostrate and were very much afraid. But Jesus came and touched them, saying, "Rise, and do not be afraid." And when the disciples raised their eyes, they saw no one else but Jesus alone.

As they were coming down from the mountain, Jesus charged them, "Do not tell the vision to anyone until the Son of Man has been raised from the dead."

MATTHEW 17: 1-9

BLESSED ELIZABETH OF THE TRINITY

In the third day of her retreat entitled Heaven on Faith Blessed Elizabeth, quoting Scripture and John of the Cross, writes:

"'Because I love my Father, I do always the things that are pleasing to Him.' Thus spoke our holy Master, and every soul who wants to live close to Him must also live this maxim. The divine good pleasure must be its food, its daily bread; it must let itself be immolated by all the Father's wishes in likeness of His adored Christ. Each incident, each event, each suffering, as well as each joy, is a sacrament which gives God to us; so it no longer makes a distinction between these things; it surmounts them, goes beyond them to rest in its Master, above all things. It 'exalts' Him high on the 'mountain of the heart.' Yes, 'higher than His gifts, His consolation, higher than the sweetness that descends upon

Him.' 'The property of love is never to seek self, to keep back nothing, but to give everything to the one it loves.'"

Complete Works, vol. 1: 9

REFLECTION

Peter, James, and John are intimate friends of Jesus but they still had much to learn. They had yet to "exalt" Jesus, "on the high mountain of the heart." Understandably they were overwhelmed by the experience and wanted to stay in the joy and consolation of this awesome event—"to build three tents," to stay rooted in the moment. But there was still a long journey ahead for them. A bright cloud intervened and a voice from the cloud seared itself into their hearts. "This is my Beloved Son with whom I am well pleased; listen to Him." They had not *listened* when Jesus spoke of His impending death. They had refused to hear with the heart that such a thing would happen to Him. A crucified Messiah did not fit their image, that of a triumphant hero conqueror. When they opened their eyes, "they saw no one else but Jesus alone." In spite of the cloud, the voice, the presence of Moses and Elijah, they had yet to recognize Jesus as God's beloved Son; they had yet to truly hear His message of self-giving love that would take Him to His death.

Elizabeth of the Trinity penetrated the mystery of Jesus. Hers was a *listening heart*. Since childhood, God's grace had cultivated this in her so that she was ready to give everything to the One she loved. Unlike Peter and the others who would stay transfixed in the awesomeness of the moment to avoid Jesus prediction of suffering, for Elizabeth "each incident, each event, each suffering as well as each joy" were all like a sacrament that *communicated* God to her. Like Jesus who offered everything to His Father, she gave everything to the One she loved.

Peter, James, and John were fearful in the strange awesomeness of the moment. In our own lives, for many reasons, we too experience fear. When things go well, we fear lest it not last. We fear suffering, loss of health, financial loss, loss of loved ones—life has many tragedies. But if we heed the Father's voice and learn to *listen* to Jesus, we will not be tempted to settle in on the mountain of our joys, but neither will we despair when in the dark valleys of our pain. Like the disciples, we will feel the touch of Jesus inviting us to rise and not be afraid for He is ever near.

Is mine a heart that really hears other persons when they speak? Are my thoughts focused instead on my contribution to the conversation? Do I assume I already know what the other person is going to say so that instead of really listening, impatiently I let my thoughts be elsewhere? Do I truly hear the words of Jesus spoken through the Gospels so my life, like His, will ultimately be transfigured in glory?

PRAYER

Blessed Elizabeth, obtain for me the grace of a listening heart. Draw me into inner stillness to hear Jesus' Indwelling Spirit guiding me to holiness of life. May the words spoken of Jesus echo within: "You are my beloved with whom I am well pleased." As always, I pray in Jesus' name. Amen.

Second Sunday of Lent — Year B

GOSPEL

Jesus took Peter, James and John and led them up a high mountain apart by themselves. And he was transfigured before them, and his clothes became dazzling white, such as no fuller on earth could bleach them. Then Elijah appeared to them along with Moses, and they were conversing with Jesus. Then Peter said to Jesus in reply, "Rabbi, it is good that we are here! Let us make three tents: one for you, one for Moses, and one for Elijah." He hardly knew what to say, they were so terrified. Then a cloud came, casting a shadow over them; from the cloud came a voice, "This is my beloved Son. Listen to him." Suddenly, looking around, they no longer saw anyone but Jesus alone with them.

As they were coming down from the mountain, he charged them not to relate what they had seen to anyone, except when the Son of Man had risen from the dead. So they kept the matter to themselves, questioning what rising from the dead meant.

MARK 9: 2-10

BLESSED ELIZABETH OF THE TRINITY

On November 21, the Feast of Mary's Presentation in the Temple, a day on which the Carmelites of Dijon had gathered in the Oratory to renew their religious vows, Elizabeth wrote her well-known prayer to the Trinity, given here in part:

"O Eternal Word, Word of my God, I want to spend my life in listening to You, to become wholly teachable that I may learn all from You. Then through all nights, all voids, all helplessness, I want to gaze on You always and remain in Your great light. O my beloved Star, so fascinate me that I may not withdraw from Your radiance."

Complete Works, vol. 1: 183

REFLECTION

No wonder the apostles were terrified. In Jewish history, the brilliant white light, the cloud, the mountain, were manifestations of the Holy One of Israel whose name was too sacred to voice. Then, Moses and Elijah appear, great Israelite prophets both of whom encountered God on the mountain. God appeared to Moses in the midst of thunder and lightning and in a heavy cloud—while for Elijah, the Lord was not in the wind, the earthquake and the fire. These passed by. The Lord came, "in the whisper of a gentle breeze" or as it is sometimes translated, "in the sound of sheer silence" (1 Kings 19: 11ff).

Different from these theophanies of former times, on the mountain of Transfiguration, God proclaimed the divine presence to be in our midst in Christ—"This is my beloved Son, listen to Him." God is not in some remote distant heaven, but intimately near in Christ. God not only sustains us in being, but through God's indwelling Trinitarian Presence invites us into a relationship of intimacy as lover to the beloved. For such intimacy with God to be actualized in us, we need a listening heart. To truly listen, the heart needs the protection of silence. Silence creates space for the Word of God to be heard. Jesus speaks to us through all the events of each day as Elizabeth experienced so profoundly. Through "all her nights, all voids, all helplessness," as she suffered interior darkness and physical pain, she maintained a silent, listening heart. In a letter to a friend (Letter 164), Elizabeth expresses a reality ever present in her heart: "May our life flow into His. May this truly be our dwelling place on earth. There let us be silent that we may listen to Him who has so much to tell us."

The overabundance of communication technologies easily noise out that sacred place of inner silence. It is not a void but is the place where Christ is to be found. Early Christian writers, as is a practice in other spiritual traditions, encourage the practice of attentiveness to one's breathing as a means of quieting the mind and entering into the inner silence of the heart. As we intentionally spend fifteen or twenty minutes each day just being attentive to our life breath as it goes in and out—perhaps using a sacred word to sustain the rhythm of our breathing—"in the sound of sheer silence," with Elizabeth, we "will learn all from God."

Have you ever reflected back to your earliest remembered awakening to the reality of God? Who are the people in your life who best image God for you? Where, or in what circumstances, do you feel closest to God?

PRAYER

Jesus, Beloved of God, draw me inward to that place of stillness where you speak words of love, mercy, forgiveness, and encouragement even in my life's darkest moments. Help me not to clutter my life with attachments to today's multiple demands for immediate communication. Help me to use wisely the many technologies that easily pollute my heart with noise so that like Elijah, I will be able to hear your voice in the sound of sheer silence. With Elizabeth, may I learn all from you, Lord Jesus as I pray in your name. Amen.

Second Sunday of Lent — Year C

GOSPEL

Jesus took Peter, John, and James and went up the mountain to pray. While he was praying his face changed in appearance and his clothing became dazzling white. And behold, two men were conversing with him, Moses and Elijah, who appeared in glory and spoke of his exodus that he was going to accomplish in Jerusalem. Peter and his companions had been overcome by sleep, but becoming fully awake, they saw his glory and the two men standing with him. As they were about to part from him, Peter said to Jesus, "Master, it is good that we are here; let us make three tents, one for you, one for Moses, and one for Elijah." But he did not know what he was saying. While he was still speaking, a cloud came and cast a shadow over them, and they became frightened when they entered the cloud. Then from the cloud came a voice that said, "This is my chosen Son; listen to him." After the voice had spoken, Jesus was found alone. They fell silent and did not at that time tell anyone what they had seen.

LUKE 9: 28B-36

BLESSED ELIZABETH OF THE TRINITY

Blessed Elizabeth writes to her sister:

"My dear little sister, let us awaken our faith, let us recall that He is there, within and that He wants us to be very faithful. So, when you feel as if you are about to lose your patience or say something against charity, bring yourself back to Him, let go of this natural inclination in order to please Him. How many acts of self-denial can be offered to Him, known to Him alone! Let us not waste them, my little sister. It seems to me that saints are souls who forget themselves all the time, who so lose themselves in Him whom they love, without looking at self, without a glance at the creature, that they can say with Saint Paul: 'It is no longer I who live, it is Jesus Christ who lives in me!'"

Complete Works, vol. 2: 127

REFLECTION

In all three of the Synoptic Gospels the account of Jesus' transfiguration is preceded by Jesus' first prediction of His passion. In this context, Jesus places before His followers the conditions for true discipleship. Jesus does not invite them to worldly success, but rather that they be willing to forfeit all so that God might be glorified in and through them as they live and proclaim the kingdom of God. God's kingdom involves denying oneself, carrying the cross of opposition and enduring hardships. Many of his followers would be martyred for their faith in Christ.

As Jesus is transfigured before Peter, James and John, Moses and Elijah also appear in glory. Both of them had suffered much in their fidelity to Israel's God. They understood that the road to glory was often through suffering as they "spoke of his exodus that he was going to accomplish in Jerusalem." Understandably, Peter wished to stay in the bliss of the moment but as the Gospel comments, "he did not know what he was saying." A voice from the cloud reminded the disciples of their need to *listen* and really *hear* what Jesus was saying to them. It was through his "exodus," his journey through suffering and death that in his resurrection, he would reveal the "glory" already his.

Our relationship with Christ is not about having warm feelings in prayer. Christ's indwelling presence is there to strengthen us in dark times and to help us to remain firm in our faith in the midst of the sufferings that life inevitably brings. Blessed Elizabeth encourages us to remain true to Christ by a vibrant faith in His abiding presence. Faith connects us with Christ who is always present and who enables us to let go of our natural inclinations if these would be against charity. Paul writes to the Romans, that: "faith is the *realization* of what is hoped for and *evidence* of things not seen." Faith makes our future fullness in Christ to be present in every passing moment. What is yet to be mysteriously is already ours. Like Elizabeth, we can be forgetful of self in service of others because we find our true identity in Christ. This is different from a psychologically destructive loss of self; rather it is a profound realization of who we truly are. From this reality does Elizabeth write: "I live now not I but Christ liveth in me." Our own "exodus" through the ups and downs of life is pregnant with the promise of future glory. Christ's transfiguration is realized in us as daily we move beyond self-centeredness into loving service of others. Through such denial of self do we become rooted in our true identity in Christ. Elizabeth could be completely oblivious of self because she was lost in Him whom she loved.

Do I ever reflect on the meaning of the sacrament of my Baptism? Through it I have been *incorporated* in Christ; become in a mysterious way, *bodily, corporeally* connected with Christ. ("Incorporation" derives from the Latin, "corpus" meaning "a body.") Am I able to withhold my natural inclinations when it is the loving thing to do? Am I able to deny myself when this is appropriate so that Christ might live more fully in me?

PRAYER

Lord Jesus, if I am to grasp the profound realty of *incorporation* in you, I need the special light of your Transfigured Presence. Deepen my faith so that I can move beyond being concerned only for myself and my own needs and interests to a greater concern for others. Help me to understand that it is in self-forgetfulness that I come to realize my true self in you. Help me to see your transfigured presence in all the persons that you place in my life so that I may always treat them with gracious, reverent care. Trusting your life in me, I offer this prayer. Amen.

SECOND WEEK OF LENT — MONDAY

GOSPEL

JESUS SAID TO HIS DISCIPLES:

"Be merciful, just as your Father is merciful.

"Stop judging and you will not be judged. Stop condemning and you will not be condemned. Forgive and you will be forgiven. Give and gifts will be given to you; a good measure, packed together, shaken down, and overflowing, will be poured into your lap. For the measure with which you measure will in return be measured out to you."

LUKE 6: 36-38

BLESSED ELIZABETH OF THE TRINITY

On the ninth day of her retreat entitled Heaven in Faith, in her second prayer Blessed Elizabeth creates a mosaic of texts from Ruysbroeck and Isaiah as she integrates these into her own reflections. She writes:

"Sin is such a terrifying evil that in order to seek any good whatsoever, or to avoid any evil whatsoever, no sin should be committed.' 'Now we have committed very many.' How can we keep from 'fainting in adoration when we plunge into the abyss of mercy and the eyes of our soul are fixed upon this fact: God has taken away our sins.' He said so Himself. 'I will blot out all their iniquities and I will no longer remember their sins.'

"The Lord in His mercy willed to turn our sins against themselves to our advantage; He found a way to make them useful for us, to convert them in our hands into a means of salvation. But do not let this diminish in any way our horror of sinning, now our sorrow for having sinned. But our sins become a source of humility for us.'"

Complete Works, vol. 1: 109

REFLECTION

The heart of this short Gospel passage contains Jesus' continued invitation to let our lives and our actions reflect God's image—the image of our true self. God is merciful; we are to be merciful both toward others and also toward ourselves. Unfortunately, within our hearts, along with the unique image of God that each of us is, there often exists a false self. Among other things, this false self would have us believe that we are no good; that we never do things right. Or conversely, that we are better, more holy than others, etc. If we tend to be harsh in judging ourselves, most likely we will project this kind of judgment on others.

Blessed Elizabeth is aware "that sin is a terrifying evil." But instead of harsh judgments on others she would have us, in adoration, "plunge into the abyss of mercy and keep our eyes fixed upon the fact that God, in Christ, has taken away our sins and made them a means toward our salvation, if they become a source of humility for us." Humility helps us to realize that none of us is without sin, yet each of us is infinitely loved by God. This awesome truth would have us fall down in adoration before the mystery of God's love for humankind. Humility is truth. The truth of ourselves is that we are indeed finite, fragile and sinful. At the same time, the incredible reality is, that God accepts us lovingly, and by God's invitation to conversion of heart, enlarges our heart to be loving and forgiving toward others as God has lovingly forgiven us. Just as God no longer remembers our sins, we will no longer dwell judgmentally on the sins of others as the light of a loving God transforms the darkness that creates the false self.

What grace do I need to pray for in order that my heart may be merciful as God is merciful? Do I judge myself harshly when I fail and then harshly judge others—forgetting that we are both infinitely loved by God—forgetting that God's love is a healing, forgiving love?

PRAYER

Ever-loving Father of our Lord Jesus Christ, as my heart becomes more free and open to receive the full measure of your love, unite my feeble efforts to share your merciful love with others with Christ's saving, redeeming gift of himself on the cross. May my life become increasingly one with the flow of his redeeming love. In his name, I pray. Amen.

SECOND WEEK OF LENT — TUESDAY

GOSPEL

Jesus spoke to the crowds and to his disciples, saying, "The scribes and the Pharisees have taken their seat on the chair of Moses. Therefore, do and observe all things whatsoever they tell you, but do not follow their example. For they preach but they do not practice. They tie up heavy burdens hard to carry and lay them on people's shoulders, but they will not lift a finger to move them. All their works are performed to be seen. They widen their phylacteries and lengthen their tassels. They love places of honor at banquets, seats of honor in synagogues, greetings in marketplaces, and the salutation 'Rabbi.' As for you, do not be called 'Rabbi.' You have but one teacher, and you are all brothers. Call no one on earth your father; you have but one Father in heaven. Do not be called 'Master'; you have but one master, the Christ. The greatest among you must be your servant. Whoever exalts himself will be humbled; but whoever humbles himself will be exalted."

MATTHEW 23: 1-12

BLESSED ELIZABETH OF THE TRINITY

Following yesterday's selection from her retreat *Heaven in Faith*, in her second prayer of the ninth day, Blessed Elizabeth continues:

"'If anyone should affirm to me that to find the bottom of the abyss is to be immersed in humility, I would not contradict him. However it seems to me that to be plunged into humility is to be plunged into God, for God is the bottom of the abyss. That is why humility, like charity, is always capable of increasing.'

"'Since a humble heart is the vessel needed, the vessel capable of containing the grace God wants to pour into it,' let us be 'humble.'

"'The humble can never rank God high enough nor themselves low enough. But here is the wonder: their weakness turns into wisdom, and the imperfections of their acts, always insufficient in their eyes, will be the greatest delight of their life. Whoever possesses humility has no need

of many words to be instructed: God tells him more things than he can learn; such was the case with the Lord's disciples.'"

Complete Works, vol. 1: 109–10

REFLECTION

The Pharisees used external things such as marks of distinction on their clothing, seeking places of honor, etc., to impress others with their importance. As could also be true of us in our life today, perhaps feelings of inadequacies before the overpowering Roman government resulted in their making greater efforts, both to impress others, and to bolster their own inadequate sense of self. As Jesus demonstrated through his own life and teachings, such external signs did not make the Pharisees credible teachers. Their proud behavior taught a doctrine of false values.

The writings of the great Flemish mystic, Ruysbroeck, resonated with Blessed Elizabeth. Here she continues to make his words her own. They echo what is in her heart regarding the virtue of humility: "To be plunged into humility is to be plunged into God." When the heart is plunged in God, Christ through His indwelling Spirit becomes himself our teacher who gently guides us so that our words and our actions are in harmony with what is in the heart.

"The humble can never rank God high enough nor themselves low enough." This reality is not about a lack of self-esteem or "putting oneself down." Rather than a putdown of self, the deeper we are "plunged into God," as interiorly we stand in mystery before the abyss of the God's incomprehensible love for us, what we are able to be or accomplish ourselves, fades into insignificance. We see with clarity that it is the flow of God's love through our lives and our endeavors that gives them value and makes them of benefit for others. Not in external show, but in humility of heart comes the source of true greatness. We need not fear our weakness, for as Blessed Elizabeth reminds us, "God turns our weakness into wisdom."

Christ challenges us with his words: "Do not be called 'Master'; you have but one master, the Christ." Do superficial realities "master" my life and constrict my freedom by my attachments to them? Do I define myself by my personal gifts and accomplishments? Does it ever occur to me to pray for humility of heart?

PRAYER

Jesus, open my heart to welcome you as my true Master and Teacher. Guide me to the realization that it is humility that illumines the truth of my deepest self. My inner being has its truest identity as an echo of you, the Father's Eternal Word. Deepen my awareness of this profound reality and may it lead me to an ever-greater acceptance of myself with all my imperfections. Help me to realize that my imperfections are not an issue with you as long as "plunging in humility," I "be plunged in you." I offer my prayer to you, trusting in your merciful love. Amen.

SECOND WEEK OF LENT — WEDNESDAY

GOSPEL

As Jesus was going up to Jerusalem, he took the Twelve disciples aside by themselves, and said to them on the way, "Behold, we are going up to Jerusalem, and the Son of Man will be handed over to the chief priests and the scribes, and they will condemn him to death, and hand him over to the Gentiles to be mocked and scourged and crucified, and he will be raised on the third day."

Then the mother of the sons of Zebedee approached Jesus with her sons and did him homage, wishing to ask him for something. He said to her, "What do you wish?" She answered him, "Command that these two sons of mine sit, one at your right and the other at your left, in your kingdom." Jesus said in reply, "You do not know what you are asking. Can you drink the chalice that I am going to drink?" They said to him, "We can." He replied, "My chalice you will indeed drink, but to sit at my right and at my left, this is not mine to give but is for those for whom it has been prepared by my Father." When the ten heard this, they became indignant at the two brothers. But Jesus summoned them and said, "You know that the rulers of the Gentiles lord it over them, and the great ones make their authority over them felt. But it shall not be so among you. Rather, whoever wishes to be great among you shall be your servant; whoever wishes to be first among you shall be your slave. Just so, the Son of Man did not come to be served but to serve and to give his life as a ransom for many."

MATTHEW 20: 17-28

BLESSED ELIZABETH OF THE TRINITY

On the fifth day of her last retreat, Blessed Elizabeth writes:

"The soul that wants to serve God day and night in His temple—I mean this inner sanctuary of which St. Paul speaks when he says: 'The temple of God is holy and you are that temple,' this soul must be resolved to share fully in its Master's passion. It is one of the redeemed who in turn must redeem others, and for that reason it will sing on its lyre: 'I glory in

the Cross of Jesus Christ.' 'With Christ I am nailed to the Cross . . .' And again, 'I suffer in my body what is lacking in the passion of Christ for the sake of His body, which is the Church.'"

Complete Works, vol. 1: 146

REFLECTION

Is it possible that the human struggle to be important in the eyes of others, to have authority over them, as was the wish of the two disciples in today's Gospel, is in fact a misplacement of an unrecognized existing reality, a lack of awareness of how important we already are? Signs of distinction in society are superficial compared to the inner reality that each person, created in the divine image and likeness, is infinitely loved by God. The prophet Isaiah assures us that, "God *delights* in us" (Isaiah 62:4). Blessed Elizabeth reminds us, quoting St. Paul, "The temple of God is holy and you are that temple."

Jesus compares himself to a mother hen who draws her chicks to herself. So would Jesus draw us to himself and embrace us in love to assure us of our importance in his eyes. He takes on our human nature to teach us how to live as members of God's family. Jesus immersed himself within the human condition with its propensity toward evil and sin. He surrendered to the injustice that resulted in his death with divinely heroic self-giving love.

The contagious energies of this incredible love were more than adequate to redeem a million worlds. It is such love that the Spirit would pour into the hearts of each one of us, the spark of which would gladly ignite into flames of love if our heart could be disposed for it. We have no need to climb the arduous ladder of success to be important before others. If we realized the gift that is already ours, willingly would we drink "the chalice" that each day offers. Jesus instructs his disciples in the meaning of true greatness. To be great is to place oneself at the service of others. To have the dignity of being first means willingness to be as available to others as a slave to its owner. We do this motivated by love and not by ambition for self-importance.

Loving service toward others takes many forms. Blessed Elizabeth holds *prayer itself as a form of service*. In prayer we "serve God day and night in the temple of the heart." Without prayer, we too quickly become weary in our service toward others and love falters and grows cold. Prayer instills courage to bear the cross of fidelity in the midst of the many hardships of daily living. Christ prays in us in the sanctuary of the heart and unites our acts of loving service and our prayer with his own redeeming love. In this sense, we share in the redemptive mission of Christ as we make the words of Paul, quoted by Blessed Elizabeth our own: "I suffer in my body what is lacking in the passion of Christ for the sake of His body, which is the Church."

How I spend my time indicates what is most valuable to me. Are my days so filled with "climbing the ladder of success" that I neglect family, friends and even God? Am I able to put aside my own concerns to be of service to others? Am I able to drink the chalice of daily living, with the trials and sufferings it often brings, as a privileged sharing in the sufferings of Christ? Instead, do I let myself be drawn into the dark pit of self-pity?

PRAYER

Compassionate Lord Jesus, you open to me the meaning of true greatness by embracing me in your redeeming love. Give me courage to drink the chalice of life in union with you. Open my heart to willing service of others without neglecting the service of prayer so that your divine life can freely flow through me. I offer my prayer to you with confidence in your mercy. Amen.

SECOND WEEK OF LENT — THURSDAY

GOSPEL

JESUS SAID TO THE PHARISEES:

"There was a rich man who dressed in purple garments and fine linen and dined sumptuously each day. And lying at his door was a poor man named Lazarus, covered with sores, who would gladly have eaten his fill of the scraps that fell from the rich man's table. Dogs even used to come and lick his sores. When the poor man died, he was carried away by angels to the bosom of Abraham. The rich man also died and was buried, and from the netherworld, where he was in torment, he raised his eyes and saw Abraham far off and Lazarus at his side. And he cried out, 'Father Abraham, have pity on me. Send Lazarus to dip the tip of his finger in water and cool my tongue, for I am suffering torment in these flames.' Abraham replied, 'My child, remember that you received what was good during your lifetime while Lazarus likewise received what was bad; but now he is comforted here, whereas you are tormented. Moreover, between us and you a great chasm is established to prevent anyone from crossing who might wish to go from our side to yours or from your side to ours.' He said, 'Then I beg you, father, send him to my father's house, for I have five brothers, so that he may warn them, lest they too come to this place of torment.' But Abraham replied, 'They have Moses and the prophets. Let them listen to them.' He said, 'Oh no, father Abraham, but if someone from the dead goes to them, they will repent.' Then Abraham said, 'If they will not listen to Moses and the prophets, neither will they be persuaded if someone should rise from the dead.'"

LUKE 16: 19-31

BLESSED ELIZABETH OF THE TRINITY

On the tenth day of her retreat Heaven in Faith, Blessed Elizabeth again makes the words of Ruysbroeck her own:

"For, as a pious author says, if contemplation 'continues toward praise and toward the eternity of its Lord, it possesses unity and will not lose it. If an order from heaven arrives, contemplation turns toward men sympathizes with their needs, is inclined toward all their miseries; it must cry and be fruitful. It illuminates like fire, and like it, it burns, absorbs and devours, lifting up to Heaven what is has devoured. And when it has finished its work here below, it rises burning with its fire, and takes up again the road on high.'"

Complete Works, vol. 1: 104

REFLECTION

Ultimately, everything that we have in life comes to us as a gift from God. It seems that the rich man became self-centered and oblivious to the needs of other. His riches became his identity. He felt no sense of connectedness with, or responsibility toward the poor beggar at his gate. His sense of self-sufficiency obscured his intrinsic relatedness both to God and to others so the eyes of his soul were blind to the beggar as a person in need. Instead of being moved to share his abundance with the beggar, perhaps he perceived this man covered with unsightly sores, as an object of embarrassment to be ignored or pushed aside.

Although the rich man considered himself a son of Abraham, and most likely he worshiped at the temple in Jerusalem, his inner and his outer life were in discontinuity. Elizabeth, on the contrary, through the words of "the pious author" again underscores the interconnectedness between active service toward those in need and the service of God through prayer. The fire of God's love directs our gaze outward as well as inward as the situation suggests. In this way everything that we do—be it prayer or active service—becomes transformed. The beggar at the gate, although humanly repulsive with his running sores, shines with the face of Christ for those who have eyes to see. All too late did a flow of compassion have the rich man ask that his five brothers be warned that they not follow him into the place of torment.

Elizabeth had a willing ear to listen to those who speak words of life-giving truth. The Pharisees, to whom Jesus addressed this parable, listened, but did not heed the words of Moses and the prophets who spoke of the promised Messiah, so neither would they listen and be converted when Jesus, in whom all the words of the prophets were fulfilled, would be risen from the dead.

Whose are the voices that I listen to and heed? Are they voices that open me to sympathize with the needs of others? Do I hear the voice of God inviting me to praise and to contemplation so that I might rise from all that I do, "burning with fire?"

PRAYER

Lord Jesus, the rich man closed his ears to the cry of Lazarus, open the ears of my heart to hear your voice in the many ways in which you speak to me. You speak to me through the scriptures, through the sacraments, and especially through the Eucharist. You also speak to me through others—through those who love me: family, friends, but also through those who, for whatever reason, make loving them more difficult. May I never wait until it is too late to reach out in compassion toward someone who has become distant from me so that I "may continue toward praise and toward the eternity of the Lord." I pray in your name with confident trust. Amen.

Second Week of Lent — Friday

Gospel

Jesus said to the chief priests and the elders of the people:

"Hear another parable. There was a landowner who planted a vineyard, put a hedge around it, dug a wine press in it, and built a tower. Then he leased it to tenants and went on a journey. When vintage time drew near, he sent his servants to the tenants to obtain his produce. But the tenants seized the servants and one they beat, another they killed, and a third they stoned. Again he sent other servants, more numerous than the first ones, but they treated them in the same way. Finally, he sent his son to them, thinking, 'They will respect my son.' But when the tenants saw the son, they said to one another, 'This is the heir. Come, let us kill him and acquire his inheritance.' They seized him, threw him out of the vineyard, and killed him. What will the owner of the vineyard do to those tenants when he comes?" They answered him, "He will put those wretched men to a wretched death and lease his vineyard to other tenants who will give him the produce at the proper times." Jesus said to them, "Did you never read in the Scriptures:

The stone that the builders rejected
*   has become the cornerstone;*
by the Lord has this been done,
*   and it is wonderful in our eyes?*

Therefore, I say to you, the Kingdom of God will be taken away from you and given to a people that will produce its fruit."

When the chief priests and the Pharisees heard his parables, they knew that he was speaking about them. And although they were attempting to arrest him, they feared the crowds, for they regarded him as a prophet.

Matthew 21: 33-43, 45-46

BLESSED ELIZABETH OF THE TRINITY

In the first prayer of the seventh day of her retreat Heaven in Faith, Blessed Elizabeth adds a contemporary challenge to the Gospel of the landowner and his vineyard. Interspersing the words of her favorite author Ruysbroeck with her own, Elizabeth writes:

"'Our created essence asks to be rejoined with its principle.' The Word, 'the splendor of the Father, is the eternal archetype after which creatures are designed on the day of their creation.' This is 'why God wills that, freed from ourselves, we should stretch out our arms toward our exemplar and possess it,' 'rising' above all things 'toward our model.' 'This contemplation opens' the soul 'to unexpected horizons.' 'In a certain manner it possesses the crown toward which it aspires.' 'The immense riches that God possesses by nature, we may possess by virtue of love, by His dwelling in us and by our dwelling in Him.'"

Complete Works, vol. 1: 103

REFLECTION

The parable of the vineyard in today's Gospel challenges us on many different levels. In Jesus' time, the vineyard in the parable would be understood to symbolize the people of Israel, many of whom were rejecting Jesus, the "Son," whom God, the owner of the vineyard, sent to them. They put to death the greatest of God's gift; God's Beloved, present in their midst who looked to them to bear good fruit.

God has placed us as tenants on our planet earth to tend and keep it in its pristine beauty. Like the chief priests and elders of the people who failed to produce fruit, is it possible that in our own way, we too deny God, the owner of our earthly vineyard, by greedy overconsumption of its natural resources? We have helped make toxic the air we breathe which is the breath of God sustaining us in being. The clear waters from the fountain of God that fill our oceans, rivers and streams, we cloud with pollution.

Ancient forests, reflecting the agelessness of God, have been leveled to satisfy our increasing wants. As we kill the life of our ecosystem, are we any different than the tenants of the vineyard who killed the owner's son?

Elizabeth's great love of nature is not reflected in this passage and ecological consciousness has yet to take hold. Never the less, her reflection penetrates the depths of today's challenge. What meaning can we find for today that, "our created essence asks to be rejoined with its principle?" According to John of the Cross, chapter 11 of the Spiritual Canticle, no. 3: "God's presence by essence gives all things life and being. Should this presence be lacking to them, they would be annihilated." Elizabeth reminds us that contemplation opens the soul to unexpected horizons. The realization that God's essential presence holds in existence all things from the mountain heights that reach toward the heavens to the minutest particle of matter, that all of nature has its life from God and is sustained in existence by God—such realization is indeed a contemplative experience. The heart recognizes that "The immense riches that God possesses by nature, we may possess by virtue of love, by His dwelling in us and by our dwelling in Him."

Elizabeth writes of "rising above all things toward our model." In this parable Christ models for us today the need for reverent care of God's Vineyard, our planet earth. To do so we need to rise above our selfish wants and live in respectful harmony with nature, contemplatively aware that God's essential presence holds all things in existence.

Am I conscious of how my use of things might be impacting the environment? Am I careful to recycle what can be re-used for other purposes? Do I take time to simply stand in awe before the splendor of the setting sun, to admire the beauty of a flower, or the smile of a child?

PRAYER

Creator God, grace me with a contemplative vision that I might experience the awesome reality of your ever-sustaining Presence. The ground under my feet, each tiny blade of grass, the air that I breathe, the wind on my face, are pregnant with your abiding Presence. May I so possess you, "the crown toward which all things aspire," so that your "sustaining love" enables me to sustain with reverent care all the wonders of the vineyard of earth. I offer my prayer through your Son in whom all things came to be. Amen.

Second Week of Lent — Saturday

Gospel

Tax collectors and sinners were all drawing near to listen to Jesus, but the Pharisees and scribes began to complain, saying, "This man welcomes sinners and eats with them." So to them Jesus addressed this parable. "A man had two sons, and the younger son said to his father, 'Father, give me the share of your estate that should come to me.' So the father divided the property between them. After a few days, the younger son collected all his belongings and set off to a distant country where he squandered his inheritance on a life of dissipation. When he had freely spent everything, a severe famine struck that country, and he found himself in dire need. So he hired himself out to one of the local citizens who sent him to his farm to tend the swine. And he longed to eat his fill of the pods on which the swine fed, but nobody gave him any. Coming to his senses he thought, 'How many of my father's hired workers have more than enough food to eat, but here am I, dying from hunger. I shall get up and go to my father and I shall say to him, "Father, I have sinned against heaven and against you. I no longer deserve to be called your son; treat me as you would treat one of your hired workers."' So he got up and went back to his father. While he was still a long way off, his father caught sight of him, and was filled with compassion. He ran to his son, embraced him and kissed him. His son said to him, 'Father, I have sinned against heaven and against you; I no longer deserve to be called your son.' But his father ordered his servants, 'Quickly, bring the finest robe and put it on him; put a ring on his finger and sandals on his feet. Take the fattened calf and slaughter it. Then let us celebrate with a feast, because this son of mine was dead, and has come to life again; he was lost, and has been found.' Then the celebration began. Now the older son had been out in the field and, on his way back, as he neared the house, he heard the sound of music and dancing. He called one of the servants and asked what this might mean. The servant said to him, 'Your brother has returned and your father has slaughtered the fattened calf because he has him back safe and sound.' He became angry, and when he refused

> to enter the house, his father came out and pleaded with him. He said to his father in reply, 'Look, all these years I served you and not once did I disobey your orders; yet you never gave me even a young goat to feast on with my friends. But when your son returns who swallowed up your property with prostitutes, for him you slaughter the fattened calf.' He said to him, 'My son, you are here with me always; everything I have is yours. But now we must celebrate and rejoice, because your brother was dead and has come to life again; he was lost and has been found.'"
>
> LUKE 15: 1-3, 11-32

BLESSED ELIZABETH OF THE TRINITY

In a letter to her friend Canon Angles a year before her death, Blessed Elizabeth writes:

"I am going to tell you a very personal secret: my dream is to be 'the praise of His glory,' I read that in St. Paul and my Bridegroom made me understand that this was to be my vocation while in exile, waiting to go to sing the eternal Sanctus in the City of the saints. But that requires great fidelity, for in order to be a praise of glory, one must be dead to all that is not He, so as to be moved only by His touch, and the worthless Elizabeth does such foolish things to her Master; but like a tender Father He forgives her, His divine glance purifies her and, like Saint Paul, she tries 'to forget what lies behind and press on toward what is ahead.'"

Complete Works, vol. 2: Letter 256

REFLECTION

As Elizabeth writes of herself, the younger son, having come to his senses, was able "to forget what lies behind" and move ahead in trust. He knew by experience of his father's generous heart. "How many of my father's hired workers have more than enough food to eat," so he would return and ask the father's forgiveness, and in humility, gladly take his place as servant among the other servants. In deep contrition he would entrust himself to the father's care.

The faithful older son had yet to penetrate the depth of the father's abundant love. Instead he justified himself on the work he did and judged his brother unfit to be loved. He went so far as to disclaim him as his brother—he said to his father on hearing the music and the dancing, "when *your son* returns who swallowed up your property"—whereas the father lovingly attempts to reconnect them—"*your brother was dead and has come to life.*"

If we look deeply into our own heart most likely we discover that like the younger son, as Elizabeth says: "we do such foolish things to our Master." We need to turn to the Father to be "purified by His divine glance" and like the prodigal son, experience the forgiveness of His welcoming embrace.

Are there not also times when like the older son, we are unsympathetic and judgmental toward others "when we do foolish things?" With Elizabeth, as we are: "waiting to sing the eternal Sanctus in glory" in eternal communion with all the saints, here "in exile," we belong to the communion of sinners. The behavior of both the younger and the older son invite us to grow in humility and self-knowledge without fear or discouragement. The father in the parable welcomed both of them: "Son, all I have is yours."

The Pharisees and the scribes complained that Jesus welcomed sinners and ate with them. Jesus is always present to us, even "in our foolishness." As one who never distains the company of sinners, Jesus not only eats with us, but is our nourishment in the transformed bread of the Eucharist.

Enriched as I am with God's extravagant love, what are the ways in which I squander it in superficial or sinful living? In my efforts to be faithful, what are the situations that tempt me to be judgmental or condemning of others in prideful self-righteous? Does God's welcoming love for sinners inspire me, with Elizabeth to be "the praise of His glory?"

PRAYER

Jesus, you said, "Who sees me sees the Father." Help me to keep my eyes fixed on you so that in your purifying gaze, I might see others through the eyes of your compassionate, merciful love and always be open to forgiveness and reconciliation. I offer my prayer to you, Lord Jesus, through whom the Father is manifest to me. Amen.

THIRD WEEK OF LENT

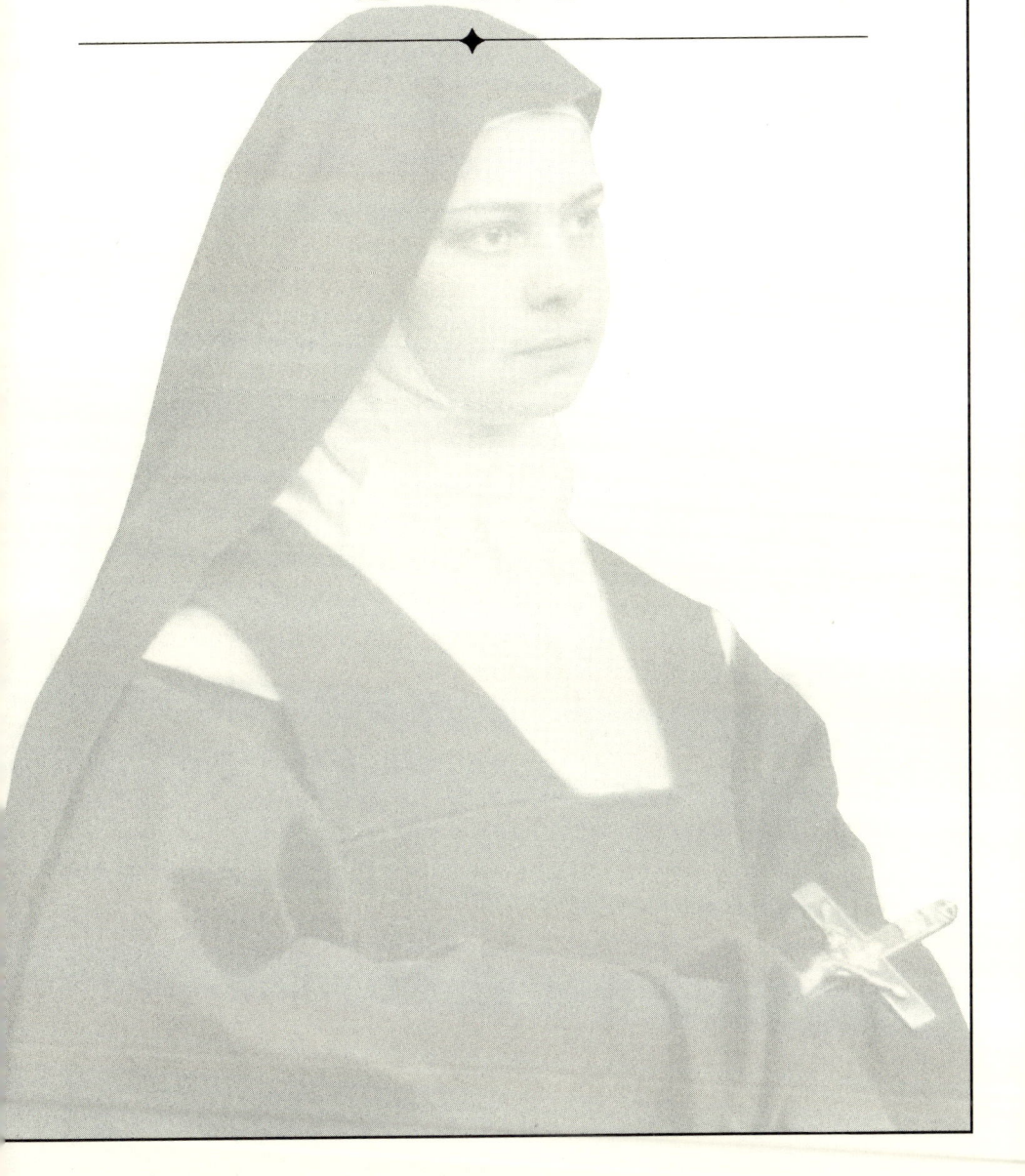

Third Sunday of Lent — Year A

Gospel

Jesus came to a town of Samaria called Sychar, near the plot of land that Jacob had given to his son Joseph. Jacob's well was there. Jesus, tired from his journey, sat down there at the well. It was about noon.

A woman of Samaria came to draw water. Jesus said to her, "Give me a drink." His disciples had gone into the town to buy food. The Samaritan woman said to him, "How can you, a Jew, ask me, a Samaritan woman, for a drink?" — For Jews use nothing in common with Samaritans. — Jesus answered and said to her, "If you knew the gift of God and who is saying to you, 'Give me a drink,' you would have asked him and he would have given you living water." The woman said to him, "Sir, you do not even have a bucket and the cistern is deep; where then can you get this living water? Are you greater than our father Jacob, who gave us this cistern and drank from it himself with his children and his flocks?" Jesus answered and said to her, "Everyone who drinks this water will be thirsty again; but whoever drinks the water I shall give will never thirst; the water I shall give will become in him a spring of water welling up to eternal life." The woman said to him, "Sir, give me this water, so that I may not be thirsty or have to keep coming here to draw water."

Jesus said to her, "Go call your husband and come back." The woman answered and said to him, "I do not have a husband." Jesus answered her, "You are right in saying, 'I do not have a husband.' For you have had five husbands, and the one you have now is not your husband. What you have said is true." The woman said to him, "Sir, I can see that you are a prophet. Our ancestors worshiped on this mountain; but you people say that the place to worship is in Jerusalem." Jesus said to her, "Believe me, woman, the hour is coming when you will worship the Father neither on this mountain nor in Jerusalem. You people worship what you do not understand; we worship what we understand, because salvation is from the Jews. But the hour is coming, and is now here, when true worshipers will worship the Father in Spirit and truth; and indeed the Father seeks such people to worship him. God is Spirit, and those who worship him must worship in Spirit and truth." The woman said to him, "I know that the Messiah is coming, the one called the Christ; when he comes, he will tell us everything." Jesus said to her, "I am he, the one speaking with you."

At that moment his disciples returned, and were amazed that he was talking with a woman, but still no one said, "What are you looking for?" or "Why are you talking with her?" The woman left her water jar and went into the town and said to the people, "Come see a man who told me everything I have done. Could he possibly be the Christ?" They went out of the town and came to him. Meanwhile, the disciples urged him, "Rabbi, eat." But he said to them, "I have food to eat of which you do not know." So the disciples said to one another, "Could someone have brought him something to eat?" Jesus said to them, "My food is to do the will of the one who sent me and to finish his work. Do you not say, 'In four months the harvest will be here'? I tell you, look up and see the fields ripe for the harvest. The reaper is already receiving payment and gathering crops for eternal life, so that the sower and reaper can rejoice together. For here the saying is verified that 'One sows and another reaps.' I sent you to reap what you have not worked for; others have done the work, and you are sharing the fruits of their work."

Many of the Samaritans of that town began to believe in him because of the word of the woman who testified, "He told me everything I have done." When the Samaritans came to him, they invited him to stay with them; and he stayed there two days. Many more began to believe in him because of his word, and they said to the woman, "We no longer believe because of your word; for we have heard for ourselves, and we know that this is truly the savior of the world."

JOHN 4: 5-42

Shorter form: JOHN 4:5-15, 19b-26, 39a, 40-42
Longer form may be optionally read on any day in the third week of Lent

BLESSED ELIZABETH OF THE TRINITY

On the ninth day, the first prayer of her retreat Heaven in Faith, in the following passage Elizabeth reflects on today's Gospel:

"Christ said one day to the Samaritan woman that 'the Father seeks true adorers in spirit and truth.' To give joy to His Heart, let us be these true adorers. Let us adore Him in 'spirit,' that is, with our hearts and our thoughts fixed on Him, and our mind filled with His knowledge imparted by the light of faith. Let us adore Him in 'truth,' that is, by our works for it is above all by our actions that we show we are true: this is to do always what is pleasing to the Father whose children we are. And finally, let us 'adore in spirit and in truth,' that is, through Jesus Christ and with Jesus Christ, for He alone is the true Adorer in spirit and truth."

Complete Works, vol. 1: 108

REFLECTION

In today's Gospel, the Samaritan woman expresses surprise that Jesus, a Jew, would speak to her—a woman and a Samaritan—even to ask a favor of her. As the Gospel writer tells us, Jews had nothing in common with Samaritans.

Whatever the historic situation that gave rise to this narrative, the Evangelist who wrote this Gospel could now penetrate its meaning from the perspective of Jesus' shameful death and triumphant resurrection from the dead. This experience led to a deeper penetration into the mystery of Jesus. Jesus is Lord! Jesus, having returned to his Father, was no longer physically present among them but as he had promised, they had been empowered by the outpouring of his Spirit on Pentecost. As they themselves became "adorers in spirit and in truth" they desired to draw others into this reality. Jesus' encounter with the Samaritan woman taught the disciples that all persons regardless of race, gender, or religion were all invited to drink of God's life-giving waters.

Blessed Elizabeth takes us beyond the superficial to the heart of this Gospel—that Christ invites each one of us, as he invited the Samaritan woman, to be "adorers in spirit and in truth." But how can this be realized in us? Like a skilled teacher, Blessed Elizabeth guides us through three important steps. First, we must become true adorers, which is to adore God in spirit, that is, *mindfully* with our heart and thoughts fixed on God who enlightens our faith with knowledge of God and of God's ways with us.

Second, we are to adore God in truth by our actions and good works. Actions witness to inner realities. Actions demonstrate that we do indeed *truly* adore God. To welcome the immigrant, the person whose language and culture differs from ours, as Jesus welcomed the Samaritan woman, to reach out to persons in need, is to become a *true* adorer.

Finally, Elizabeth would have us adore, both *in spirit and in truth,* that is, "*through* Jesus Christ and with Jesus Christ, for He alone is the true Adorer in spirit and in truth." It is Christ who adores the Father in us and it is His truth that we express in our actions as we reach out in love toward others. This deep reality invites prayerful pondering during this Lenten season so that the prayer of the Church in the first preface for Lent be realized in us: *Through the celebration of the Paschal Mystery you bring to perfection the image of your Son in us.*

Am I inclined to keep certain persons outside the sphere of my relationships because of prejudice toward their race or religion? Are my religious beliefs congruent with my behaviors? Do I pray for the grace of a closer relationship with Christ whose image is etched within and whose life I share through the grace of my Baptism?

PRAYER

Lord Jesus, as I reflect on your encounter with the Samaritan woman, I feel drawn to adore you in spirit and in truth. You place in my heart a desire to realize my true life in you. Come anew each day as "Adorer, as Restorer and as Savior" as Elizabeth prays in her prayer to the Trinity, that my life may a radiance of your life in me and that your image in me be brought to perfection. In your name I pray. Amen.

THIRD SUNDAY OF LENT — YEAR B

GOSPEL

Since the Passover of the Jews was near, Jesus went up to Jerusalem. He found in the temple area those who sold oxen, sheep and doves, as well as the money changers seated there. He made a whip out of cords and drove them all out of the temple area, with sheep and oxen, and spilled the coins of the money changers and overturned their tables, and to those who sold doves he said, "Take these out of here, and stop making my Father's house a marketplace." His disciples recalled the words of Scripture, *Zeal for your house will consume me.* At this the Jews answered and said to him, "What sign can you show us for doing this?" Jesus answered and said to them, "Destroy this temple and in three days I will raise it up." The Jews said, "This temple has been under construction for forty-six years, and you will raise it up in three days?" But he was speaking about the temple of his body. Therefore, when he was raised from the dead, his disciples remembered that he had said this, and they came to believe the Scripture and the word Jesus had spoken.

While he was in Jerusalem for the feast of Passover, many began to believe in his name when they saw the signs he was doing. But Jesus would not trust himself to them because he knew them all, and did not need anyone to testify about human nature. He himself understood it well.

JOHN 2: 13-25

BLESSED ELIZABETH OF THE TRINITY

"The soul that wants to serve God day and night in His temple—I mean this inner sanctuary of which St. Paul speaks when he says, 'The temple of God is holy and you are that temple,' this soul must be resolved to share fully its Master's passion. It is one of the redeemed who in its turn must redeem other souls, and for that reason it will sing on its lyre, 'I glory in the Cross of Jesus Christ,' 'With Christ I am nailed to the Cross'—and again, 'I suffer in my body what is lacking in the passion of Christ for the sake of His body, which is the Church.'"

Complete Works, vol. 1: 146

REFLECTION

The temple at Jerusalem was considered the sanctuary of God's dwelling in the midst of the Israelites, God's Chosen People. The ritual of sacrifice was integral to temple worship. The sheep, the oxen and the doves were sold there and then offered in sacrifice. Unfortunately, the buying and selling of the animals had become a lucrative business for those involved. Perhaps through greed, they lost a sense of the sacredness of their transactions. The holiness of the temple area was being desecrated. Consumed with zeal for His Father's House, Jesus instinctively cried out in protest as He encountered the Temple become like a marketplace. He gave a prophetic witness to His indignation by turning over the tables of the money changers and ordering those who sold doves to leave the temple area.

When challenged to reveal the meaning of this prophetic act, Jesus gave the sign of His impending death and resurrection. *Destroy this temple and in three days I will rebuild it.* Through his death on the cross, and His rising from the dead three days later, His Glorified Body would replace the Jerusalem Temple. He Himself would be an Eternal Temple sacred for all humankind.

Jesus would draw all of us into this unfathomable mystery. Through the gift of God's indwelling Presence, in Christ, our body, our entire being in Christ, becomes a temple, holy to the Lord. Rightly should we reverence the divine in one another.

Like Elizabeth, we too are called to serve God day and night in God's temple—this "inner sanctuary"—which is ourselves. This reality is possible right within whatever might be our life calling. It does not abstract us from daily living but is integral to it. Everything that life offers; our joys, and especially our sorrows and the many sufferings that inevitable come our way, these are all integral to the temple's "construction" as was Jesus' passion, death and resurrection to his own glorified body. As was true for Blessed Elizabeth, what is lacking in the sufferings of Christ is our unique participation in the drama of the cross through the sufferings, small or great, that are ours as members of His Body.

By cleansing the temple of Jerusalem, Jesus invites us to cleanse the inner temple of the heart. Is my inner being a market place, always frenetically busy, multi-tasking and rushing around from one thing to the next? What in my life keeps me from awareness of the Sacred within? Do I ever reflect on the reality that my list of things to do will never come to an end? There is always more that we can do. Do I take time for others with reverent care, especially to be present to loved ones? Does this Gospel inspire me to ask Jesus to cleanse my inner being so that I become a holy temple for God?

PRAYER

Blessed Elizabeth, by the example of your inspiring life, teach me the sacred art of mindfulness that I might realize the preciousness of each moment and the invitation it offers me to remain in the temple of the heart, even in the midst of everyday concerns.

Lord Jesus, strengthen me to glory in the sufferings that each day brings so that united with your sufferings, whatever happens will serve to cleanse the temple of my heart. Trusting in the intercession of Blessed Elizabeth I offer this prayer to you. Amen.

Third Week of Lent — Year C

GOSPEL

Some people told Jesus about the Galileans whose blood Pilate had mingled with the blood of their sacrifices. Jesus said to them in reply, "Do you think that because these Galileans suffered in this way they were greater sinners than all other Galileans? By no means! But I tell you, if you do not repent, you will all perish as they did! Or those eighteen people who were killed when the tower at Siloam fell on them – do you think they were more guilty than everyone else who lived in Jerusalem? By no means! But I tell you, if you do not repent, you will all perish as they did!"

And he told them this parable: "There once was a person who had a fig tree planted in his orchard, and when he came in search of fruit on it but found none, he said to the gardener, 'For three years now I have come in search of fruit on this fig tree but have found none. So cut it down. Why should it exhaust the soil?' He said to him in reply, 'Sir, leave it for this year also, and I shall cultivate the ground around it and fertilize it; it may bear fruit in the future. If not you can cut it down.'"

Luke 13: 1-9

BLESSED ELIZABETH OF THE TRINITY

At a time when her friend was experiencing "terrible voids" and other forms of mental and physical suffering, Blessed Elizabeth writes:

"When your soul is burdened and fatigued by the weight of your body, do not be discouraged, rather go by faith and love to Him who said: 'Come to me and I will refresh you.' As for your spirit, never let yourself be depressed by the thought of your sufferings. The great Saint Paul says: 'Where sin abounds, grace abounds all the more. It seems to me the weakest even the guiltiest soul is the one that has the most reason for hope; and the act of forgetting self and throwing oneself into the arms of God glorifies Him and gives Him more joy than all the turning inward and all the self-examinations that make one live with one's own infirmities, though the soul possesses at its very center a Savior who wants at every moment to purify it."

Complete Works, vol. 2: Letter 249

REFLECTION

Passed on from previous generations, in the time of Jesus people believed that suffering and misfortune were the result of one's personal sins or misdeeds, or those of one's parents or forebears. For Jesus, what is important is that we repent of our sins and come to Him who offers pardon and mercy. His hearers knew that the parable of the fig tree was about them and their nation. Unfortunately, they did not allow the life-giving words of Jesus to penetrate the soil of their hearts. When the early Christians listened to this Gospel, the city of Jerusalem referred to in scripture as "the vineyard of the Lord" had already been "cut down" by the Romans and their sacred temple destroyed never to be rebuilt. Even after frequent fertilization by the prophets, it had failed to bear fruit.

Jesus' invitation to repentance echoes through this Gospel. Blessed Elizabeth helps us toward this by reminding us, "Where sin abounds, grace abounds still more." Grace, the gift of God's abiding Presence, is the fertilizer that makes possible the tiny leaf of repentance to bear fruit in hope. As Blessed Elizabeth writes: "The weakest even the guiltiest soul is the one that has the most reason for hope." Christ would have us forget self and throw oneself into the arms of God instead of turning inward with excessive self-examination. Excessive self-concern paralyzes the heart whereas, "the soul possesses at its very center a Savior who wants at every moment to purify it."

In former times when the city of Jerusalem was in danger of being destroyed, the prophet Isaiah advised the King, "Your salvation lay in conversion and tranquility, your strength in complete trust" (Isaiah 30:15).

Do I pray for the gift of complete trust when my life is in turmoil and my sins seem beyond forgiveness? Do I truly believe that Jesus welcomes my turning to him, and in this is my strength? Instead of being discouraged, are the ears of my heart open to hear his encouraging words, "Come to me and I will refresh you?"

PRAYER

St. Paul writes to the early Christians, "May the God of all consolation keep your heart and your mind in Christ Jesus Our Lord." Jesus, ever present, realize this prayer in me so that I may always be mindful of and open to your gift of repentance. May I not give way to discouragement even when I have seriously failed you. Help me to forget myself by throwing myself into your welcoming arms allowing you to "fertilize" my heart and my mind and so know the consolation of your saving, healing love. With confidence I offer this prayer to you. Amen.

Third Week of Lent — Monday

GOSPEL

JESUS SAID TO THE PEOPLE IN THE SYNAGOGUE AT NAZARETH:

"Amen, I say to you, no prophet is accepted in his own native place. Indeed, I tell you, there were many widows in Israel in the days of Elijah when the sky was closed for three and a half years and a severe famine spread over the entire land. It was to none of these that Elijah was sent, but only to a widow in Zarephath in the land of Sidon. Again, there were many lepers in Israel during the time of Elisha the prophet; yet not one of them was cleansed, but only Naaman the Syrian." When the people in the synagogue heard this, they were all filled with fury. They rose up, drove him out of the town, and led him to the brow of the hill on which their town had been built, to hurl him down headlong. But he passed through the midst of them and went away.

LUKE 4: 24-30

BLESSED ELIZABETH OF THE TRINITY

To her friend Germaine whom Elizabeth calls her "dear little sister," Blessed Elizabeth writes:

"To prove to Jesus how much you love Him, learn how to forget yourself always in order to make your dear ones happy, and be very faithful to your duties and all your resolutions. Live more by will than by imagination. If you feel your weakness, my dear little Germaine, God wants you to use it to make acts of the will that you offer Him like so many acts of love rising up to His Heart to move it with delight. He loves you so much, little sister, He so wants you to be His, whatever might be the way you are to follow here below."

Complete Works, vol. 2: Letter 278

REFLECTION

One might wonder how this selection from Blessed Elizabeth connects with today's Gospel reading. In this Gospel, Jesus voices his feelings of rejection by his own people and especially by those in the town where he spent his early years. They thought they knew all about him—he was Jesus the son of Joseph the carpenter and Mary was his mother. If he has become this great wonder-worker, why does he not perform a miracle for them to witness! Jesus reminds them of a well-known saying, "no prophet is accepted in his own native place." Instead of hearing his words as a call to repentance, their rejection turns to violence as they drive him out intending to hurl him down the brow of the hill on which their town was built. We can only imagine the pain Jesus felt in His heart at being so misunderstood by His own townspeople.

In contrast to the Gospel selection for today, Blessed Elizabeth understands the love Jesus has for each one of us and she encourages her friend to open her heart in loving response. We do this, not by extraordinary deeds of wonder, but by fidelity in doing the ordinary things expected of us. Such expressions of love are not about feelings of devotions. Often we need "to live more by will than by imagination." Blessed Elizabeth challenges us to be less concerned about ourselves but instead, that we "learn how to forget ourselves always in order to make our dear ones happy."

Am I able to let myself be loved by God? What is my understanding of love—is it contingent on being consoled by Jesus in difficult times? Instead, am I able, while doing ordinary things, to make acts of the will that rise up to delight the heart of Christ?

PRAYER

Ever-loving Lord Jesus, you suffered the pain of rejection by your very own people. As I look at my own experience of rejection, real or imagined, it tends to close me off from love. Your willingness to experience the human condition even to dying a shameful death, abandoned by all, was on the contrary, an expression of your infinite, never ceasing love for me and for each one of us. Open my heart to love with your very own love so that I can willingly and without discrimination, in simple and ordinary ways, share this love with others. I offer my prayer to you, Lord Jesus, trusting in your abiding presence. Amen.

Third Week of Lent — Tuesday

Gospel

Peter approached Jesus and asked him, "Lord, if my brother sins against me, how often must I forgive him? As many as seven times?" Jesus answered, "I say to you, not seven times but seventy-seven times. That is why the Kingdom of heaven may be likened to a king who decided to settle accounts with his servants. When he began the accounting, a debtor was brought before him who owed him a huge amount. Since he had no way of paying it back, his master ordered him to be sold, along with his wife, his children, and all his property, in payment of the debt. At that, the servant fell down, did him homage, and said, 'Be patient with me, and I will pay you back in full.' Moved with compassion the master of that servant let him go and forgave him the loan. When that servant had left, he found one of his fellow servants who owed him a much smaller amount. He seized him and started to choke him, demanding, 'Pay back what you owe.' Falling to his knees, his fellow servant begged him, 'Be patient with me, and I will pay you back.' But he refused. Instead, he had him put in prison until he paid back the debt. Now when his fellow servants saw what had happened, they were deeply disturbed, and went to their master and reported the whole affair. His master summoned him and said to him, 'You wicked servant! I forgave you your entire debt because you begged me to. Should you not have had pity on your fellow servant, as I had pity on you?' Then in anger his master handed him over to the torturers until he should pay back the whole debt. So will my heavenly Father do to you, unless each of you forgives your brother from your heart."

Matthew 18: 21-35

BLESSED ELIZABETH OF THE TRINITY

In this excerpt from a letter to her friend, Canon Angles, Blessed Elizabeth asks him to pray that she be totally identified with Christ.

"What a sublime mission the Carmelite has; she is to be mediatrix with Jesus Christ, to be another humanity for Him in which He can perpetuate His life of reparation, sacrifice, praise, and adoration. O, ask Him that I may be equal to my vocation and not abuse the graces He lavishes on me; if you knew how fearful that makes me sometimes.... Then I cast myself on Him whom Saint John calls, 'the faithful and true' and I beg Him to be Himself my fidelity!"

Complete Works, vol. 2: Letter 256

REFLECTION

Today's Gospel reading of the king who decides to settle accounts with his servants is an invitation to each one of us. The compassion that the king shows to the debtor who owed him much, images Christ who even on the cross prays for forgiveness for those responsible for his death. In keeping with the king's Christ-like heart of compassion, Elizabeth also desires to be another humanity in which Christ can perpetuate His life in her. The wicked servant, instead of taking on the compassionate mind of his master, demands full payment from a fellow servant who owed him a trifling compared to the debt of which he had been pardoned.

Jesus challenges us to forgive "from your heart." An unforgiving heart becomes a breeding ground for feelings of anger and resentment. Such feelings inevitably find their way into our behavior, into how we treat others; especially those whom we feel owe us something. Elizabeth was conscious of her weakness and human fragility as she writes to her friend, "if you knew how fearful that makes me sometimes." But she also trusts in the presence of Christ and in the desire He places in her heart to be for Him another humanity in which He can continue His mission of love and mercy. She knows that through prayer, Christ who is faithful and true will strengthen her, so she asks her friend to pray that she not abuse the graces Christ lavishes on her.

The wicked servant was handed over to the torturers until he paid the last debt. Anger, bitterness and resentment torture the heart. Only through conversion, seeking God's forgiveness in the sacrament of reconciliation, and seeking the forgiveness of others, can we pay the debt incurred by our unforgiving heart. Elizabeth understood well that only by praying to be another humanity for Christ could she forgive, not seven times, but seventy times seven.

What is my "forgiving average?" Do I harbor resentment or bitterness over past hurts? Do I stay estranged from family members or friends because of my unwillingness to forgive them or unwillingness to ask them for forgiveness? In this parable, do I hear Christ calling me to conversion of heart and inviting me to be transformed into his way of compassion and forgiveness?

PRAYER

Ever-loving compassionate One, like the wicked servant whose heart was lacking in compassion and forgiveness, and like Blessed Elizabeth who feared to abuse the graces bestowed on her, my own feelings of weakness stir me to pray for the gift of a forgiving heart. Is it possible that I too might be another humanity for you to perpetuate your life of "reparation, sacrifice, praise, and adoration?" This desire stirs my heart to pray for the grace that it be realized in me. I give thanks to you and pray in your name knowing that from you all blessings flow. Amen.

Third Week of Lent — Wednesday

GOSPEL

JESUS SAID TO HIS DISCIPLES:

"Do not think that I have come to abolish the law or the prophets. I have come not to abolish but to fulfill. Amen, I say to you, until heaven and earth pass away, not the smallest letter or the smallest part of a letter will pass from the law, until all things have taken place. Therefore, whoever breaks one of the least of these commandments and teaches others to do so will be called least in the Kingdom of heaven. But whoever obeys and teaches these commandments will be called greatest in the Kingdom of heaven."

MATTHEW 5: 17-19

BLESSED ELIZABETH OF THE TRINITY

Shortly before her death, to her dear friend Antoinette, Blessed Elizabeth writes these words:

"Dear Antoinette, in the light of eternity the soul sees things as they really are. Oh! How empty is all that has not been done for God and with God! I beg you, oh, mark everything with the seal of love! It alone endures. How serious life is: each minute is given us in order to 'root' us deeper in God, as Saint Paul says, so the resemblance to our divine Model may be more striking, the union more intimate. But to accomplish this plan, which is that of God Himself, here is the secret: forget self, give up self, ignore self, look at the Master, look only at Him, accept as coming directly from His love both joy and suffering; this places the soul on such serene heights!"

Complete Works, vol. 2: Letter 333

REFLECTION

These profound words of Blessed Elizabeth open up for us the depth of today's Gospel. This Gospel selection can only be understood within the context of what has preceded it. Jesus, seeing the crowd following him, had gone up the mountain to a level place. Like a new Moses, he began to speak words of deep wisdom to his followers. The Law of Moses that guided their lives began to take on new and more profound meaning. It was not in rigid adherence to regulations about diet or even circumcision—this misunderstanding initially divided the early Jewish Christian community—instead the poor in spirit, the meek, and the merciful were the ones who were blessed. In showing mercy, God's light would shine before others.

Jesus insisted that he did not come to abolish the law but to bring it to perfection, to its true fulfillment in the lives of each of his hearers. The law was about living in a God-like manner. God, the eternal Lawgiver, was here present in the person of Jesus. As the true light of the world, Jesus was drawing His hearers, through his words and example, into the law's true meaning. Enlightened by the light of Christ, the task of his followers was to obey and teach the commandments by their very lives. In this they would truly live the law so the smallest letter and smallest part of the letter would take place and they would be called greatest in the kingdom of heaven.

Blessed Elizabeth understood well how empty all our actions are, "if they are not done for God and with God." Only that which is marked with the seal of love endures because it is by love that we resemble our divine Model. Resemblance to God, to Christ is the heart of the law's observance. Instead of rigidly following the minutia of observance, Elizabeth would have us follow her plan of living so that resemblance to Jesus becomes a reality. Her method is simple: forget self; ignore self. But to do so has meaning and bears good fruit provided that *our gaze is on the divine Master and it is this that causes us to be forgetful of self.* If our eyes are fixed on Jesus, who promised to be with us always, we will be enabled to accept all that life brings as coming directly "from His love and we will be serene" and the law will, without distortion, become a living reality in our lives.

What is my attitude toward law? Do I interpret the law in the light of Jesus' Gospel of love and mercy? Do I keep my eyes fixed on Jesus? Am I able to forget myself in love and compassion when a need arises? Like Blessed Elizabeth, am I convinced that only that which is marked with the seal of love endures? Do I ever reflect on the seriousness of life—that each moment of life is an unrepeatable gift—that *each minute* is given us in order to "root" us deeper in God?

PRAYER

Jesus, our true and eternal law-giver, strengthen my desire to keep my eyes fixed on you so that self-centeredness not keep me rigid and unbending. Open my heart to love with your own love. As I become rooted in you, may all my words and actions be in conformity with your commandments so that others might be inspired to be faithful to you. As I offer my prayer in your name, remind me that each day is your gift that I will never have to live again. Amen.

THIRD WEEK OF LENT — THURSDAY

GOSPEL

Jesus was driving out a demon that was mute, and when the demon had gone out, the mute man spoke and the crowds were amazed. Some of them said, "By the power of Beelzebul, the prince of demons, he drives out demons." Others, to test him, asked him for a sign from heaven. But he knew their thoughts and said to them, "Every kingdom divided against itself will be laid waste and house will fall against house. And if Satan is divided against himself, how will his kingdom stand? For you say that it is by Beelzebul that I drive out demons. If I, then, drive out demons by Beelzebul, by whom do your own people drive them out? Therefore they will be your judges. But if it is by the finger of God that I drive out demons, then the Kingdom of God has come upon you. When a strong man fully armed guards his palace, his possessions are safe. But when one stronger than he attacks and overcomes him, he takes away the armor on which he relied and distributes the spoils. Whoever is not with me is against me, and whoever does not gather with me scatters."

LUKE 11: 14-23

BLESSED ELIZABETH OF THE TRINITY

This letter is a continuation of yesterday's selection. It continues Blessed Elizabeth's farewell words to her dear friend.

"My beloved Antoinette, I leave you my faith in the presence of God, of the God who is all Love dwelling in our souls. I confide to you: it is this intimacy with Him 'within' that has been the beautiful sun illuminating my life, making it already an anticipated heaven; it is what sustains me today in my suffering. I do not fear my weakness; that's what gives me confidence. For the Strong One is within me and His power is almighty. It is able to do, says the Apostle, abundantly more than we can hope for."

Complete Works, vol. 2: Letter 333

REFLECTION

In today's Gospel Jesus reminds us of the need to allow Him to be the center and focus of our lives so that the kingdom of God be manifest. Jesus is the One who will drive out all that is discordant within. Jesus reminds us not to "scatter" what is most precious—the invitation to be "with" Jesus. As was true of Blessed Elizabeth, Jesus would draw us into intimacy and become "the beautiful sun illuminating our life." At the same time, the experience of our weakness stirs inner demons of fear and doubt; feelings of guilt and anxiety at times plunges us into inner darkness. Demons of self-pity and mistrust of God's abiding love often plunges us into turmoil, and so we are divided against ourselves.

In such times of inner conflict the simple but profound words of Blessed Elizabeth reach out to us what she says in her letter to her friend, she says to each one of us; "I leave you my faith in the presence of God, of the God who is all Love dwelling in our souls." Christ within is the "Strong One" who drives out our demons and offers peace to the struggling heart. Christ is also the Stronger One who removes the armor of our guarded hearts, making room for faith to expand. When our inner kingdom is no longer divided against itself, our weakness becomes our strength. Blessed Elizabeth reminds us through the words of the Apostle, the power of God is almighty, and is able to do abundantly more than we can hope for.

In times of inner conflict do I look to Jesus to be the finger of God pointing at my darkness inviting me to trust in His healing love? Do I really believe that my weakness is not a problem for God but attracts Jesus toward me—as did the mute man's need for healing draw Jesus toward him? Do my inner demons keep me mute instead of speaking out against issues of social injustice, especially toward the poor and needy—against abortion, against the horrors of war, against capital punishment, and the many other issues that keep the kingdom of God divided against itself?

PRAYER

Jesus, Compassionate One, you know the depth of my weakness. You know the many things that keep my heart divided against itself and therefore not in harmony with your Kingdom. I pray that Blessed Elizabeth would leave me as she did her friend, "her faith in the presence of God, of the God who is all love dwelling in our souls." I pray for the grace of such deep intimacy with you that I may have complete confidence in your love. Fill me with courage to be one of your "gathers" and not one who "scatters." In your name I pray that your kingdom come in and through me. Amen.

Third Week of Lent — Friday

GOSPEL

One of the scribes came to Jesus and asked him, "Which is the first of all the commandments?" Jesus replied, "The first is this: *Hear, O Israel! The Lord our God is Lord alone! You shall love the Lord your God with all your heart, with all your soul, with all your mind, and with all your strength.* The second is this: *You shall love your neighbor as yourself.* There is no other commandment greater than these." The scribe said to him, "Well said, teacher. You are right in saying, *He is One and there is no other than he.* And *to love him with all your heart, with all your understanding, with all your strength, and to love your neighbor as yourself* is worth more than all burnt offerings and sacrifices." And when Jesus saw that he answered with understanding, he said to him, "You are not far from the Kingdom of God." And no one dared to ask him any more questions.

Mark 12: 28-34

BLESSED ELIZABETH OF THE TRINITY

On the tenth day of her retreat entitled Heaven in Faith, Blessed Elizabeth continues to reflect on what it means to "be a praise of glory." This is her heart's deepest desire and she continues to penetrate its depths. She writes:

"A praise of glory is a soul that lives in God that loves Him with a pure and disinterested love, without seeking itself in the sweetness of this love; that loves Him beyond all His gifts and even though it would not have received anything from Him, it desires the good of the Object thus loved. Now how do we effectively desire and will good to God if not in accomplishing His will since this will orders everything for His greater glory? Thus the soul must surrender itself to this will completely, passionately, so as to will nothing else but what God wills."

Complete Works, vol. 1: 112

REFLECTION

Unknown to him, the scribe in today's Gospel was, like Elizabeth, "a praise of glory." His was a disinterested love; a love that responded whole heartedly to God whose love for the scribe stirred the scribe to return God's love with all his heart, understanding and strength and to love his neighbor as himself. God's love is an inclusive love. To truly love God is to love with God's own love, excluding no one.

That the scribe understood the commandment to love as worth more than all burnt offerings and sacrifices was a remarkable insight considering how important sacrifice and burnt offerings were to Jewish temple worship. We can picture Jesus, with an affirming smile, assuring the scribe that he is not far from the Kingdom of God.

God's Kingdom was soon to have its ultimate realization in the passion, death and resurrection of Jesus. His death would herald the definitive and eternal sacrifice offered once, and yet daily renewed in sacrament through the celebration of the Eucharist.

The challenge of loving one's neighbor with a disinterested love, not expecting anything in return, is its own burnt offering as Blessed Elizabeth knew from her own experience. For her it meant sacrificing on the altar of love self-centered attachments that shrink the heart's capacity to love with God's love. In surrendering herself completely to God's will, in receiving the Eucharist, like Christ, Elizabeth becomes "bread for others." It is to this that she invites us through these Lenten reflections.

What changes would I need to make in my life if I were to love God beyond God's gifts? Does my behavior reflect the intricate connection between my love for God and the love and care that I extend to my neighbor? Are the sacrifices I am making this Lent motivated by love; Christ's love for me manifest in His passion and death?

PRAYER

Ever-loving God, of old you gave your commandments to Moses on Mount Sion. It was on Mount Calvary, through your Incarnate Word that you renewed your covenant of love and gave us a living example of your will for us—that with Christ and like Blessed Elizabeth, we love you with our whole heart, mind, soul and strength, with a pure and disinterested love. Jesus, in your eternal sacrifice, you modeled the all embracing, forgiving love that I desire to extend to others. Help me to love with your own love so that like the scribe, I might not be far from the Kingdom established by you. I offer this prayer to you, my beloved Lord and Savior. Amen.

THIRD WEEK OF LENT — SATURDAY

GOSPEL

Jesus addressed this parable to those who were convinced of their own righteousness and despised everyone else. "Two people went up to the temple area to pray; one was a Pharisee and the other was a tax collector. The Pharisee took up his position and spoke this prayer to himself, 'O God, I thank you that I am not like the rest of humanity—greedy, dishonest, adulterous—or even like this tax collector. I fast twice a week, and I pay tithes on my whole income.' But the tax collector stood off at a distance and would not even raise his eyes to heaven but beat his breast and prayed, 'O God, be merciful to me a sinner.' I tell you, the latter went home justified, not the former; for everyone who exalts himself will be humbled, and the one who humbles himself will be exalted."

LUKE 18: 9-14

BLESSED ELIZABETH OF THE TRINITY

The following excerpt is taken from a lengthy text entitled *The Greatness of Our Vocation* written for her friend, whom she affectionately calls Framboise,

"Framboise, all the movements of pride that you feel within yourself, only become faults when the will takes part in them! Without that, although you may suffer much, you are not offending God. Doubtless self-love is at the bottom of those faults which, as you say, you commit without thinking, but that, my poor darling, is, in a way, part of us . . . what God asks of you is never to entertain deliberately any thought of pride, and never to act on the inspiration of pride, for this is wrong. And yet, if you find yourself doing either of these, you must not become discouraged, for again, it is pride which is irritated. You must 'display your misery' like Magdalene at the Master's feet, and ask Him to set you free. He so loves to see a soul recognize its weakness. Then, as a great saint said, 'The abyss of God's immensity encounters the abyss of the creature's nothingness,' and God embraces this nothingness."

Complete Works, vol. 1: 125–26

REFLECTION

The Gospel tells us that Jesus addresses this parable to those who are convinced of their own righteousness and despise everyone else. In the light of this Gospel passage, Blessed Elizabeth would be assuring her friend who is struggling with movements of pride, that these temptations are not like that of the Pharisee who was convinced of his own righteousness. The Pharisee was "deliberately entertaining thoughts of pride" as he *condemned the rest of humanity* and thanked God that he was not like *them*. In a sweeping statement he accuses *others* of ever manner of vice and exalts himself for what he considers his virtuous life.

Elizabeth reminds us that we are *all like them*. We all struggle at time with movements of pride and self-love easily contaminates the best of our endeavors. The tax collector was aware of his sinfulness and he willed to do better. He "displayed his misery"—as Blessed Elizabeth encouraged her friend to do—and in recognizing his weakness, the tax collector trusted God's mercy to set him free. God "embraced his nothingness" and so the tax collector, rather than the Pharisee, went home justified.

To truly love oneself is to be humble. Humility grounds us in the truth of ourselves as finite, fragile and prone toward sin. At the same time, it keeps us attuned to the abyss of God whose love reaches out to embrace our nothingness as we turn toward God in humble prayer for mercy. The distorted self-love against which Elizabeth cautions her friend is what so consumed the Pharisee that he forgot "the abyss of the creature's nothingness" and displayed himself an equal to God who alone is without sin.

Do I tend to become discouraged in the face of my many failures? Am I critical and judgmental toward others either in thought or word, forgetting my own human fragility? Can I trustfully "display my miseries" in the sacrament of reconciliation with confidence in God's mercy so that like the tax collector, I will "go home justified?" At the same time am I grateful for the many acts of kindness and compassion toward others that God encourages in me?

PRAYER

Ever-gracious God, in the abyss of your Trinitarian Love you came among us in Jesus the Christ to enfold us in his humanity so that nothing that is human is now beyond redemption if we but open ourselves to the abyss of your merciful love. Grant me the grace never to doubt your love and your willingness to embrace me in your forgiving love if I but turn to you in sincere repentance. Through the grace of your Indwelling Spirit keep me aware of my critical and judgmental thoughts that the "Pharisee," alive in me, be forgiven, healed and finally transformed. I pray in your name that you grant me genuine humility of heart and a genuine love for others. Amen.

FOURTH WEEK OF LENT

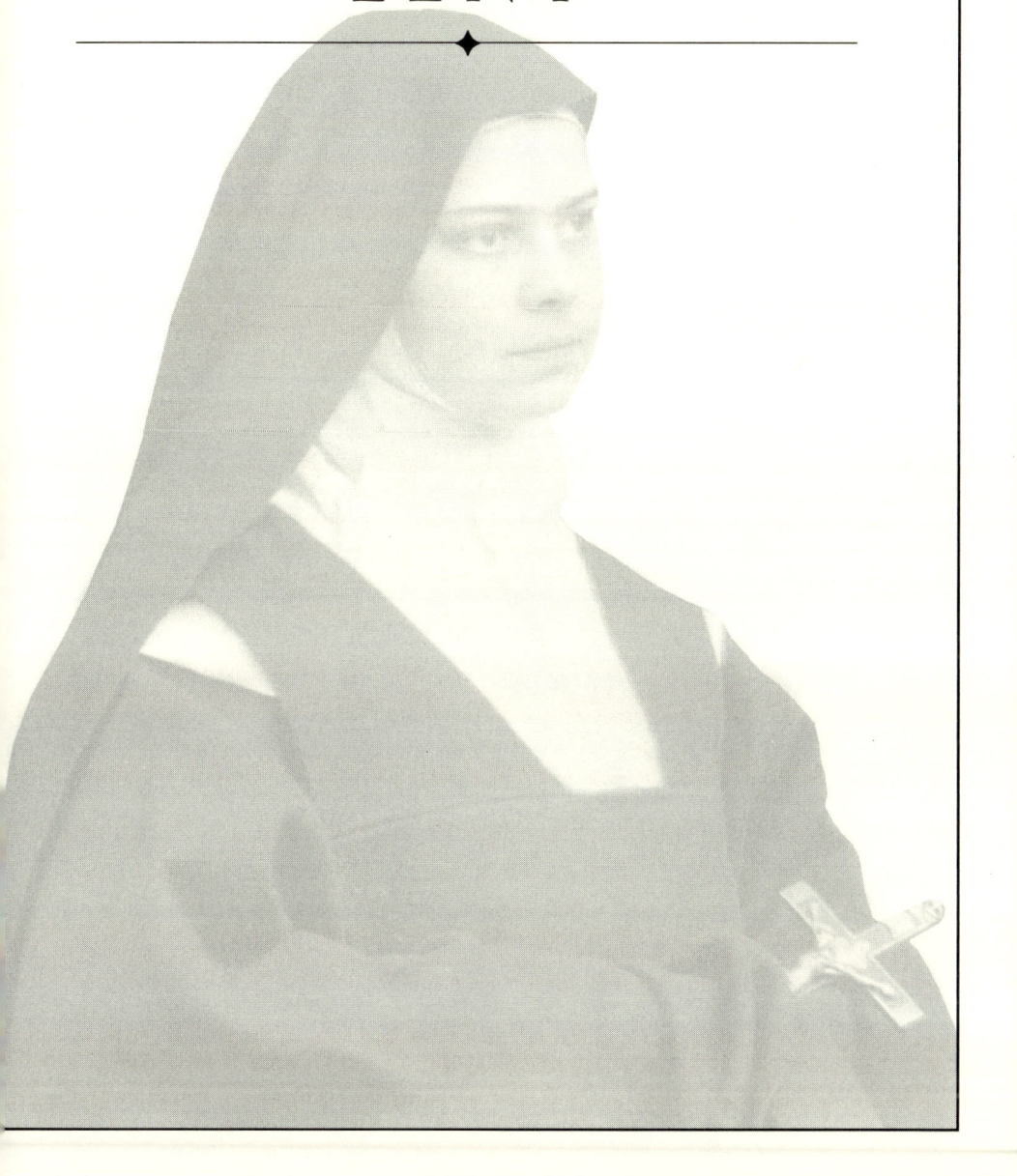

Fourth Sunday of Lent — Year A

Gospel

As Jesus passed by he saw a man blind from birth. His disciples asked him, "Rabbi, who sinned, this man or his parents, that he was born blind?" Jesus answered, "Neither he nor his parents sinned; it is so that the works of God might be made visible through him. We have to do the works of the one who sent me while it is day. Night is coming when no one can work. While I am in the world, I am the light of the world." When he had said this, he spat on the ground and made clay with the saliva, and smeared the clay on his eyes, and said to him, "Go wash in the Pool of Siloam" —which means Sent—. So he went and washed, and came back able to see.

His neighbors and those who had seen him earlier as a beggar said, "Isn't this the one who used to sit and beg?" Some said, "It is," but others said, "No, he just looks like him." He said, "I am." So they said to him, "How were your eyes opened?" He replied, "The man called Jesus made clay and anointed my eyes and told me, 'Go to Siloam and wash.' So I went there and washed and was able to see." And they said to him, "Where is he?" He said, "I don't know."

They brought the one who was once blind to the Pharisees. Now Jesus had made clay and opened his eyes on a sabbath. So then the Pharisees also asked him how he was able to see. He said to them, "He put clay on my eyes, and I washed, and now I can see." So some of the Pharisees said, "This man is not from God, because he does not keep the sabbath." But others said, "How can a sinful man do such signs?" And there was a division among them. So they said to the blind man again, "What do you have to say about him, since he opened your eyes?" He said, "He is a prophet."

Now the Jews did not believe that he had been blind and gained his sight until they summoned the parents of the one who had gained his sight. They asked them, "Is this your son, who you say was born blind? How does he now see?" His parents answered and said, "We know that this is our son and that he was born blind. We do not know how he sees now, nor do we know who opened his eyes. Ask him, he is of age; he can speak for himself." His parents said this because they were afraid of the Jews, for the Jews had already agreed that if anyone acknowledged him as the Christ, he would be expelled from the synagogue. For this reason his parents said, "He is of age; question him."

So a second time they called the man who had been blind and said to him, "Give God the praise! We know that this man is a sinner." He replied, "If he is a sinner, I do not know. One thing I do know is that I was blind and now I see." So they said to him, "What did he do to you? How did he open your eyes?" He answered them, "I told you already and you did not listen. Why do you want to hear it again? Do you want to become his disciples, too?" They ridiculed him and said, "You are that man's disciple; we are disciples of Moses! We know that God spoke to Moses, but we do not know where this one is from." The man answered and said to them, "This is what is so amazing, that you do not know where he is from, yet he opened my eyes. We know that God does not listen to sinners, but if one is devout and does his will, he listens to him. It is unheard of that anyone ever opened the eyes of a person born blind. If this man were not from God, he would not be able to do anything." They answered and said to him, "You were born totally in sin, and are you trying to teach us?" Then they threw him out.

When Jesus heard that they had thrown him out, he found him and said, "Do you believe in the Son of Man?" He answered and said, "Who is he, sir, that I may believe in him?" Jesus said to him, "You have seen him, the one speaking with you is he." He said, "I do believe, Lord," and he worshiped him. Then Jesus said, "I came into this world for judgment, so that those who do not see might see, and those who do see might become blind."

Some of the Pharisees who were with him heard this and said to him, "Surely we are not also blind, are we?" Jesus said to them, "If you were blind, you would have no sin; but now you are saying, 'We see,' so your sin remains."

JOHN 9: 1-41

Shorter form: JOHN 9:1, 6-9, 13-17, 34-38
Longer form may be optionally read on any day in the fourth week of Lent

BLESSED ELIZABETH OF THE TRINITY

In this second prayer of the sixth day of her retreat entitled Heaven in Faith, Blessed Elizabeth internalizes the words of Ruysbroeck as she reflects on the meaning of simplicity. She writes:

"'If your eye is single, your whole body will be full of light.' What is this single eye of which the Master speaks but this 'simplicity of intention' which 'gathers into unity all the scattered forces of the soul and unites the spirit itself to God. It is simplicity which gives God honor and praise; it is simplicity which presents and offers the virtues to Him. . . . I call simplicity of intention that which seeks only God and refers all things to Him.'"

Complete Works, vol. 1: 102

REFLECTION

This passage has direct bearing on today's Gospel selection, the lengthy reading from the Gospel of John about the man born blind. This man demonstrates the simplicity that Blessed Elizabeth reflects on. When asked to go and wash in the Pool of Siloam, unlike his predecessor Naaman the leper, who when told by the prophet Elisha to wash seven times in the Jordan, at first refused to do so in the expectation of a more dramatic cure (2 Kings 5:14), the man born blind simply did as he was told in confident expectancy. When the Pharisees approached him, again in simplicity, he spoke of what he knew without being intimidated by the aggressiveness of the Pharisees.

Before their insistence that Jesus could not be of God since he cured on the Sabbath, with "singleness of eye" and "simplicity of intention" the cured man told his story. More than this, not only were his eyes opened, his "whole body was full of light." He recognized and proclaimed Jesus to be a prophet. As Jesus points out, the Pharisees in denying what is before their eyes, the marvelous cure of the man born blind, are the ones who are truly blind.

Today, faith in Christ and in His Church is challenged not only by the critical voices of those who do not believe but also by the failures and sinfulness of those who are considered faithful followers. All of us have occasion to experience how "scattered are the forces of the soul."

This Gospel challenges us to seek the simplicity of heart which "gives God honor and praise" and "which refers all things to God." We do this by first recognizing our own blindness and our need for Christ's healing light. The Pharisees called Jesus, the all holy one, "a sinner." Without Christ's healing light we easily judge and condemn others. In doing so, our own faith in Christ and in the Church tends to be weakened.

Fortunately we need not stay in our blindness for Christ is ever present with His healing light. Instead of condemning others and perhaps even ourselves, which is a form of inner violence, with simplicity of heart, we need only turn to Him in prayer asking that, "our eye be single and our body lightsome." As Christ's healing energies flows through us, like the man born blind, we can proclaim Christ to others and ourselves become a source of light and healing for our Church and world.

What helps me to remain faithful in the face of today's challenging darkness?

Do I have the mind of Christ that sees not the darkness but the need for healing? How can I be a healing presence before my own darkness and that of the world around me?

Does desire for this stir me to prayer? The desire itself is God's gift inviting me deeper into the compassionate heart of God.

PRAYER

Ever-present Compassionate Jesus, you are our light and our salvation. Instead of condemning me for my blindness, with mercy and love you reach out to touch the eyes of my heart to enable me to see others through your own compassionate eyes. Transform my darkness with your light and make me, not a condemning, but a gentle, healing presence to all those whom you place in my life. As always, I make this prayer in your name trusting in your love to hear my heart's desires. Amen.

Fourth Sunday of Lent — Year B

GOSPEL

Jesus said to Nicodemus:

"Just as Moses lifted up the serpent in the desert, so must the Son of Man be lifted up, so that everyone who believes in him may have eternal life."

For God so loved the world that he gave his only Son, so that everyone who believes in him might not perish but might have eternal life. For God did not send his Son into the world to condemn the world, but that the world might be saved through him. Whoever believes in him will not be condemned, but whoever does not believe has already been condemned, because he has not believed in the name of the only Son of God. And this is the verdict, that the light came into the world, but people preferred darkness to light, because their works were evil. For everyone who does wicked things hates the light and does not come toward the light, so that his works might not be exposed. But whoever lives the truth comes to the light, so that his works may be clearly seen as done in God.

John 3: 14-21

BLESSED ELIZABETH OF THE TRINITY

The following reflection is taken from a "spiritual treatise" written to a young friend Francoise de Sourdon, with whom Blessed Elizabeth maintained a strong bond of friendship.

"Be strengthened in faith, that is, never act except in the great light of God, never according to impressions of your imagination. Believe that He loves you, that He wants to help you in the struggles you have to undergo. Believe in His love, His exceeding love, as St. Paul says [Ephesians 2:4]. *Nourish your soul on the great thoughts of faith, which will reveal to you all its richness and the end for which God has created you! 'He loved me*

and gave Himself up for me' [Galatians 2:20]. *That, my little child, is what it means to be true."*

Complete Works, vol. 1: 128

REFLECTION

To enter deeply into today's Gospel, try to listen to Jesus and hear His words as if for the first time. Hear them addressed to you personally. Hear Jesus inviting you to a deeper faith in Him, inviting you to let His light shine through all the dark regions of your heart. Allow Jesus to make "lightsome" the dark corners of your unbelief so that the immensity of His love, flowing from His having been "lifted up" on the Cross, might flow through you so that all your works "may be clearly seen as done in God."

For this reason does Blessed Elizabeth invite her friend to be strong in faith. Allow her words like those of Jesus to be imprinted in your heart—never act except in the great light of God—believe in His exceeding love for you—nourish your soul on the great thoughts of faith—that He love me and gave Himself up for me. As Blessed Elizabeth so wisely says, this is what it means to be true—letting our actions confirm the words of Jesus; that whoever lives the truth comes to the light.

Is Jesus truly the Light of my life? Is my behavior such that others recognize that what I do is done in and for God? What grace do I need to pray for that belief in God's exceeding love for me and for each person in my life finds expression and can be seen by others as an evident reality?

PRAYER

Jesus, you are the Light of the World. Enlighten my darkness with the gift of your abiding presence. Your works were clearly seen as done in God. May this same reality find expression in me. May I not prefer the darkness; instead may I nourish my soul on thoughts of faith. Help me to remember the end for which you created me and keep me from critically condemning those whom you came to save. Always keep me true to your life in me as I pray in your name. Amen.

Fourth Sunday of Lent — Year C

Gospel

Tax collectors and sinners were all drawing near to listen to Jesus, but the Pharisees and scribes began to complain, saying, "This man welcomes sinners and eats with them." So to them Jesus addressed this parable: "A man had two sons, and the younger son said to his father, 'Father, give me the share of your estate that should come to me.' So the father divided the property between them. After a few days, the younger son collected all his belongings and set off to a distant country where he squandered his inheritance on a life of dissipation. When he had freely spent everything, a severe famine struck that country, and he found himself in dire need. So he hired himself out to one of the local citizens who sent him to his farm to tend the swine. And he longed to eat his fill of the pods on which the swine fed, but nobody gave him any. Coming to his senses he thought, 'How many of my father's hired workers have more than enough food to eat, but here am I, dying from hunger. I shall get up and go to my father and I shall say to him, "Father, I have sinned against heaven and against you. I no longer deserve to be called your son; treat me as you would treat one of your hired workers."' So he got up and went back to his father. While he was still a long way off, his father caught sight of him, and was filled with compassion. He ran to his son, embraced him and kissed him. His son said to him, 'Father, I have sinned against heaven and against you; I no longer deserve to be called your son.' But his father ordered his servants, 'Quickly, bring the finest robe and put it on him; put a ring on his finger and sandals on his feet. Take the fattened calf and slaughter it. Then let us celebrate with a feast, because this son of mine was dead, and has come to life again; he was lost, and has been found.' Then the celebration began. Now the older son had been out in the field and, on his way back, as he neared the house, he heard the sound of music and dancing. He called one of the servants and asked what this might mean. The servant said to him, 'Your brother has returned and your father has slaughtered the fattened calf because he has him back safe and sound.' He became angry, and when he refused to enter the house, his father came out and pleaded with him. He said to his father in reply, 'Look, all these years I served you and not once did I disobey your orders; yet you never gave me even a young goat to feast on with my friends. But when your son returns who swallowed up your property with prostitutes, for him you slaughter the fattened calf.' He said to him, 'My son, you are here with me always; everything I have is yours. But now we must celebrate and rejoice, because your brother was dead and has come to life again; he was lost and has been found.'"

LUKE 15: 1-3, 11-32

BLESSED ELIZABETH OF THE TRINITY

In a letter to her friend, Madame Angles, Blessed Elizabeth offers this word of encouragement:

"Do not say that this is not for you, that you are too wretched; on the contrary that is only one more reason for going to Him who saves. We will be purified, not by looking at this wretchedness, but by looking at Him who is all purity and holiness. Saint Paul says that 'He has predestined us to be conformed to His image.' In the saddest times, think that the divine artist is using a chisel to make His work more beautiful, and remain at peace beneath the hand that is working on you."

Complete Works, vol. 2: 230

REFLECTION

Today's Gospel begins with the Pharisees, intending criticism, unwittingly proclaiming an essential message about God revealed in Jesus: "This man welcomes sinners and eats with them." As Blessed Elizabeth reminds her friend: "Do not say that you are too wretched; on the contrary that is one more reason for going to Him who saves." Sinners felt at home with Jesus. Looking at Jesus, rather than at their wretchedness, gave them a sense of their own dignity and worth before God as Jesus welcomed them to a shared meal and conversed with them.

The parable of the prodigal son and his welcoming father is a story about God "the divine artist" who desires to make beautiful the divine image and likeness in which we are created. Tax collectors and sinners could draw near to Jesus because Jesus communicated by His very being His Father's welcoming embrace of each person. God's love for us is not contingent on our being perfect, but it is in responding with confidence to God's welcoming embrace that we are transformed into persons capable of loving with God's own love.

The son in this parable did not have love for himself or for his father. With selfish intent, he claimed what he felt was his and went off to find fulfillment. He soon discovered that fulfillment based on self-satisfaction alone leads to emptiness and futility. He ended in the deepest degradation for a Jew—feeding swine. Swine were considered unclean animals and Jews were forbidden even to touch them.

In a moment of grace, the younger son was enabled to look beyond his own self-centered wants. He recalled his father's loving care not only of his family, but also of the hired workers. "Looking beyond his wretchedness" was an important step in returning home to his father's house and to what was deepest within the house of his soul.

What did the son discover on his return? That even in his saddest times the divine artist had been creatively speaking in the depth of his being inviting him home to himself. This transformation merited celebration. He was now capable of wearing the finest robe and eating the best of food—can we see here symbols of Baptism and Eucharist?

Unfortunately the older son failed to recognize the "wretchedness" of his self-righteous attitude—he too was lost to himself and needed to be found, he was dead and needed to come to the truth of his inner life in God. The father reaches out to him—as God does to each of us—inviting him to his inner truth: "My son, you are here with me always; everything I have is yours." Did he allow his wretchedness to be transformed by the father's sensitive care? Was he then able to join this festivity of sinners and eat with them? The Gospel does not tell us.

Does this parable help me place my wretchedness before the divine artist and with humility readily join the festivity of sinners with Jesus in our midst? What is my experience of receiving the Eucharist? Do I approach this sacrament as a festive meal with Jesus who would transform me into Himself?

PRAYER

Ever-loving God of surprises, Jesus reveals you as a God who delights in our company. It seems that our wretchedness attracts you to us and is like the raw material for your transforming action in our lives. I pray for the grace to be honest with myself. Do not let a sense of unworthiness keep me from you and may prideful arrogance not cause me to be disdainful of others. Instead, help me to remain at peace beneath your loving hand as like a divine artist you make me more beautiful in conforming me to the image of Your Beloved Son, Jesus in whose hands I place this prayer. Amen.

FOURTH WEEK OF LENT — MONDAY

GOSPEL

At that time Jesus left [Samaria] for Galilee. For Jesus himself testified that a prophet has no honor in his native place. When he came into Galilee, the Galileans welcomed him, since they had seen all he had done in Jerusalem at the feast; for they themselves had gone to the feast.

Then he returned to Cana in Galilee, where he had made the water wine. Now there was a royal official whose son was ill in Capernaum. When he heard that Jesus had arrived in Galilee from Judea, he went to him and asked him to come down and heal his son, who was near death. Jesus said to him, "Unless you people see signs and wonders, you will not believe." The royal official said to him, "Sir, come down before my child dies." Jesus said to him, "You may go; your son will live." The man believed what Jesus said to him and left. While the man was on his way back, his slaves met him and told him that his boy would live. He asked them when he began to recover. They told him, "The fever left him yesterday, about one in the afternoon." The father realized that just at that time Jesus had said to him, "Your son will live," and he and his whole household came to believe. Now this was the second sign Jesus did when he came to Galilee from Judea.

JOHN 4: 43-54

BLESSED ELIZABETH OF THE TRINITY

To her friend Antoinette, Blessed Elizabeth writes:

"May the God who is all love be your unchanging dwelling place, your cell, and your cloister in the midst of the world; remember that He dwells in the deepest center of your soul as if in a sanctuary where He wants always to be loved to the point of adoration. He remains there to fill you to overflowing with his graces, to transform you in Himself. Oh, when you sense your weakness, go to Him; He is the Strong One, the One who gives

victory through the holiness at His right hand as the Psalmist sings. He covers you with his shadow. Trust in His love completely."

Complete Works, vol. 2: 246

REFLECTION

These words of Blessed Elizabeth might at first seem disconnected from today's Gospel reading about the royal official whose son is ill. But a closer look uncovers some of the deeper realities that Jesus calls forth from the royal official. The official, for all his authority, was unable to cure his own son. He "sensed his own weakness" and went to Jesus as the "Strong One." The official trusted that Jesus had the power to cure his son. When Jesus challenged him, "Unless you see signs and wonders," the official remained persistent in his belief. "Come down before my child dies." When Jesus simply told him to go to his son who would live, the man believed what Jesus said and left. When he discovered that it was at the very hour that his son was cured, he and his entire household were "filled to overflowing with grace." Unknown to themselves, they were being transformed by their newfound faith into the One who "so desired to be loved by them even to the point of adoration."

We do not know if the royal official and his household remained faithful followers of Jesus through his death and resurrection, but if they did not lose faith in him, they would have come to know Jesus' promise to be with them always, "to dwell in the deepest center of their soul as in a sanctuary."

We are blessed with a faith-filled knowledge that Jesus is always with us as "our unchanging dwelling place" as the one who responds to our needs. He "covers us with his shadow" and instills complete "trust in His love." Today's Gospel challenges our faith, not only when petitioning for our needs it also challenges our faith in Jesus' abiding presence with us. Wherever we go, his healing presence is with us.

If I were truly to live my faith in Jesus indwelling presence, what difference would it make in my life? When I sense my own weakness does it leave me discouraged or does it draw me closer to "the Strong One?" Do I pray for inner healing?

PRAYER

Ever-present Holy One, you are all love. Be my unchanging dwelling place, my cell, and my inner cloister in the midst of this world. Help me to remember that you dwell in the deepest center of my soul. Fill me to overflowing with your grace that I may, like Jesus, be a healing presence to all whom I hold dear. I offer this prayer to you in the name of your beloved Son in whom you are well pleased. Amen.

Fourth Week of Lent — Tuesday

Gospel

There was a feast of the Jews, and Jesus went up to Jerusalem. Now there is in Jerusalem at the Sheep Gate a pool called in Hebrew Bethesda, with five porticoes. In these lay a large number of ill, blind, lame, and crippled. One man was there who had been ill for thirty-eight years. When Jesus saw him lying there and knew that he had been ill for a long time, he said to him, "Do you want to be well?" The sick man answered him, "Sir, I have no one to put me into the pool when the water is stirred up; while I am on my way, someone else gets down there before me." Jesus said to him, "Rise, take up your mat, and walk." Immediately the man became well, took up his mat, and walked.

Now that day was a sabbath. So the Jews said to the man who was cured, "It is the sabbath, and it is not lawful for you to carry your mat." He answered them, "The man who made me well told me, 'Take up your mat and walk.'" They asked him, "Who is the man who told you, 'Take it up and walk'?" The man who was healed did not know who it was, for Jesus had slipped away, since there was a crowd there. After this Jesus found him in the temple area and said to him, "Look, you are well; do not sin any more, so that nothing worse may happen to you." The man went and told the Jews that Jesus was the one who had made him well. Therefore, the Jews began to persecute Jesus because he did this on a sabbath.

John 5: 1-16

BLESSED ELIZABETH OF THE TRINITY

In a letter to her mother Blessed Elizabeth writes:

"Darling Mama, live with him. Ah, I wish I could tell all souls what sources of strength, of peace, and of happiness they would find if they would only consent to live in this intimacy. Only they don't know how to wait: if God does not give Himself in some perceptible way, they leave His holy presence, and when He comes to them laden with all His gifts, He finds no one there, the soul is outside in external things, it is not living in its depths! Recollect yourself from time to time, little Mama, and then you will be quite close to your Sabeth."

Complete Works, vol. 2: 313

REFLECTION

The man in today's Gospel had been ill for a long time but he continued to wait, hoping to be healed. Until Jesus came into his life no one helped him. Others reached the healing waters ahead of him. His waiting was rewarded, not by being helped into the healing waters but by Jesus who quietly said: "Rise, take up your mat, and walk." He was healed of a bodily affliction but something deeper occurred. Jesus said to him, "You are well; do not sin anymore, so that nothing worse may happen to you." It seems "his soul had been outside in external things" which adversely affected his body with illness. His many years of waiting prepared him to receive Jesus who "came to him laden with gifts of healing both of body and of soul."

If we look deeply into our soul we see our own need for Jesus healing presence. Expectations that Jesus reveal his presence "in some perceptible way," "in external things" like the man ill in the Gospel who expected healing by having someone put him in the pool when the waters were stirred up—can easily keep us from recognizing Jesus' silent, healing presence in the depths of our being.

Blessed Elizabeth repeatedly invites us to live in intimacy with God "as our source of strength, of peace and of happiness." Jesus comes to each one of us laden with his gifts but if "He finds no one there," if our soul is outside in external things, we will miss his healing presence. Jesus often comes in imperceptible ways so we simply wait with expectation, believing that He is truly with us.

Am I able to persevere in faith when prayer seems dry and when I have no perceptible sense of Jesus' indwelling presence? Do I then abandon prayer instead of humbly waiting for Him to heal my inner being? Am I habitually living "outside of myself," immersed in external things, in order to escape the challenge of attentiveness to His presence within?

PRAYER

Divine Healer, You know how readily I live outside of my true self, seeking diversion in external things. My darkness keeps me from awareness of your abiding presence and of the peace you offer. Heal my soul's "lameness" so that I may always walk with you who are the source of my strength, my peace and my happiness. Help me to leave behind my sinful ways knowing that when human help fails, I need only to wait believing that you are truly with me transforming me into yourself. With humility of heart and grateful trust I offer this prayer to you. Amen.

FOURTH WEEK OF LENT — WEDNESDAY

GOSPEL

Jesus answered the Jews: "My Father is at work until now, so I am at work." For this reason they tried all the more to kill him, because he not only broke the sabbath but he also called God his own father, making himself equal to God.

Jesus answered and said to them, "Amen, amen, I say to you, the Son cannot do anything on his own, but only what he sees the Father doing; for what he does, the Son will do also. For the Father loves the Son and shows him everything that he himself does, and he will show him greater works than these, so that you may be amazed. For just as the Father raises the dead and gives life, so also does the Son give life to whomever he wishes. Nor does the Father judge anyone, but he has given all judgment to the Son, so that all may honor the Son just as they honor the Father. Whoever does not honor the Son does not honor the Father who sent him. Amen, amen, I say to you, whoever hears my word and believes in the one who sent me has eternal life and will not come to condemnation, but has passed from death to life. Amen, amen, I say to you, the hour is coming and is now here when the dead will hear the voice of the Son of God, and those who hear will live. For just as the Father has life in himself, so also he gave to the Son the possession of life in himself. And he gave him power to exercise judgment, because he is the Son of Man. Do not be amazed at this, because the hour is coming in which all who are in the tombs will hear his voice and will come out, those who have done good deeds to the resurrection of life, but those who have done wicked deeds to the resurrection of condemnation.

"I cannot do anything on my own; I judge as I hear, and my judgment is just, because I do not seek my own will but the will of the one who sent me."

JOHN 5: 17-30

BLESSED ELIZABETH OF THE TRINITY

Blessed Elizabeth writes the following advice to a person undergoing interior trials. Her words reflect her own conduct during such a painful period in her own life:

"Do you remember those beautiful words of Jesus to His Father: 'Thou hast given Him power over all flesh that He may give eternal life to all whom Thou hast given Him?' That is what He wants to do in us. He wishes you to go out of self, to give up all that preoccupies you, in order to retire into the solitude He has chosen as His dwelling place in the depths of your heart. He is always there, although you do not realize it. He is waiting for you, and wishes to establish with you a wonderful intercourse, admirabile commercium *as the Liturgy terms it, the intercourse of bride and Bridegroom. By His continual contact with you He will free you from your weakness and your faults and from all that troubles you. Nothing ought to prevent our going to Him."*

The Praise of Glory, 84

REFLECTION

We can thank Jesus' accusers for this lengthy Gospel passage in which Jesus describes his relationship with his Father. The intimacy and oneness of life between Father and Son reflects the intimacy to which each one of us is called by the grace of our Baptism. By *our incorporation in Christ* through Baptism, we become sharers in the *very life of God*. We need frequently to remind ourselves of this profound truth. This is the reality that Blessed Elizabeth repeatedly holds before us. While it may seem that she lives more in heaven than on earth, she too was schooled by trials. Her efforts to sustain inner stillness were often challenged by the tumult of her imagination and by her highly sensitive feelings.

A deeper look into the meaning of today's Gospel selection suggests that we can connect Jesus' words with the soul's desire to be freed of its weakness. For just as the Father raises the dead and gives life, so also does Jesus bring to life all that is dead in our inner being. For this to be realized, we need only to open ourselves to the divine invitation to share in the intimacy that Jesus shares with His Father.

A single flow of divine love energy unites Father and Son. Jesus necessarily uses analogous human concepts such as the father-son relationships in speaking of what ultimately is best titled: "Incomprehensible Mystery." At the same time, we do see the Father in seeing Jesus and we *honor* the Father in *honoring* the Son. Whoever *hears* Jesus words, and *believes* in the one who sent Jesus, *already possesses* eternal life and *will not come to condemnation* because the Father beholds us being increasingly transformed into the likeness of His Son. This *seeing, honoring, hearing and believing* is what it means to "go out of self"—that dimension of our being that keeps us preoccupied, "entombed" as it were in superficiality, instead of sharing in Jesus' Risen Life.

The *admirabile commercium,* the life of intimacy with Christ is Lent's deepest challenge and most essential "practice." Fasting and almsgiving have their truest meaning when they deepen our life in Christ and our trust in God's never failing love. As Blessed Elizabeth writes: "Nothing aught to prevent our going to Him." What in my life prevents me from going to Jesus in prayer? Can I name that which keeps me "entombed," and therefore not open to the flow of energy, which is that of Christ's Risen Life? Do specific scriptural ways of naming God keep me from going deeper into Divine Mystery and into the *admirabile commercium* of divine intimacy?

PRAYER

God of incomprehensible mystery, draw me into intimacy with you. Open my heart to seeing, honoring hearing and believing all that your Son opens before me in the Scriptures. Help me to hear his words, to believe in you who sent him and so with him to pass from death to the glories of his Risen Life. In his name I pray. Amen.

FOURTH WEEK OF LENT — THURSDAY

GOSPEL

JESUS SAID TO THE JEWS:

"If I testify on my own behalf, my testimony is not true. But there is another who testifies on my behalf, and I know that the testimony he gives on my behalf is true. You sent emissaries to John, and he testified to the truth. I do not accept human testimony, but I say this so that you may be saved. He was a burning and shining lamp, and for a while you were content to rejoice in his light. But I have testimony greater than John's. The works that the Father gave me to accomplish, these works that I perform testify on my behalf that the Father has sent me. Moreover, the Father who sent me has testified on my behalf. But you have never heard his voice nor seen his form, and you do not have his word remaining in you, because you do not believe in the one whom he has sent. You search the Scriptures, because you think you have eternal life through them; even they testify on my behalf. But you do not want to come to me to have life.

"I do not accept human praise; moreover, I know that you do not have the love of God in you. I came in the name of my Father, but you do not accept me; yet if another comes in his own name, you will accept him. How can you believe, when you accept praise from one another and do not seek the praise that comes from the only God? Do not think that I will accuse you before the Father: the one who will accuse you is Moses, in whom you have placed your hope. For if you had believed Moses, you would have believed me, because he wrote about me. But if you do not believe his writings, how will you believe my words?"

JOHN 5: 31-47

BLESSED ELIZABETH OF THE TRINITY

On the fourth day of her last retreat, Blessed Elizabeth writes:

"If I want my interior city to have some similarity and likeness to that 'of the King of eternal ages' and to receive this great illumination from God, I must extinguish every other light and, as in the holy city, the Lamb must be 'its only light.'

> *"Here faith, the beautiful light of faith appears. It alone should light my way as I go to meet the Bridegroom. The psalmist sings that He 'hides Himself in darkness,' then in another place he seem to contradict himself by saying that 'light surrounds Him like a cloak.'*
>
> *"It was said of Moses that he was 'unshakable in his faith, as if he had seen the Invisible.' It seems to me that this should be the attitude of a praise of glory who wishes to continue her hymn of thanksgiving through everything: 'unshakable in her faith as if she had seen the Invisible'; unshakable in her faith in His 'exceeding love.' 'We have known the love of God for us, and we have believed in it.'"*
>
> Complete Works, vol. 1: 145

REFLECTION

The words, *testify* and *testimony* appears ten times in today's Gospel passage. Like John the Baptist who testified to the truth, and with her own great depth of insight, like an echo of the Father's testimony on Jesus behalf, Blessed Elizabeth here gives her own testimony as she "rejoices in His light." Her desire is to "extinguish every other light" so that Christ would be her only light. Unlike those who refused to hear his voice—as Jesus laments in this poignant section of John's Gospel—Blessed Elizabeth both hears his voice and she responds in faith so that she herself becomes a burning and shining lamp to enlighten us as we ponder her words.

Faith is another word for belief. In not believing in Jesus in spite of the many works that testify on His behalf, how can belief in Moses, who led the people out of slavery into the Promised Land, be a possibility? Moses prefigured Jesus, the light that illumined the night for the Israelites like a pillar of fire as they fled from their pursuers. Moses both heard and believed in the voice that spoke to him in the burning bush and, like Elizabeth, became "a praise of glory" as he testified to the One True God before all the people.

We feel the sadness in Jesus because the love of God is not in those who do not accept Jesus. To reject Jesus is to reject the Father who sent Him. Blessed Elizabeth invites us, like Moses, to be "unshakable in faith" even in times when God seems hidden in darkness. The light of faith will illumine our darkness as the testimony of Jesus finds an increasing welcome in our hearts and His words remain in us. This lengthy Gospel, along the words of Blessed Elizabeth, leaves much for us to ponder. Pray for the grace to ponder its many layers of meaning in your life.

I ask myself: have I been a "praise of glory" in the times when it seemed that God's inner light guided me through a difficult or perplexing situation? Or did I just take God for granted? I pray to recognize the situations in my life when, like the disbelievers of Jesus time, I listened to the arguments of human reasoning instead of being faithful to Jesus' testimony of truth.

PRAYER

God and Father of Our Lord Jesus Christ, you accomplish in Jesus the works you give him to perform. Help me to be attentive to the voice of your indwelling Spirit that I too do only that which is pleasing to you and give testimony by my life to my faith in you and in your beloved Son. Help me in my moments of darkness and disbelief that I never lose faith in you. At such times, "may your light surround me like a cloak" that I may be "unshakeable in my faith" and "in your exceeding love." With a grateful heart I pray in Jesus name. Amen.

GOSPEL

Jesus moved about within Galilee; he did not wish to travel in Judea, because the Jews were trying to kill him. But the Jewish feast of Tabernacles was near.

But when his brothers had gone up to the feast, he himself also went up, not openly but as it were in secret.

Some of the inhabitants of Jerusalem said, "Is he not the one they are trying to kill? And look, he is speaking openly and they say nothing to him. Could the authorities have realized that he is the Christ? But we know where he is from. When the Christ comes, no one will know where he is from." So Jesus cried out in the temple area as he was teaching and said, "You know me and also know where I am from. Yet I did not come on my own, but the one who sent me, whom you do not know, is true. I know him, because I am from him, and he sent me." So they tried to arrest him, but no one laid a hand upon him, because his hour had not yet come.

JOHN 7: 1-2, 10, 25-30

BLESSED ELIZABETH OF THE TRINITY

In the tenth day of her retreat, Heaven in Faith, Blessed Elizabeth, referring to the Blessed Virgin, writes:

"'If you knew the gift of God . . .' There is one who knew this gift of God, one who did not lose one particle of it, one who was so pure, so luminous that she seemed to be the Light itself: 'Speculum justitiae.' One whose life was so simple, so lost in God that there is hardly anything we can say about it. 'Virgo fidelis': that is, Faithful Virgin, 'who kept all these things in her heart.'"

Complete Works, vol. 1: 110

REFLECTION

This selection from the Gospel of John can best be understood by recalling that John's Gospel comes to us from the end of the first century and it displays the ongoing reflection of the Christian community and their deepened understanding of who Jesus is. Perhaps the sadness and frustration we see in Jesus as he cries out in lament over the many who hear his words and witness his saving deeds, but who reject him, gives expression to the sadness of the early Christians as persons continued to reject Jesus like some of the inhabitants of Jerusalem. In knowing Jesus' human background, where he was from, the town where he grew up, their minds were closed to any further reality. They were not able to see beyond their limited factual knowledge. They failed to recognize in Jesus the human face of God, so attempts are made to arrest him. But their plans could not be realized: "no one laid hands on him, because his hour had not yet come." Jesus remains in charge of his destiny. At the same time, we can imagine the pain in the heart of Jesus knowing that there were those who were plotting to kill him.

With all the intensity of his desire to be truly known and in confirmation of his own inner truth, Jesus cries out: "Yet I did not come on my own, but the one who sent me, whom you do not know, is true. I know him, because I am from him, and he sent me." Was Jesus' pain even more intense because in not *knowing* him, they did not *know* the One who sent him? Jesus did not come on his own; he lived in the presence of another whom Jesus knew to be one with himself.

Today many continue to reject Jesus. Blessed Elizabeth reminds us that there was one who truly *knew* the gift of God. It is to her that we can turn as perhaps we too sorrow over a dear one who fails to recognize God's gift in Jesus who comes forth from God and who unveils the face of God for humankind. Mary remains the Faithful Virgin in spite of the circumstances that challenged her faith. She watched Jesus being rejected, his life threatened and his seeming defeat in death and yet she remained faithful. She continued to believe in Jesus whom she knew to be the gift of God in spite of human rejection.

As members of Christ's Church, we often fail by our lack of Christ-like behavior to make *known* the face of God. The Faithful Virgin remains as our great intercessor before God. She helps us to be faithful as we search to truly *know* Jesus and to give expression to this *knowing* through our compassionate and caring behavior toward others. As members of his Body the Church, Jesus continues to live in us, and Mary, *Speculum Justitiae,* Mirror of Justice, continues her mission as Mother of God by mothering Christ's life in each one of us.

Since I have been baptized *in Christ* and I receive him in the Eucharist, does my Christ-like behavior inspire others to desire to *know* Christ and the one who sent him? Do I treat others with respect even when their moral values are different from mine? Others may be *unknown* to me because of their different culture, ethnicity, or religious beliefs. Do I unjustly discriminate against them, or consider them inferior and show this my behavior?

PRAYER

Ever-Faithful Virgin, who valiantly stood at the painful "death bed" of you Son on the Cross, the ultimate in rejection, I pray for the grace to reflect Jesus and the One who sent him through all my words and actions. Help me not to reject others because they do not fit my expectations, or by thinking I know them and showing my disapproval when in reality we are truly known only by God. When like Jesus, I feel sad and lonely that those dear to me seem at times not to know me in greater depth, be my comfort, support and strength. I pray in the name of your Son, our Lord and God. Amen.

FOURTH WEEK OF LENT — SATURDAY

GOSPEL

Some in the crowd who heard these words of Jesus said, "This is truly the Prophet." Others said, "This is the Christ." But others said, "The Christ will not come from Galilee, will he? Does not Scripture say that the Christ will be of David's family and come from Bethlehem, the village where David lived?" So a division occurred in the crowd because of him. Some of them even wanted to arrest him, but no one laid hands on him.

So the guards went to the chief priests and Pharisees, who asked them, "Why did you not bring him?" The guards answered, "Never before has anyone spoken like this man." So the Pharisees answered them, "Have you also been deceived? Have any of the authorities or the Pharisees believed in him? But this crowd, which does not know the law, is accursed." Nicodemus, one of their members who had come to him earlier, said to them, "Does our law condemn a man before it first hears him and finds out what he is doing?" They answered and said to him, "You are not from Galilee also, are you? Look and see that no prophet arises from Galilee."

Then each went to his own house.

JOHN 7: 40-53

BLESSED ELIZABETH OF THE TRINITY

This reflection is taken from the fifth day of Blessed Elizabeth's retreat *Heaven in Faith*.

"'Behold, I stand at the door and knock. If any man listens to My voice and opens the door to Me, I will come in to him and sup with him, and he with Me.' Blessed the ears of the soul alert enough, recollected enough to hear this voice of the Word of God; blessed also the eyes of this soul which in the light of a deep and living faith can witness the 'coming' of the Master in to His intimate sanctuary. But what then is this coming? 'It is an unceasing generation, an enduring hymn of praise.' Christ 'comes

with His treasures, but such is the mystery of the divine swiftness that He is continually coming, always for the first time as if He had never come; for His coming, independent of time, consists of an eternal 'now.'"

Complete Works, vol. 1: 99

REFLECTION

This Gospel continues the account of Jesus hostile encounters with the Pharisees, a hostility that builds through chapters 5 to 11 in the Gospel of John and culminates with John's description of the high priest Caiaphas as he prophesies that Jesus must die for the good of the people.

Some in the crowd "listened" and heard the voice of Jesus knocking at the door of the heart and could proclaim: "this is truly the Prophet" or "this is the Christ." Others however, disdainfully considering themselves of superior knowledge, responded: the Christ does not come from Galilee. Jesus did not fit their preconceived notions of a Messiah who would liberate them from the power of Roman domination and reign as king in the style of the great king David. Nicodemus was someone who struggled to be open. In defending Jesus, he too suffered a haughty response.

Today's Gospel powerfully illustrates the harm we do to ourselves when "the ears of the soul are *not alert enough, recollected enough to hear this voice of the Word of God.*" Jesus "is continually coming, always for the first time as if He had never come; for His coming, independent of time, consists of an eternal *"now."*

Each moment offers fresh opportunities to welcome Christ as we learn to listen with quiet, open hearts to others. Each person is Christ "standing at the door and knocking for entrance into the heart by our attentive listening. Each person is Christ laden with treasures of our need to be more patience, treasures of deeper humility so that our preconceived ideas do not close off another like the chief priests and the Pharisees who condemned Jesus without having truly *listened* and heard his words. How sad to think that the disfavor of the Pharisees might have frightened away those in the crowd who did truly listen and who proclaimed Jesus to be the Christ.

Have I ever listened disdainfully to someone who shared their struggles with the Church and by my superior attitude drove them into further alienation? Have I ever reflected that the eternal now is in every passing moment and that Christ truly speaks to me through things both pleasant and unpleasant? Do I trust Christ to give me the courage like Nicodemus, to speak for the truth when occasion presents itself?

PRAYER

Jesus, you knew what it was like to feel distained and rejected by the scorn of others. Help me to turn to you at such difficult moments in my own life. Grace me to recognize your transforming presence in each passing moment, whether agreeable or disagreeable. Through the intercession of Blessed Elizabeth may the ears of my soul be open enough, recollected enough to hear and proclaim you as my Lord and my God as in your name I pray. Amen.

FIFTH WEEK OF LENT

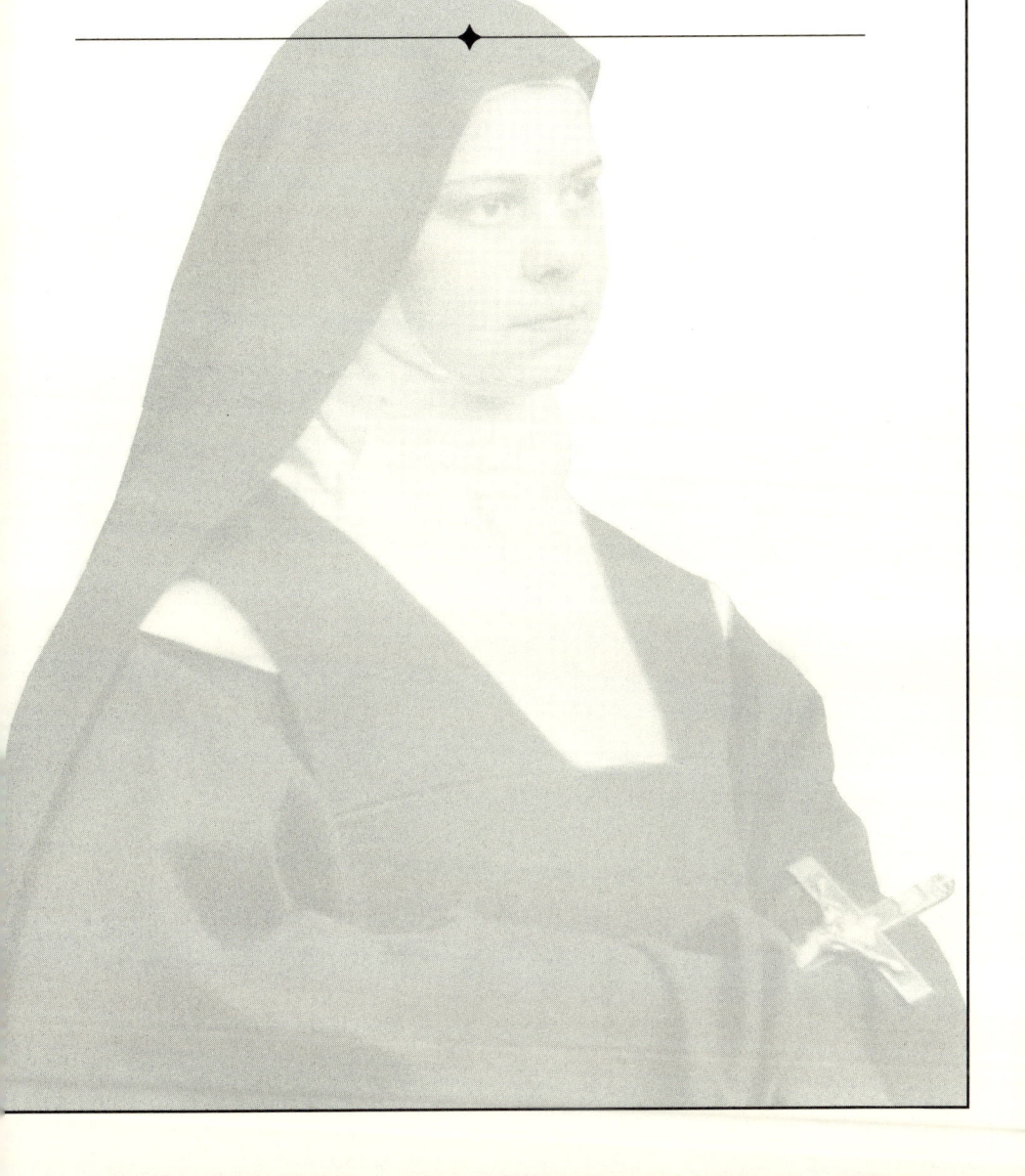

Fifth Sunday of Lent — Year A

Gospel

Now a man was ill, Lazarus from Bethany, the village of Mary and her sister Martha. Mary was the one who had anointed the Lord with perfumed oil and dried his feet with her hair; it was her brother Lazarus who was ill. So the sisters sent word to Jesus saying, "Master, the one you love is ill." When Jesus heard this he said, "This illness is not to end in death, but is for the glory of God, that the Son of God may be glorified through it." Now Jesus loved Martha and her sister and Lazarus. So when he heard that he was ill, he remained for two days in the place where he was. Then after this he said to his disciples, "Let us go back to Judea." The disciples said to him, "Rabbi, the Jews were just trying to stone you, and you want to go back there?" Jesus answered, "Are there not twelve hours in a day? If one walks during the day, he does not stumble, because he sees the light of this world. But if one walks at night, he stumbles, because the light is not in him." He said this, and then told them, "Our friend Lazarus is asleep, but I am going to awaken him." So the disciples said to him, "Master, if he is asleep, he will be saved." But Jesus was talking about his death, while they thought that he meant ordinary sleep. So then Jesus said to them clearly, "Lazarus has died. And I am glad for you that I was not there, that you may believe. Let us go to him." So Thomas, called Didymus, said to his fellow disciples, "Let us also go to die with him."

When Jesus arrived, he found that Lazarus had already been in the tomb for four days. Now Bethany was near Jerusalem, only about two miles away. And many of the Jews had come to Martha and Mary to comfort them about their brother. When Martha heard that Jesus was coming, she went to meet him; but Mary sat at home. Martha said to Jesus, "Lord, if you had been here, my brother would not have died. But even now I know that whatever you ask of God, God will give you." Jesus said to her, "Your brother will rise." Martha said to him, "I know he will rise, in the resurrection on the last day." Jesus told her, "I am the resurrection and the life; whoever believes in me, even if he dies, will live, and everyone who lives and believes in me will never die. Do you believe this?" She said to him, "Yes, Lord. I have come to believe that you are the Christ, the Son of God, the one who is coming into the world."

When she had said this, she went and called her sister Mary secretly, saying, "The teacher is here and is asking for you." As soon as she heard this, she rose quickly and went to him. For Jesus had not yet come into the village, but was still where Martha had met him. So when the Jews who were with her in the house comforting her saw Mary get up quickly and go out, they followed her, presuming that she was going to the tomb to weep there. When Mary came to where Jesus was and saw him, she fell at his feet and said to him, "Lord, if you had been here, my brother would not have died." When Jesus saw her weeping and the Jews who had come with her weeping, he became perturbed and deeply troubled, and said, "Where have you laid him?" They said to him, "Sir, come and see." And Jesus wept. So the Jews said, "See how he loved him." But some of them said, "Could not the one who opened the eyes of the blind man have done something so that this man would not have died?"

So Jesus, perturbed again, came to the tomb. It was a cave, and a stone lay across it. Jesus said, "Take away the stone." Martha, the dead man's sister, said to him, "Lord, by now there will be a stench; he has been dead for four days." Jesus said to her, "Did I not tell you that if you believe you will see the glory of God?" So they took away the stone. And Jesus raised his eyes and said, "Father, I thank you for hearing me. I know that you always hear me; but because of the crowd here I have said this, that they may believe that you sent me." And when he had said this, he cried out in a loud voice, "Lazarus, come out!" The dead man came out, tied hand and foot with burial bands, and his face was wrapped in a cloth. So Jesus said to them, "Untie him and let him go."

Now many of the Jews who had come to Mary and seen what he had done began to believe in him.

JOHN 11: 1-45

Shorter form: JOHN 11:3-7, 17, 20-27, 33b-45
Longer form may be optionally read on any day in the fifth week of Lent

BLESSED ELIZABETH OF THE TRINITY

On April 27, 1904, just two years before her own death, Blessed Elizabeth consoles her friend, Abbe Chevignard, whose father had died the day before.

"I had just written to you when I learned of the painful sacrifice God is asking of your heart and my soul needs to tell yours how united it is to you in this trial. It seems to me that at such times, the Master alone can speak, He whose divinely loving Heart "was troubled" at the tomb of Lazarus. So we can mix our tears with his and, leaning on Him find strength and peace once again. . . . Monsieur l'Abbe, let us follow him by faith into those regions of peace and love. Sursum corda, everything must end in God; one day He will say His 'veni' to us too; then like a little baby on the heart of its mother, we will fall asleep in Him, and 'in His light we will see light.'"

Complete Works, vol. 2: Letter 200

REFLECTION

Today's lengthy narrative, unique to John's Gospel, brings together significant theological themes found in all the Synoptic Gospels. Along with Jesus calling forth Lazarus from the tomb of death at the prayer of his sisters, *we could reflect on the many other instances in the Gospels where Jesus responds to prayer*. Another theme is that of *friendship* and how Jesus relates with his friends and followers. A very important theological message in this Gospel is Martha's profound *affirmation of faith:* "Yes Lord. I have come to believe that you are the Christ, the Son of God, the one who is coming into the world." These all invite reflection, but it is Blessed Elizabeth who focuses our *attention on Jesus and the reality of death.*

The raising of Lazarus to life is the most detailed of such instances in the Gospels. We see Jesus wait for two days before responding to the Martha and Mary's urgent appeal. It is only after Lazarus dies that Jesus goes to them. While we cannot pretend to fathom Jesus response, we know how it issued in one of Jesus' great *I AM* proclamations.

I Am the resurrection and the life; whoever believes in me, even if he dies, will live, and everyone who lives and believes in me will never die.

Martha responds with a proclamation of faith that echoes the voice of the Church that will resonate through the ages after Jesus himself rises from the entombment of his own death: *You are the Christ, the Son of God, the one who is coming into the world.*

It is Blessed Elizabeth who focuses us on Christ as she offers help and consolation to her friend as Jesus did to his. In the raising of Lazarus we see Jesus humanity in a way not always evident in John's Gospel as it is in the other Synoptic Gospels. Here, Jesus weeps with grief over Lazarus and is visibly *perturbed* perhaps at people's insensitive comments: why did he wait so long in coming?

As Blessed Elizabeth writes: "His divinely loving Heart 'was troubled' at the tomb of Lazarus." Jesus loved Lazarus and his sisters and his tears mix with theirs. When our loved ones die, we can believe in faith that Jesus also weeps with us. Like Lazarus and like the father of Elizabeth's friend, God will one day say his "Veni," [his, come] to us too. Hopefully Elizabeth words inspire in us deep desires that in our own moment of death, "like a little baby in the heart of its mother," peacefully, we will fall asleep in Him.

Do I live in such a way that when death draws near I will be ready to surrender my life to God with absolute trust that Christ will walk with me through death and guide me to fullness of life? Do I need to be called forth from the tomb of my sinful habits in order to be freed for friendship with Christ, the source of life here and in eternity?

PRAYER

Lord Jesus, you are the Resurrection and the Life. Call me forth out of my darkness into the light of your faithful, caring friendship and love. Increase my faith. Help me to believe that you weep with me in my sorrow when my loved ones die, and help me to be your compassionate presence to others in their loss of loved ones through death.

Help me, like Blessed Elizabeth, to lift up my heart to you—Sursum Corda—rejoicing, as I pray in your name, that my life will one day realize its fullness in your Divine Presence forever. Amen.

Fifth Sunday of Lent — Year B

GOSPEL

Some Greeks who had come to worship at the Passover Feast came to Philip, who was from Bethsaida in Galilee, and asked him, "Sir, we would like to see Jesus." Philip went and told Andrew; then Andrew and Philip went and told Jesus. Jesus answered them, "The hour has come for the Son of Man to be glorified. Amen, amen, I say to you, unless a grain of wheat falls to the ground and dies, it remains just a grain of wheat; but if it dies, it produces much fruit. Whoever loves his life loses it, and whoever hates his life in this world will preserve it for eternal life. Whoever serves me must follow me, and where I am, there also will my servant be. The Father will honor whoever serves me.

"I am troubled now. Yet what should I say? 'Father, save me from this hour'? But it was for this purpose that I came to this hour. Father, glorify your name." Then a voice came from heaven, "I have glorified it and will glorify it again." The crowd there heard it and said it was thunder; but others said, "An angel has spoken to him." Jesus answered and said, "This voice did not come for my sake but for yours. Now is the time of judgement on this world; now the ruler of this world will be driven out. And when I am lifted up from the earth, I will draw everyone to myself." He said this indicating the kind of death he would die.

John 12: 20-33

BLESSED ELIZABETH OF THE TRINITY

In a text entitled *The Greatness of Our Vocation*, Blessed Elizabeth writes:

"This way to Calvary I climb each day seems to me more like the path of Beautitude! Have you ever seen those pictures depicting death reaping with his sickle? Well, that is my condition; I seem to feel myself being destroyed like that. Sometimes it is painful for nature and I can assure you that if I were to remain at that level, I would feel only my cowardice in the face of suffering. But that is looking at things from the human point of view! Very quickly 'I open the eye of my soul in the light of faith.' And this faith tells me that it is love who is destroying me, who is slowly consuming me; then I feel a tremendous joy, and I surrender myself to Him as His prey."

Complete Works, vol. 1: 126

REFLECTION

Blessed Elizabeth felt her cowardice in the face of suffering. Jesus also struggled as he neared his own dark hour. Our heart takes us to the scene in the Garden of Gethsemane, vividly presented in each of the Synoptic Gospels. In this Gospel, in John's unique way, Jesus is "sorrowful to the point of death" and he prays that this cup of suffering might pass him by. *"Now my soul is troubled and what shall I say? Father save me from this hour! No this is why I came to this hour. Father, glorify thy name!"* It is Jesus' surrender to "His Hour" that prevails so that the Father might be glorified in him. His and his Father's great love for humankind moves Jesus to surrender to the burden of suffering, so inevitable to the human condition. Jesus is willing to lose his life as an example for us. United with him, as we too lose our life through suffering and death, we gain it for all eternity because it is Love who consumes us if we surrender ourselves to him.

As Jesus said of himself, Blessed Elizabeth also is like the grain of wheat that falls to the ground and dies in order to bear much fruit. She is willing to lose her life in this world in order to preserve it for eternal life. She overcomes her cowardice in the face of suffering so that her faith might bear fruit in love.

Jesus knew that when lifted up on His Cross of suffering, he would draw all people to himself. How can we look at our Crucified Lord and not be drawn into His all-embracing love, and in our own times of suffering not be moved to desire that our lives, like that of Jesus, would also draw others to love? As persons who serve and follow Christ, we are invited to accept the inevitable suffering that life brings. We might "feel our cowardice in the face of suffering" but if we "go beyond the human point of view" and open the eyes of our soul, we will willingly unite what is difficult or painful in our life with the sufferings of Jesus.

Quiet reflection on the crucifixion, death and resurrection of Jesus imperceptibly opens the heart to suffering's transforming power. As His followers, where Jesus is, we also desire to be whatever that might mean for each one of us.

What is my attitude toward suffering? When suffering comes my way do I open the eye of my soul in the light of faith to see Love transforming me through this inevitable facet of human life? Am I patient and caring toward others in their suffering or do I avoid them and love's invitation to enter into their pain with compassion and an empathetic heart?

PRAYER

Our Father in heaven, so lovingly named by Jesus, help me to unite myself with your divine Son through all the trials and sufferings that life brings. Help me to accept suffering as part of serving and following Jesus so that united with him, like the grain of wheat buried in the ground, my life might bear abundant fruit for others. In his name I offer this prayer to you, trusting in his abiding presence. Amen.

Fifth Sunday of Lent — Year C

Gospel

Jesus went to the Mount of Olives. But early in the morning he arrived again in the temple area, and all the people started coming to him, and he sat down and taught them. Then the scribes and the Pharisees brought a woman who had been caught in adultery and made her stand in the middle. They said to him, "Teacher, this woman was caught in the very act of committing adultery. Now in the law, Moses commanded us to stone such women. So what do you say?" They said this to test him, so that they could have some charge to bring against him. Jesus bent down and began to write on the ground with his finger. But when they continued asking him, he straightened up and said to them, "Let the one among you who is without sin be the first to throw a stone at her." Again he bent down and wrote on the ground. And in response, they went away one by one, beginning with the elders. So he was left alone with the woman before him. Then Jesus straightened up and said to her, "Woman, where are they? Has no one condemned you?" She replied, "No one, sir." Then Jesus said, "Neither do I condemn you. Go, and from now on do not sin any more."

JOHN 8: 1-11

BLESSED ELIZABETH OF THE TRINITY

On the twelfth day of her last retreat Blessed Elizabeth writes:

"And if I fall at every moment, in a wholly confident faith I will be helped up by Him. I know that He will forgive me, that He will cancel out everything with a jealous care, and even more, He will 'despoil' me, He will 'free' me from all my miseries, from everything that is an obstacle to the divine action."

Complete Works, vol. 1: 156

REFLECTION

We think of the temple area as a sacred space dedicated to worship of Israel's God whom the Israelites believed to be Lord of heaven and of earth. Here they would offer sacrifice to God who had delivered them from the slavery of Egypt and who claimed them as His Chosen People. Unfortunately, some of the Pharisees became more concerned with ritual observance and strict following of the Law than on learning humility of heart. They lost touch with their own sinfulness. They became self-righteous and easily condemned others.

While the act of adultery involves two persons, it is only the woman who is brought before Jesus. They were prepared to stone her to death even as they hoped to find reason to also condemn Jesus for not upholding the Law of Moses. But Jesus, seeing their duplicity, challenged the one without sin to throw the first stone. Did they experience the look of Jesus penetrating their soul and seeing through their hypocrisy, so that one by one they went away?

With their overzealous observance of the Law, these Pharisees failed to come to know in their hearts God, the Eternal Law-giver, so how could they recognize Jesus as God's beloved Son present in their midst? Through Jesus' compassionate response to the woman, Jesus unveils for this sinful woman the face of His Father as infinite, compassionate, forgiving Love.

Blessed Elizabeth is one who truly knew God, having contemplated deeply the heart of Jesus. She knew that her "miseries" were not an obstacle for Jesus' healing love. She needed only to turn to him with absolute confidence. With a holy daring, she not only expected forgiveness, but she trusted Christ to transform her by "despoiling" her of her "miseries" so that God's Trinitarian Life might flow freely through her. Her "miseries" became a special place of encounter with Christ.

Can we not dare to hope that the same became true for the woman taken in adultery as her frightened eyes met the compassionate look of Jesus and heard him say: "neither do I condemn you?"

This Gospel again invites us to take a prayerful look deep into our heart. Do we have the humility to seek forgiveness from God for our own offenses and at the same time to forgive others who have offended us? To truly forgive another is not to deny that we have been wronged, instead, genuine forgiveness takes us beyond our hurts and grievances, beyond the residue of anger or other emotions festering in the heart, into the loving Heart of Christ. Centered in Christ, our ears become attuned to truly hear His words of forgiveness to the woman taken in adultery as they echo through the ages: "Neither do I condemn you. Go, and from now on do not sin any more."

Do I have the humility to acknowledge the self-righteousness present in my critical judgments on others? Is there a person or situation in my life that still awaits the healing balm of Christ's forgiveness to be channeled through me?

PRAYER

Compassionate Heart of Christ, your willingness to forgive infinitely exceeds the human mind's ability to grasp. Enlarge my heart so that your compassionate understanding of our human fragility and sinfulness might flow through me toward others. Shape my heart in your likeness so that, as Blessed Elizabeth prays, I might be for you another humanity in which to live your mysteries. Amen.

FIFTH WEEK OF LENT — MONDAY — YEAR A & B

GOSPEL

Jesus went to the Mount of Olives. But early in the morning he arrived again in the temple area, and all the people started coming to him, and he sat down and taught them. Then the scribes and the Pharisees brought a woman who had been caught in adultery and made her stand in the middle. They said to him, "Teacher, this woman was caught in the very act of committing adultery. Now in the law, Moses commanded us to stone such women. So what do you say?" They said this to test him, so that they could have some charge to bring against him. Jesus bent down and began to write on the ground with his finger. But when they continued asking him, he straightened up and said to them, "Let the one among you who is without sin be the first to throw a stone at her." Again he bent down and wrote on the ground. And in response, they went away one by one, beginning with the elders. So he was left alone with the woman before him. Then Jesus straightened up and said to her, "Woman, where are they? Has no one condemned you?" She replied, "No one, sir." Then Jesus said, "Neither do I condemn you. Go, and from now on do not sin any more."

JOHN 8: 1-11

BLESSED ELIZABETH OF THE TRINITY

Blessed Elizabeth felt a deep sense of gratitude toward her prioress, Mother Germaine. One month before her death, writing as if the words came from Christ Himself, Blessed Elizabeth expresses her deep desires for Mother Germaine.

"*Let yourself be loved more than these!* That is, without fearing that any obstacle will be a hindrance to it, for I am free to pour out My love on whom I wish! '*Let yourself be loved more than these*' is your vocation. It is in being faithful to it that you will make Me happy for you will magnify *the power of My love. This love can rebuild what you have destroyed. Let yourself be loved more than these.'"*

Complete Works, vol. 1: 179

REFLECTION

In today's Gospel the compassionate, forgiving response of Jesus to the woman taken in adultery offers a visible manifestation of God's unconditional love for each one of us. Christ forgave her without a word on her part. Was it the beseeching look in her eyes as her glance rested on this man whose caring look was so different from that hard, accusing look of the Pharisees that gave birth to a glimmer of hope in her heart? Would her life somehow be spared? We can only imagine the terror she felt at that moment, exposed in her shame, with no one to defend her—where was the man who engaged her in adultery?

Jesus asks the searching question: Who is the one without sin? Let them cast the first stone. Is the issue here less about sin, which is so much a part of our fragile humanity, than about mentally or verbally casting stones at others without recognizing our duplicity—that we are all sinners in need of forgiveness? Is this the teaching Jesus wishes to engrave in our heart so that, like Jesus we would have compassionate forgiveness for one another?

Blessed Elizabeth takes us into the heart of Christ as he sees this woman. The enduring, infinity of divine love flowed through him and became the lens through which he saw her—that same love which he would gladly extend to the Pharisees. All that is needed is a receptive, willingness to receive. Did Jesus have the Pharisees in mind when lamenting over Jerusalem he had cried out in His anguish: How often I would have gathered you together as a mother hen gathers her brood under her wings but you refused? (Lk.13:34) Blessed Elizabeth encourages us, as she did her prioress: Let yourself be loved—do not fear even the obstacle of sin, which needs only our openness to receive forgiveness and the outpouring of God's faithful love. God's love heals, restores and rebuilds what sin has destroyed in us. So let yourself be loved. God's loving thought holds us in existence. Were God to forget us for an instant, we would no longer be!

Am I able to acknowledge the ways in which I excuse my own shortcomings and at the same time am demanding and critical of others? Or do I do violence to myself by putting myself down as unworthy of consideration by God, or by others? Instead, reflect on the reality of your preciousness to God. Pray for the grace to truly believe that the God of Incomprehensible Mystery has loved you into existence. Frequently thank God for the mystery of the Incarnation—God enfleshed in our humanity, whose love for you, and for each person individually, is made known in Christ.

PRAYER

Ever-loving Christ, like a mother hen you would gather us to yourself. Help me to show my gratitude for your abundant love by being loving and compassionate toward others. Rebuild in me, and in others, what my critical mind may have destroyed. May your Indwelling Spirit alert me to the times when I assume the role of the Pharisee toward myself or toward others so that with a repentant heart and empowered with your grace, I will go, and from now on, will sin no more. With confident trust, I offer this prayer to you. Amen.

Fifth Week of Lent — Monday — Year C

In Year C, when the preceding Gospel is read on Sunday, the following text is used.

GOSPEL

Jesus spoke to them again, saying, "I am the light of the world. Whoever follows me will not walk in darkness, but will have the light of life." So the Pharisees said to him, "You testify on your own behalf, so your testimony cannot be verified." Jesus answered and said to them, "Even if I do testify on my own behalf, my testimony can be verified, because I know where I came from and where I am going. But you do not know where I come from or where I am going. You judge by appearances, but I do not judge anyone. And even if I should judge, my judgment is valid, because I am not alone, but it is I and the Father who sent me. Even in your law it is written that the testimony of two men can be verified. I testify on my behalf and so does the Father who sent me." So they said to him, "Where is your father?" Jesus answered, "You know neither me nor my Father. If you knew me, you would know my Father also." He spoke these words while teaching in the treasury in the temple area. But no one arrested him, because his hour had not yet come.

JOHN 8: 12-20

BLESSED ELIZABETH OF THE TRINITY

Shortly before her death, to her friend Clémence Blanc, Blessed Elizabeth writes these words:

"In Heaven, I will be your Angel more than ever. I know how well my little sister needs protection in the midst of Paris, where her life is being spent. Saint Paul says that "God chose us in Him before the creation so we might be pure, immaculate in His presence, in love." Ah! How I will ask Him to accomplish this great decree of His will in you! For that purpose, listen to the advice of the same apostle: "Walk in Jesus Christ, rooted in Him, built up on Him, strengthened in faith and growing

more and more in Him." *While contemplating Ideal Beauty in its great brightness, I will ask Him to imprint it on your soul, so that already here on earth, where everything is soiled, you might be beautiful with His beauty, luminous with His Light.*

Complete Works, vol. 2: Letter 331

REFLECTION

Jesus says, "I am the light of the world. Whoever follows me will not walk in darkness, but will have the light of life." This statement by Jesus upsets the Pharisees. It challenges them. It disrupts their world and their hold on power. They ask him to prove His testimony. Today, the new Pharisees, the doubters, like to ones of old, ask us believers to prove the testimony of Jesus Christ.

Blessed Elizabeth knows Jesus is the light of the world. We know Jesus is the light of the world. She has read the Gospel and quotes the great apostle Paul who says "Walk in Jesus Christ, rooted in Him". We must walk in the ways of Jesus to be a light of God in this world. If we do, we will become His testimony.

Blessed Elizabeth prays that God will imprint on her friend the beauty of God. If we are to be lights of God, we too must pray that God brings out of us His presence of love and beauty.

PRAYER

O God, as Blessed Elizabeth has prayed before, we pray today. Make us Your lights in the world of darkness. Strengthen us with Your love and let us reflect the beauty that is always You. We ask in quiet stillness. Amen.

---

*The draft manuscript was missing today's writing selection, reflection and prayer. Sr. Vilma Seelaus, O.C.D. was ill at the time of publication, and was unable to complete the manuscript. Peter J. Mongeau, Publisher of Christus Publishing, LLC, choose the writing selection, and wrote the above reflection and prayer.

Fifth Week of Lent — Tuesday

Gospel

Jesus said to the Pharisees:

"I am going away and you will look for me, but you will die in your sin. Where I am going you cannot come." So the Jews said, "He is not going to kill himself, is he, because he said, 'Where I am going you cannot come'?" He said to them, "You belong to what is below, I belong to what is above. You belong to this world, but I do not belong to this world. That is why I told you that you will die in your sins. For if you do not believe that I AM, you will die in your sins." So they said to him, "Who are you?" Jesus said to them, "What I told you from the beginning. I have much to say about you in condemnation. But the one who sent me is true, and what I heard from him I tell the world." They did not realize that he was speaking to them of the Father. So Jesus said to them, "When you lift up the Son of Man, then you will realize that I AM, and that I do nothing on my own, but I say only what the Father taught me. The one who sent me is with me. He has not left me alone, because I always do what is pleasing to him." Because he spoke this way, many came to believe in him.

John 8: 21-30

BLESSED ELIZABETH OF THE TRINITY

These reflections are taken from the twelfth day of Blessed Elizabeth's last retreat:

"This is Christ's work in every soul of good will and it is the work that His immense love, His 'exceeding love,' is eager to do in me. He wants to be my peace so that nothing can distract me or draw me out of 'the invincible fortress of holy recollection.' It is there that He will give me 'access to the Father' and will keep me as still and as peaceful in His presence as if my soul were already in eternity. It is by the Blood of His Cross that He will make peace in my little heaven, so that it may truly be the repose of the Three."

Complete Works, vol. 1: 156

REFLECTION

Today's Gospel takes us into the heart of Jesus self-understanding. The Pharisees ask Jesus: Who are you? They failed to penetrate the depth of his person because they were unable to go beyond their preconceived expectations of what the messiah should be like. Their hopes were on the human level colored by the valiant heroes of past history who led the people to deliverance from their enemies. Their imaginative memories needed to be detached and emptied so that God's self-revelation in Jesus could find room and become the source of true hope for Israel's future. Is this what happened to the many who because he spoke this way, came to believe in him?

Such self-emptying of the "hero messiah" could only be realized through belief in Jesus' *"exceeding love"* for them. He would open them to a new understanding of God's ways in their midst—a way of compassion and love toward the needy, a way of inner peace and silent awareness of God's abiding presence. Jesus would not lead them in battle against their Roman overlords but to spiritual liberation from their attachment to preconceived notions of who God should be for them.

With a sorrowful heart Jesus tells them that if they do not believe in him they will die in their sin. Could their *sin* be a too limited self-understanding? *In revealing himself, Jesus was also revealing to them the depth of God's abiding presence to humankind.* Jesus says: The one who sent me is with me. He has not left me alone, because I always do what is pleasing to him.

Blessed Elizabeth models for us what the Pharisees failed to understand—that these words of Jesus describe our own deepest identity: that God is always with us. We are never alone. Elizabeth could be as still and as peaceful as if her soul were already in eternity, even in the midst of the severe sufferings of her last illness, because she understood herself to be united with God's Trinitarian indwelling presence.

Jesus self-revelation to the Pharisees reveals our own deepest mystery experienced by Blessed Elizabeth as a mystery of God's exceeding love. If Jesus stood before you today and asked you: Who are you? How would you respond? Do you find your identity in worldly success? Who are you? Do past experiences of hurt or failure limit your present sense of yourself? Pray for the grace of an ever-deepened faith awareness of God's abiding presence, and for self-acceptance as one who has been given access to God in and through Christ.

PRAYER

Jesus, the One who sent you is always with you and has never left you alone. Never leave me alone because without you I easily become like those blinded to the abiding offer of your infinite love. May a spark of your self-disclosure stir into recognition my own deepest identity. Give me the eyes of contemplative faith to penetrate the depth of myself as intrinsically one with you as in your name I pray. Amen.

Fifth Week of Lent — Wednesday

Gospel

Jesus said to those Jews who believed in him, "If you remain in my word, you will truly be my disciples, and you will know the truth, and the truth will set you free." They answered him, "We are descendants of Abraham and have never been enslaved to anyone. How can you say, 'You will become free'?" Jesus answered them, "Amen, amen, I say to you, everyone who commits sin is a slave of sin. A slave does not remain in a household forever, but a son always remains. So if the Son frees you, then you will truly be free. I know that you are descendants of Abraham. But you are trying to kill me, because my word has no room among you. I tell you what I have seen in the Father's presence; then do what you have heard from the Father."

They answered and said to him, "Our father is Abraham." Jesus said to them, "If you were Abraham's children, you would be doing the works of Abraham. But now you are trying to kill me, a man who has told you the truth that I heard from God; Abraham did not do this. You are doing the works of your father!" So they said to him, "We were not born of fornication. We have one Father, God." Jesus said to them, "If God were your Father, you would love me, for I came from God and am here; I did not come on my own, but he sent me."

John 8: 31-42

BLESSED ELIZABETH OF THE TRINITY

On the fourth day of her last retreat, the echo of a familiar refrain continues to sound the depth of Jesus words in today's Gospel reading:

"It was said of Moses that he was 'unshakable in his faith, as if he had seen the Invisible.' It seems to me that this should be the attitude of a praise of glory who wishes to continue her hymn of thanksgiving through everything: 'unshakable in her faith as if she had seen the Invisible'; unshaken in her faith in His 'exceeding love.' 'We have known the love of God for us, and we have believed in it.'"

Complete Works, vol. 1: 145

REFLECTION

Jesus here addresses Jews who believed in him until they heard themselves challenged by a truth about themselves beyond their present self-understanding. When they heard Jesus' words about "the truth setting them free," they became defensive, forgetful of their past history with its many years of enslavement in Egypt. In their present situation, while they were not slaves of the Romans who occupied their land, their freedom was much curtailed. Jesus however spoke about a deeper reality. Sin is what enslaves us; freedom is a matter of the heart. Their hearts were not free to truly hear the depth of Jesus message to them. God, not Abraham was their true father and if they had *truly* accepted God as their father they would not have lost their faith in Jesus. Jesus tells them what he has seen in the Father's presence. His words are what he hears from the Father who sent him. The proof that God was in truth their father would be in their love for Jesus. Instead they try to kill him.

Blessed Elizabeth would remind them of their great liberator Moses who led their ancestors out of the slavery of Egypt into freedom and into the land they inhabited. Moses was unshaken in his faith in spite of the obstacles of the journey. He was a true son of Abraham and a true son of God. Because of his "exceeding love," which kept Moses faithful in the midst of the exodus trials, Matthew in his Gospel could image Jesus as the New Moses.

Elizabeth remained unshaken in her faith because of her belief in God's love. Her self-understanding was illumined by the radiance of God's infinitely expanding love. The truth of God's love, energizing her heart from the heart of Christ, gave her the melody "to continue her hymn of thanksgiving through everything." This love-song of the heart echoes from the Gospel through all the events of her short life.

As is often true, today's Gospel again challenges me to look deeply into myself. Is there a particular sin that enslaves me? But do not stop here. Remind yourself that small or great, enslavement to sin does not define you. Your self-understanding has deeper roots. Within the caverns of your heart are sparks of divine love that stir you to conversion—that prompts your acts of kindness that are part of each day.

Ask yourself: do I truly believe that God's *exceeding love* claims me as a "family member"—as a daughter or son of God—that for this reason does Jesus invites me to say with him, *Our* Father?

Should the word *Father* be difficult for you for any reason, remind yourself that all human names for God are totally inadequate. Simply enter into the truth of Jesus' words and let the mystery of God enfold you.

PRAYER

Holy Spirit of Jesus, attune the ears of my heart to hear the strains of your love resounding in the depth of my being. Help me to recognize the melody of your love as the inspiration of all the good that I am able to do and to hear your song of love, *as you desiring me* that *I might desire you.* Pray this prayer in me as in your name I pray. Amen.

Fifth Week of Lent — Thursday

GOSPEL

Jesus said to the Jews:

"Amen, amen, I say to you, whoever keeps my word will never see death." So the Jews said to him, "Now we are sure that you are possessed. Abraham died, as did the prophets, yet you say, 'Whoever keeps my word will never taste death.' Are you greater than our father Abraham, who died? Or the prophets, who died? Who do you make yourself out to be?" Jesus answered, "If I glorify myself, my glory is worth nothing; but it is my Father who glorifies me, of whom you say, 'He is our God.' You do not know him, but I know him. And if I should say that I do not know him, I would be like you a liar. But I do know him and I keep his word. Abraham your father rejoiced to see my day; he saw it and was glad." So the Jews said to him, "You are not yet fifty years old and you have seen Abraham?" Jesus said to them, "Amen, amen, I say to you, before Abraham came to be, I AM." So they picked up stones to throw at him; but Jesus hid and went out of the temple area.

John 8: 51-59

BLESSED ELIZABETH OF THE TRINITY

On the eighth day of her retreat Heaven in Faith, Blessed Elizabeth continues to draw us ever deeper into the mystery of our inner being. She writes:

"He wants to glorify us, and for that reason, says St. Paul, He 'has made us worthy to share in the inheritance of the saints in light,' but we well be glorified in the measure in which we will have been conformed to the image of His divine Son. So let us contemplate this adored Image, let us remain unceasingly under its radiance so that it may imprint itself on us; let us go to everything with the same attitude of soul that our holy Master would have. Then we will realize the great plan by which God

has 'resolved in Himself to restore all things in Christ.'"

Complete Works, vol. 1: 105–6

REFLECTION

This section of the Gospel of John brings us farther along in the controversies Jesus continues to have with the Jews that ultimately leads to his death. At the heart of these encounters is an ongoing revelation on the part of Jesus of the mystery that shapes his person. His divine origin is beyond their ability to grasp with their intellect so they counteract with denigrating and even violent responses—they pick up stones to throw at him.

Jesus walks in their midst as an icon of God and he speaks words that cannot be understood by belligerent ears. For an icon to unveil its mystery it needs the contemplative eye of faith to see beyond the exterior. It draws one beyond the obvious into deeper realms that only the heart can understand. Whoever keeps my words will never taste death—it is my Father who glorifies me—I know Him and I keep His words—Abraham rejoiced to see my day; he saw it and was glad—before Abraham came to be, I AM.

In Exodus (3:13ff) God appears to Moses in the burning bush and announces that He is sending Moses to lead his people out of their slavery in Egypt. When Moses asks to know God's name, God replies: Tell the people I AM who I AM. The Jews of Jesus time heard as blasphemy and as coming from one possessed Jesus' words, "before Abraham came to be, I AM."

Our Christian belief holds much before us that cannot be understood by the rational mind. Only the eyes of faith can penetrate the mystery of God Incarnate in our midst, Christ's Presence in the Eucharist, and more mysterious still, God's indwelling Presence. Blessed Elizabeth reminds us that our life task is to be conformed to the image of the divine Son whose indwelling presence shapes our true self so that the radiance of Christ might shine through our every word and action. For this to be realized, she invites us to contemplate the divine image, to keep the eyes of the heart attentive to his indwelling presence and to reflect often on the scriptures so that "his attitude of soul" becomes ours.

Am I aware that while striving for psychological wholeness is important, coming to my true self includes a spiritual reality? Reflect that it is a gift already given which simply awaits my cooperation. The radiance of Christ germinates within. Christ is the divine sun who warms the heart through prayer and brings to blossom the unique image of God that I am meant to reflect. As image of God, each one of us uniquely reflects something of God in our world.

PRAYER

Jesus, the more I look at you in your Gospels, the more I marvel at your willingness to be in our midst as one of us when you were so misunderstood and so rejected by your own people. But am I any better? I need your help if I am to deepen in my faith in your abiding presence and if I am to truly live what it means to be *a Christian*—someone identified by your name. As in your name I pray, shape my inmost being into your likeness so that my life increasingly radiates your life in me. Amen.

Fifth Week of Lent — Friday

GOSPEL

The Jews picked up rocks to stone Jesus. Jesus answered them, "I have shown you many good works from my Father. For which of these are you trying to stone me?" The Jews answered him, "We are not stoning you for a good work but for blasphemy. You, a man, are making yourself God." Jesus answered them, "Is it not written in your law, 'I said, "You are gods"'? If it calls them gods to whom the word of God came, and Scripture cannot be set aside, can you say that the one whom the Father has consecrated and sent into the world blasphemes because I said, 'I am the Son of God'? If I do not perform my Father's works, do not believe me; but if I perform them, even if you do not believe me, believe the works, so that you may realize and understand that the Father is in me and I am in the Father." Then they tried again to arrest him; but he escaped from their power.

He went back across the Jordan to the place where John first baptized, and there he remained. Many came to him and said, "John performed no sign, but everything John said about this man was true." And many there began to believe in him.

John 10: 31-42

BLESSED ELIZABETH OF THE TRINITY

In the second prayer of the fourth day of her retreat Heaven in Faith, reflecting on passages from the Spiritual Canticle of John of the Cross Blessed Elizabeth writes:

"'I have come to cast fire upon the earth and how I long to see it burn.' It is the Master Himself who expresses His desire to see the fire of love enkindled. In fact, 'all our works and all our labors are nothing in His sight. We can neither give Him anything nor satisfy His only desire, which is to exalt the dignity of our soul.' Nothing pleases Him so much as to see it 'grow.' 'Now nothing can exalt it so much as to become in some *way the equal of God; that is why He demands from the soul the tribute of its love, as the property of love is to make the lover equal to the beloved as much as possible. The soul in possession of this love' 'appears on an equal footing with Christ because their mutual affection renders everything common to both.'"*

Complete Works, vol. 1: 99

REFLECTION

Today's Gospel vividly depicts the ongoing conflict between Jesus and the Jewish authorities. In his own defense, Jesus opens to them their own scriptures reminding them how they are identified with God by the keeping of the Law. "I said, 'You are gods.'" The works of Jesus are before their eyes confirming that he is the one whom the Father has consecrated and sent into the world. Rightly could Jesus claim to be the Son of God. Those who rejected Jesus had closed the eyes of the heart through which in faith they would have seen that Jesus truly is in the Father and the Father in him so they tried again to arrest him for blasphemy. In doing so, they again closed their eyes to the depth of their own truth, "I said, 'You are gods.'"

Jesus escapes and makes his way across the Jordan to where John first baptized and where Jesus heard the words at his own baptism by John, "You are my beloved, and on you my favor rests." Perhaps Jesus needed to re-visit this place to find strength for what was ahead—a place where people were more open to his message. "And many there began to believe in him."

Blessed Elizabeth is among those open to Jesus message and through a deep faith, could internalize the words of her Carmelite mentor, St. John of the Cross, that Christ would transform us into himself. As John writes: "We can neither give Him anything nor satisfy His only desire, *which is to exalt the dignity of our soul.* That is why He demands from the soul the tribute of its love, *as the property of love is to make the lover equal to the beloved as much as possible.* The soul in possession of this love *appears on an equal footing with Christ* because their mutual affection renders everything common to both."

When we are united with Christ through love, it can be said of us, "you are gods." We are "gods" by our participation in the life of Christ expressed by a love that embraces all persons without distinction. We can give nothing to God except the tribute of our love and this very love is God's gift to us, a gift that would transform us into total God-like ness.

What in my attitudes and behavior would need transformation "for me to appear on an equal footing with Christ?" Can I dare to believe that I am destined to be "God" by participation? For this to be realized am I willing to pray for the grace to love God and others with the same self-sacrificing love that Jesus mirrors to me in the Gospels?

PRAYER

Lord Jesus, you continue to amaze and fill me with awe. You are the beloved of God; you are in the Father and the Father is in you. At the same time you are fully human! You came among us as one who unveils the face of God. You also reveal the depth of our human capacity to be so united with you through your love in us that we can say of one another, "you are God." As you do your Father's works, through your indwelling presence, continue to work in and through us that the fire of your love might be enkindled in our world. With deep gratitude I offer this prayer to your Father in your name. Amen.

Fifth Week of Lent — Saturday

Gospel

Many of the Jews who had come to Mary and seen what Jesus had done began to believe in him. But some of them went to the Pharisees and told them what Jesus had done. So the chief priests and the Pharisees convened the Sanhedrin and said, "What are we going to do? This man is performing many signs. If we leave him alone, all will believe in him, and the Romans will come and take away both our land and our nation." But one of them, Caiaphas, who was high priest that year, said to them, "You know nothing, nor do you consider that it is better for you that one man should die instead of the people, so that the whole nation may not perish." He did not say this on his own, but since he was high priest for that year, he prophesied that Jesus was going to die for the nation, and not only for the nation, but also to gather into one the dispersed children of God. So from that day on they planned to kill him.

So Jesus no longer walked about in public among the Jews, but he left for the region near the desert, to a town called Ephraim, and there he remained with his disciples.

Now the Passover of the Jews was near, and many went up from the country to Jerusalem before Passover to purify themselves. They looked for Jesus and said to one another as they were in the temple area, "What do you think? That he will not come to the feast?"

John 11: 45-56

BLESSED ELIZABETH OF THE TRINITY

In the sixth day of her last retreat, in this passage Blessed Elizabeth reflects on the importance of singleness of purpose. Using scripture, especially passages from the Psalms, she writes:

"Let us say with St. Paul, 'Quotidie morior' [I die daily]. The great saint wrote to the Colossians, 'You have died and your life is hidden with Christ in God.' This is the condition: we must be dead! Without that we

may be hidden in God at certain moments; but we do not LIVE habitually in this divine Being because all our emotions, self-seekings and the rest, come to draw us out of Him. The soul that gazes steadfastly on its Master with this 'single eye which fills the whole body with light' is kept 'from the depths of iniquity within it' of which the prophet complains. The Lord has brought is into 'this spacious place' which is nothing else than Himself; there everything is pure, everything is holy."

Complete Works, vol. 1: 148

REFLECTION

Today's Gospel and the selection from Blessed Elizabeth demonstrate the importance of being in touch with that which motivates our actions. The Pharisees were single-minded in the desire to do away with this man of wisdom who worked wonders among the people. They were losing their authority so they rationalized their fears by making it a political issue. Caiaphas the high priest intervenes: "You know nothing, nor do you consider that it is better for you that one man should die instead of the people, so that the whole nation may not perish." Because the "eye was not single in a steadfast gaze on its Master" the Pharisees allowed self-seeking and "the depth of iniquity within" to overshadow the "spacious place" "which is nothing else than Himself."

Jesus, too, is single-minded in following his mission. He knows the Pharisees duplicity and their intent to put him to death so he retires to a desert place. Here Jesus, whose "single eye fills the whole body with light," draws strength in prayer to his Father that he remain faithful, knowing what will be his fate as was that of so many of the prophets before him.

Ours has been called a culture of narcissism. In our contemporary world we are often faced with situations not unlike those of Jesus' times. Like the Pharisees, self-centeredness, self-seeking in all its forms can imperceptibly draw us out of our center in Christ. When our Christian values are challenged we easily rationalize and let ourselves be swayed from a single-minded following of Christ. How important it is to honestly look at the values that motivate our actions. Are they Gospel values? We can do this only if, at least in desire, "our life is hidden with Christ in God."

We need at times to "leave the region" of our everyday lives and like Jesus, retire to a quiet place and reconnect with the possible "depth of iniquity within" as well as with, "that spacious place which is nothing else but Himself." Here in the depth of our being, the place of God's indwelling presence; we can redirect our life into a single-minded following of Christ.

What am I single-minded about? We will never be without things to do. Does my commitment to my job or my profession cause me to neglect important persons in my life, especially my family? Do I rationalize my neglect of prayer and the sacraments of the Church by claiming to be too busy?

PRAYER

Jesus, Holy Wisdom, enlighten the dark places in my heart and redirect my inner being to more single-minded commitment to you and to your Gospel of love. Draw me into that silent place within, where "gazing steadfastly" at you, I may be freed from illusion and graced with renewed fidelity to you and to the loved ones you have placed in my life. I make this prayer with trust and confidence in your guiding Wisdom. Amen.

HOLY WEEK

PALM SUNDAY – YEAR A

GOSPEL

AT THE PROCESSION WITH PALMS

When Jesus and the disciples drew near Jerusalem and came to Bethphage on the Mount of Olives, Jesus sent two disciples, saying to them, "Go into the village opposite you, and immediately you will find an ass tethered, and a colt with her. Untie them and bring them here to me. And if anyone should say anything to you, reply, 'The master has need of them.' Then he will send them at once." This happened so that what had been spoken through the prophet might be fulfilled: / *Say to daughter Zion,* / *"Behold, your king comes to you,* / *meek and riding on an ass,* / *and on a colt, the foal of a beast of burden."* / The disciples went and did as Jesus had ordered them. They brought the ass and the colt and laid their cloaks over them, and he sat upon them. The very large crowd spread their cloaks on the road, while others cut branches from the trees and strewed them on the road. The crowds preceding him and those following kept crying out and saying: / "Hosanna to the Son of David; / blessed is the he who comes in the name of the Lord; / hosanna in the highest." / And when he entered Jerusalem the whole city was shaken and asked, "Who is this?" And the crowds replied, "This is Jesus the prophet, from Nazareth in Galilee."

MATTHEW 21: 1-11

GOSPEL

MASS

One of the Twelve, who was called Judas Iscariot, went to the chief priests and said, "What are you willing to give me if I hand him over to you?" They paid him thirty pieces of silver, and from that time on he looked for an opportunity to hand him over.

On the first day of the Feast of Unleavened Bread, the disciples approached Jesus and said, "Where do you want us to prepare for you to eat the Passover?" He said, "Go into the city to a certain man and tell him, 'The teacher says, "My appointed time draws near; in your house I shall celebrate the Passover with my disciples."'"The disciples then did as Jesus had ordered, and prepared the Passover.

When it was evening, he reclined at table with the Twelve. And while they were eating, he said, "Amen, I say to you, one of you will betray me." Deeply distressed at this, they began to say to him one after another, "Surely it is not I, Lord?" He said in reply, "He who has dipped his hand into the dish with me is the one who will betray me. The Son of Man indeed goes, as it is written of him, but woe to that man by whom the Son of Man is betrayed. It would be better for that man if he had never been born." Then Judas, his betrayer, said in reply, "Surely it is not I, Rabbi?" He answered, "You have said so."

While they were eating, Jesus took bread, said the blessing, broke it, and giving it to his disciples said, "Take and eat; this is my body." Then he took a cup, gave thanks, and gave it to them, saying, "Drink from it, all of you, for this is my blood of the covenant, which will be shed on behalf of many for the forgiveness of sins. I tell you, from now on I shall not drink this fruit of the vine until the day when I drink it with you new in the kingdom of my Father." Then, after singing a hymn, they went out to the Mount of Olives.

Then Jesus said to them, "This night all of you will have your faith in me shaken, for it is written: / *I will strike the shepherd, / and the sheep of the flock will be dispersed;* / but after I have been raised up, I shall go before you to Galilee." Peter said to him in reply, "Though all may have their faith in you shaken, mine will never be." Jesus said to him, "Amen, I say to you, this very night before the cock crows, you will deny me three times." Peter said to him, "Even though I should have to die with you, I will not deny you." And all the disciples spoke likewise.

Then Jesus came with them to a place called Gethsemane, and he said to his disciples, "Sit here while I go over there and pray." He took along Peter and the two sons of Zebedee, and began to feel sorrow and distress. Then he said to them, "My soul is sorrowful even to death. Remain here and keep watch with me." He advanced a little and fell prostrate in prayer, saying, "My Father, if it is possible, let this cup pass from me; yet, not as I will, but as you will." When he returned to his disciples he found them asleep. He said to Peter, "So you could not keep watch with me for one hour? Watch and pray that you may not undergo the test. The spirit is willing, but the flesh is weak." Withdrawing a second time, he prayed again, "My Father, if it is not possible that this cup pass without my drinking it, your will be done!" Then he returned once more and found them asleep, for they could not keep their eyes open. He left them and withdrew again and prayed a third time, saying the same thing again. Then he returned to his disciples and said to them, "Are you still sleeping and taking your rest? Behold, the hour is at hand when the Son of Man is to be handed over to sinners. Get up, let us go. Look, my betrayer is at hand."

While he was still speaking, Judas, one of the Twelve, arrived, accompanied by a large crowd, with swords and clubs, who had come from the chief priests and the elders of the people. His betrayer had arranged a sign with them, saying, "The man I shall kiss is the one; arrest him." Immediately he went over to Jesus and said, "Hail, Rabbi!" and he kissed him. Jesus answered him, "Friend, do what you have come for." Then stepping forward they laid hands on Jesus and arrested him. And behold, one of those who accompanied Jesus put his hand to his sword, drew it, and struck the high priest's servant, cutting off his ear. Then Jesus said to him, "Put your sword back into its sheath, for all who take the sword will perish by the sword. Do you think that I cannot call upon my Father and he will not provide me at this moment with more than twelve legions of angels? But then how would the Scriptures be fulfilled which say that it must come to pass in this way?" At that hour Jesus said to the crowds, "Have you come out as against a robber, with swords and clubs to seize me? Day after day I sat teaching in the temple area, yet you did not arrest me. But all this has come to pass that the writings of the prophets may be fulfilled." Then all the disciples left him and fled.

Those who had arrested Jesus led him away to Caiaphas the high priest, where the scribes and the elders were assembled. Peter was following him at a distance as far as the high priest's courtyard, and going inside he sat down with the servants to see the outcome. The chief priests and the entire Sanhedrin kept trying to obtain false testimony against Jesus in order to put him to death, but they found none, though many false witnesses came forward. Finally two came forward who stated, "This man said, 'I can destroy the temple of God and within three days rebuild it.'" The high priest rose and addressed him, "Have you no answer? What are these men testifying against you?" But Jesus was silent. Then the high priest said to him, "I order you to tell us under oath before the living God whether you are the Christ, the Son of God." Jesus said to him in reply, "You have said so. But I tell you: / From now on you will see 'the Son of Man / seated at the right hand of the Power' / and 'coming on the clouds of heaven.'" / Then the high priest tore his robes and said, "He has blasphemed! What further need have we of witnesses? You have now heard the blasphemy; what is your opinion?" They said in reply, "He deserves to die!" Then they spat in his face and struck him, while some slapped him, saying, "Prophesy for us, Christ: who is it that struck you?"

Now Peter was sitting outside in the courtyard. One of the maids came over to him and said, "You too were with Jesus the Galilean." But he denied it in front of everyone, saying, "I do not know what you are talking about!" As he went out to the gate, another girl saw him and said to those who were there, "This man was with Jesus the Nazorean." Again he denied it with an oath, "I do not know the man!"

A little later the bystanders came over and said to Peter, "Surely you too are one of them; even your speech gives you away." At that he began to curse and to swear, "I do not know the man." And immediately a cock crowed. Then Peter remembered the word that Jesus had spoken: "Before the cock crows you will deny me three times." He went out and began to weep bitterly.

When it was morning, all the chief priests and the elders of the people took counsel against Jesus to put him to death. They bound him, led him away, and handed him over to Pilate, the governor.

Then Judas, his betrayer, seeing that Jesus had been condemned, deeply regretted what he had done. He returned the thirty pieces of silver to the chief priests and elders, saying, "I have sinned in betraying innocent blood." They said, "What is that to us? Look to it yourself." Flinging the money into the temple, he departed and went off and hanged himself. The chief priests gathered up the money, but said, "It is not lawful to deposit this in the temple treasury, for it is the price of blood." After consultation, they used it to buy the potter's field as a burial place for foreigners. That is why that field even today is called the Field of Blood. Then was fulfilled what had been said through Jeremiah the prophet, / *And they took the thirty pieces of silver, / the value of a man with a price on his head, / a price set by some of the Israelites, / and they paid it out for the potter's field / just as the Lord had commanded me.*

Now Jesus stood before the governor, who questioned him, "Are you the king of the Jews?" Jesus said, "You say so." And when he was accused by the chief priests and elders, he made no answer. Then Pilate said to him, "Do you not hear how many things they are testifying against you?" But he did not answer him one word, so that the governor was greatly amazed.

Now on the occasion of the feast the governor was accustomed to release to the crowd one prisoner whom they wished. And at that time they had a notorious prisoner called Barabbas. So when they had assembled, Pilate said to them, "Which one do you want me to release to you, Barabbas, or Jesus called Christ?" For he knew that it was out of envy that they had handed him over. While he was still seated on the bench, his wife sent him a message, "Have nothing to do with that righteous man. I suffered much in a dream today because of him." The chief priests and the elders persuaded the crowds to ask for Barabbas but to destroy Jesus. The governor said to them in reply, "Which of the two do you want me to release to you?" They answered, "Barabbas!" Pilate said to them, "Then what shall I do with Jesus called Christ?" They all said, "Let him be crucified!" But he said, "Why? What evil has he done?" They only shouted the louder, "Let him be crucified!" When Pilate saw that he was not succeeding at all, but that a riot was breaking out instead, he took water and washed his hands in the sight of the crowd, saying, "I am innocent of this man's blood. Look to it yourselves." And the whole people said in reply, "His blood be upon us and upon our children." Then he released Barabbas to them, but after he had Jesus scourged, he handed him over to be crucified.

Then the soldiers of the governor took Jesus inside the praetorium and gathered the whole cohort around him. They stripped off his clothes and threw a scarlet military cloak about him. Weaving a crown out of thorns, they placed it on his head, and a reed in his right hand. And kneeling before him, they mocked him, saying, "Hail, King of the Jews!" They spat upon him and took the reed and kept striking him on the head. And when they had mocked him, they stripped him of the cloak, dressed him in his own clothes, and led him off to crucify him.

As they were going out, they met a Cyrenian named Simon; this man they pressed into service to carry his cross.

And when they came to a place called Golgotha — which means Place of the Skull —, they gave Jesus wine to drink mixed with gall. But when he had tasted it, he refused to drink. After they had crucified him, they divided his garments by casting lots; then they sat down and kept watch over him there. And they placed over his head the written charge against him: This is Jesus, the King of the Jews. Two revolutionaries were crucified with him, one on his right and the other on his left. Those passing by reviled him, shaking their heads and saying, "You who would destroy the temple and rebuild it in three days, save yourself, if you are the Son of God, and come down from the cross!"

Likewise the chief priests with the scribes and elders mocked him and said, "He saved others; he cannot save himself. So he is the king of Israel! Let him come down from the cross now, and we will believe in him. He trusted in God; let him deliver him now if he wants him. For he said, 'I am the Son of God.'" The revolutionaries who were crucified with him also kept abusing him in the same way.

From noon onward, darkness came over the whole land until three in the afternoon. And about three o'clock Jesus cried out in a loud voice, *"Eli, Eli, lema sabachthani?"* which means, "My God, my God, why have you forsaken me?" Some of the bystanders who heard it said, "This one is calling for Elijah." Immediately one of them ran to get a sponge; he soaked it in wine, and putting it on a reed, gave it to him to drink. But the rest said, "Wait, let us see if Elijah comes to save him." But Jesus cried out again in a loud voice, and gave up his spirit.

Here all kneel and pause for a short time.

And behold, the veil of the sanctuary was torn in two from top to bottom. The earth quaked, rocks were split, tombs were opened, and the bodies of many saints who had fallen asleep were raised. And coming forth from their tombs after his resurrection, they entered the holy city and appeared to many. The centurion and the men with him who were keeping watch over Jesus feared greatly when they saw the earthquake and all that was happening, and they said, "Truly, this was the Son of God!" There were many women there, looking on from a distance, who had followed Jesus from Galilee, ministering to him. Among them were Mary Magdalene and Mary the mother of James and Joseph, and the mother of the sons of Zebedee.

When it was evening, there came a rich man from Arimathea named Joseph, who was himself a disciple of Jesus. He went to Pilate and asked for the body of Jesus; then Pilate ordered it to be handed over. Taking the body, Joseph wrapped it in clean linen and laid it in his new tomb that he had hewn in the rock. Then he rolled a huge stone across the entrance to the tomb and departed. But Mary Magdalene

> and the other Mary remained sitting there, facing the tomb.
>
> The next day, the one following the day of preparation, the chief priests and the Pharisees gathered before Pilate and said, "Sir, we remember that this impostor while still alive said, 'After three days I will be raised up.' Give orders, then, that the grave be secured until the third day, lest his disciples come and steal him and say to the people, 'He has been raised from the dead.' This last imposture would be worse than the first." Pilate said to them, "The guard is yours; go, secure it as best you can." So they went and secured the tomb by fixing a seal to the stone and setting the guard.
>
> MATTHEW 26: 14-75 & 27: 1-66
>
> Shorter form: MATTHEW 27:11-54

BLESSED ELIZABETH OF THE TRINITY

On June 10, 1906, five months before her actual death, Blessed Elizabeth writes to her friend, Germaine de Gemeaux:

"On the evening of Palm Sunday, I had a very severe attack, and I thought the hour had finally arrived when I was going to fly away into the infinite realms to contemplate unveiled this Trinity that has already been my dwelling place here below. In the calm and silence of that night, I received Extreme Unction and the visit of my Master. It seemed to me He was awaiting that moment to break my bonds. Oh! my little sister, what ineffable days I spent expecting the great vision!"

Complete Works, vol. 2: Letter 278

REFLECTION

Palm Sunday is a solemn day in the life of the Church. As Jesus enters Jerusalem, the crowd proclaims: Hosanna to the son of David. But soon after, as the Liturgy progresses, we hear the reading of Matthew's account of Jesus passion. Matthew's Passion Narrative begins with Jesus' gift of himself in the Eucharist and concludes with Jesus giving up his spirit in death.

The passion of Jesus gives us much to reflect upon. Jesus' suffering ended in his death but death gave way to Christ rising in glory to die no more. Death has, as it were, been mysteriously divinized as it entered into the body of one who was both human and divine. While death has not lost any of its diminishments in that human life as known on this earth no longer exists, its meaning and its seeming finality have undergone radical change. Christ's resurrection offers the unraveling of death's ultimate finality and opens the door to fullness of life in God where death no longer has a claim on us. Palm Sunday, the beginning of Holy Week, where the deepest mysteries of our faith are unveiled before us, invites us to look more deeply into the meaning of our own lives and our own eventual death.

In her short life, Blessed Elizabeth was graced to penetrate deeply into the mystery of the indwelling Presence of God. For her, death meant: "I was going to fly away into the infinite realms to contemplate unveiled this Trinity that has already been my dwelling place here below." In calm and in inner silence she could await her passage through death in to the arms of her Beloved. Her life models the reality that the mysteries of Christ are our mysteries.

Does my faith in Christ influence my attitude toward the joys and sufferings of life with its eventual death? What does death mean for me? What changes do I need to make in my life in order to have fewer regrets at the time of my death? Are there persons with whom I need to be reconciled so that neither of us dies estranged from the other?

PRAYER

Blessed Elizabeth, as once again the Church guides us through the intense journey of Holy Week, keep me mindful of Christ's indwelling Presence. Help me to realize that the mysteries I contemplate this week are not events that happened long ago. May I be ever more aware of Christ's desire to renew his life in me so that at the time of my death I may look forward to the unveiling of God's Trinitarian life in the bliss of eternity. I offer this prayer through you, Lord Jesus desiring that your love draw me ever deeper into the mystery of the indwelling Trinity. Amen.

PALM SUNDAY – YEAR B

GOSPEL

PROCESSION WITH PALMS

When Jesus and his disciples drew near to Jerusalem, to Bethpage and Bethany at the Mount of Olives, he sent two of his disciples and said to them, "Go into the village opposite you, and immediately on entering it, you will find a colt tethered on which no one has ever sat. Untie it and bring it here. If anyone should say to you, 'Why are you doing this?' reply, 'The Master has need of it and will send it back here at once.'" So they went off and found a colt tethered at a gate outside on the street, and they untied it. Some of the bystanders said to them, "What are you doing, untying the colt?" They answered them just as Jesus had told them to, and they permitted them to do it. So they brought the colt to Jesus and put their cloaks over it. And he sat on it. Many people spread their cloaks on the road, and others spread leafy branches that they had cut from the fields. Those preceding him as well as those following kept crying out: / "Hosanna! / Blessed is he who comes in the name of the Lord! / Blessed is the kingdom of our father David that is to come! / Hosanna in the highest!"

MARK 11: 1-10

Alternative: JOHN 12:12-16

Gospel

Mass

The Passover and the Feast of Unleavened Bread were to take place in two days' time. So the chief priests and the scribes were seeking a way to arrest him by treachery and put him to death. They said, "Not during the festival, for fear that there may be a riot among the people."

When he was in Bethany reclining at table in the house of Simon the leper, a woman came with an alabaster jar of perfumed oil, costly genuine spikenard. She broke the alabaster jar and poured it on his head. There were some who were indignant. "Why has there been this waste of perfumed oil? It could have been sold for more than three hundred days' wages and the money given to the poor." They were infuriated with her. Jesus said, "Let her alone. Why do you make trouble for her? She has done a good thing for me. The poor you will always have with you, and whenever you wish you can do good to them, but you will not always have me. She has done what she could. She has anticipated anointing my body for burial. Amen, I say to you, wherever the gospel is proclaimed to the whole world, what she has done will be told in memory of her."

Then Judas Iscariot, one of the Twelve, went off to the chief priests to hand him over to them. When they heard him they were pleased and promised to pay him money. Then he looked for an opportunity to hand him over.

On the first day of the Feast of Unleavened Bread, when they sacrificed the Passover lamb, his disciples said to him, "Where do you want us to go and prepare for you to eat the Passover?" He sent two of his disciples and said to them, "Go into a city and a man will meet you, carrying a jar of water. Follow him. Wherever he enters, say to the master of the house, 'The Teacher says, "Where is my guest room where I may eat the Passover with my disciples?"' Then he will show you a large upper room furnished and ready. Make the preparations for us there." The disciples then went off, entered the city, and found it just as he had told them; and they prepared the Passover.

When it was evening, he came with the Twelve. And as they reclined at table and were eating, Jesus said, "Amen, I say to you, one of you will betray me, one who is eating with me." They began to be distressed and to say to him, one by one, "Surely it is not I?" He said to them, "One of the Twelve, the one who dips with me into the dish. For the Son of Man indeed goes, as it is written of him, but woe to that man by whom the Son of Man is betrayed. It would be better for that man if he had never been born."

While they were eating, he took bread, said the blessing, broke it, and gave it to them, and said, "Take it; this is my body." Then he took a cup, gave thanks, and gave it to them, and they all drank from it. He said to them, "This is my blood of the covenant, which will be shed for many. Amen, I say to you, I shall not drink again the fruit of the vine until the day when I drink it new in the kingdom of God." Then, after singing a hymn, they went out to the Mount of Olives.

Then Jesus said to them, "All of you will have your faith shaken, for it is written: / *I will strike the shepherd, / and the sheep will be dispersed.* / But after I have been raised up, I shall go before you to Galilee." Peter said to him, "Even though all should have their faith shaken, mine will not be." Then Jesus said to him, "Amen, I say to you, this very night before the cock crows twice you will deny me three times." But he vehemently replied, "Even though I should have to die with you, I will not deny you." And they all spoke similarly.

Then they came to a place named Gethsemane, and he said to his disciples, "Sit here while I pray." He took with him Peter, James and John, and began to be troubled and distressed. Then he said to them, "My soul is sorrowful even to death. Remain here and keep watch." He advanced a little and fell to the ground and prayed that if it were possible the hour might pass by him; he said, "Abba, Father, all things are possible to you. Take this cup away from me, but not what I will but what you will." When he returned he found them asleep. He said to Peter, "Simon, are you asleep? Could you not keep watch for one hour? Watch and pray that you may not undergo the test. The spirit is willing but the flesh is weak." Withdrawing again, he prayed, saying the same thing. Then he returned once more and found them asleep, for they could not keep their eyes open and did not know what to answer him. He returned a third time and said to them, "Are you still sleeping and taking your rest? It is enough. The hour has come. Behold, the Son of Man is to be handed over to sinners. Get up, let us go. See, my betrayer is at hand."

Then, while he was still speaking, Judas, one of the Twelve, arrived, accompanied by a crowd with swords and clubs who had come from the chief priests, the scribes, and the elders. His betrayer had arranged a signal with them, saying, "The man I shall kiss is the one; arrest him and lead him away securely." He came and immediately went over to him and said, "Rabbi." And he kissed him. At this they laid hands on him and arrested him. One of the bystanders drew his sword, struck the high priest's servant, and cut off his ear. Jesus said to them in reply, "Have you come out as against a robber, with swords and clubs, to seize me? Day after day I was with you teaching in the temple area, yet you did not arrest me; but that the Scriptures may be fulfilled." And they all left him and fled. Now a young man followed him wearing nothing but a linen cloth about his body. They seized him, but he left the cloth behind and ran off naked.

They led Jesus away to the high priest, and all the chief priests and the elders and the scribes came together. Peter followed him at a distance into the high priest's courtyard and was seated with the guards, warming himself at the fire. The chief priests and the entire Sanhedrin kept trying to obtain testimony against Jesus in order to put him to death, but they found none. Many gave false witness against him, but their testimony did not agree. Some took the stand and testified falsely against him, alleging, "We heard him say, 'I will destroy this temple made with hands and within three days I will build another not made with hands.'" Even so their testimony did not agree. The high priest rose before the assembly and questioned Jesus, saying, "Have you no answer? What are these men testifying against you?" But he was silent and answered nothing. Again the high priest asked him and said to him, "Are you the Christ, the son of the Blessed One?" Then Jesus answered, "I am; / and you will see the Son of Man / seated at the right hand of the Power / and coming with the clouds of heaven." /

At that the high priest tore his garments and said, "What further need have we of witnesses? You have heard the blasphemy. What do you think?" They all condemned him as deserving to die. Some began to spit on him. They blindfolded him and struck him and said to him, "Prophesy!" And the guards greeted him with blows.

While Peter was below in the courtyard, one of the high priest's maids came along. Seeing Peter warming himself, she looked intently at him and said, "You too were with the Nazarene, Jesus." But he denied it saying, "I neither know nor understand what you are talking about." So he went out into the outer court. Then the cock crowed. The maid saw him and began again to say to the bystanders, "This man is one of them." Once again he denied it. A little later the bystanders said to Peter once more, "Surely you are one of them; for you too are a Galilean." He began to curse and to swear, "I do not know this man about whom you are talking." And immediately a cock crowed a second time. Then Peter remembered the word that Jesus had said to him, "Before the cock crows twice you will deny me three times." He broke down and wept.

As soon as morning came, the chief priests with the elders and the scribes, that is, the whole Sanhedrin held a council. They bound Jesus, led him away, and handed him over to Pilate. Pilate questioned him, "Are you the king of the Jews?" He said to him in reply, "You say so." The chief priests accused him of many things. Again Pilate questioned him, "Have you no answer? See how many things they accuse you of." Jesus gave him no further answer, so that Pilate was amazed.

Now on the occasion of the feast he used to release to them one prisoner whom they requested. A man called Barabbas was then in prison along with the rebels who had committed murder in a rebellion. The crowd came forward and began to ask him to do for them as he was accustomed. Pilate answered, "Do you want me to release to you the king of the Jews?" For he knew that it was out of envy that the chief priests had handed him over. But the chief priests stirred up the crowd to have him release Barabbas for them instead. Pilate again said to them in reply, "Then what do you want me to do with the man you call the king of the Jews?" They shouted again, "Crucify him." Pilate said to them, "Why? What evil has he done?" They only shouted the louder, "Crucify him." So

Pilate, wishing to satisfy the crowd, released Barabbas to them and, after he had Jesus scourged, handed him over to be crucified.

The soldiers led him away inside the palace, that is, the praetorium, and assembled the whole cohort. They clothed him in purple and, weaving a crown of thorns, placed it on him. They began to salute him with, "Hail, King of the Jews!" and kept striking his head with a reed and spitting upon him. They knelt before him in homage. And when they had mocked him, they stripped him of the purple cloak, dressed him in his own clothes, and led him out to crucify him.

They pressed into service a passer-by, Simon, a Cyrenian, who was coming in from the country, the father of Alexander and Rufus, to carry his cross.

They brought him to the place of Golgotha—which is translated Place of the Skull—. They gave him wine drugged with myrrh, but he did not take it. Then they crucified him and divided his garments by casting lots for them to see what each should take. It was nine o'clock in the morning when they crucified him. The inscription of the charge against him read, "The King of the Jews." With him they crucified two revolutionaries, one on his right and one on his left. Those passing by reviled him, shaking their heads and saying, "Aha! You who would destroy the temple and rebuild it in three days, save yourself by coming down from the cross." Likewise the chief priests, with the scribes, mocked him among themselves and said, "He saved others; he cannot save himself. Let the Christ, the King of Israel, come down now from the cross that we may see and believe." Those who were crucified with him also kept abusing him.

At noon darkness came over the whole land until three in the afternoon. And at three o'clock Jesus cried out in a loud voice, *"Eloi, Eloi, lema sabachthani?"* which is translated, "My God, my God, why have you forsaken me?" Some of the bystanders who heard it said, "Look, he is calling Elijah." One of them ran, soaked a sponge with wine, put it on a reed and gave it to him to drink saying, "Wait, let us see if Elijah comes to take him down." Jesus gave a loud cry and breathed his last.

Here all kneel and pause for a short time.

The veil of the sanctuary was torn in two from top to bottom. When the centurion who stood facing him saw how he breathed his last he said, "Truly this man was the Son of God!" There were also women looking on from a distance. Among them were Mary Magdalene, Mary the mother of the younger James and of Joses, and Salome. These women had followed him when he was in Galilee and ministered to him. There were also many other women who had come up with him to Jerusalem.

When it was already evening, since it was the day of preparation, the day before the sabbath, Joseph of Arimathea, a distinguished member of the council, who was himself awaiting the kingdom of God, came and courageously went to Pilate and asked for the body of Jesus. Pilate was amazed that he was already dead. He summoned the centurion and asked him if Jesus had already died. And when he learned of it from the centurion, he gave the body to Joseph. Having bought a linen cloth, he took him down, wrapped him in the linen cloth, and laid him in a tomb that had been hewn out of the rock. Then he rolled a stone against the entrance to the tomb. Mary Magdalene and Mary the mother of Joses watched where he was laid.

MARK 14: 1-72 & 15: 1-47

Shorter form: MARK 15:1-39

BLESSED ELIZABETH OF THE TRINITY

On the fourteenth day of her last retreat, Blessed Elizabeth continues to reflect on her desire to forfeit everything so that she may gain Christ.

"Then, when her hour of humiliation, of annihilation comes, she will recall this little phrase, 'Jesus autem tacebat' [Jesus remained silent] and she will be silent, 'keeping all her strength for the Lord'; this strength which 'we draw from silence.' And when the hour of abandonment, of desertion, and of anguish comes, the hour that drew from Christ this loud cry, 'why have You abandoned Me?' she will recall this prayer: 'that they may have in themselves the fullness of My joy'; and drinking to the dregs 'the cup prepared by the Father,' she will find a divine sweetness in its bitterness."

Complete Works, vol. 1: 159

REFLECTION

The Passion Narrative in Mark is the starkest of all the Gospels. Other than Jesus cry of abandonment, "God my God, why have you forsaken me?" no words of Jesus are recorded. Mark's focus seems to be that of the constant shame and humiliation that Jesus suffered. The betrayal of Judas, Peter's denial; the release of someone who was a thief and a murderer while Jesus the innocent one is handed over to be crucified; the mockery of the soldiers; Jesus' weakness under the weight of the cross; being crucified between two revolutionaries; the taunting of the by standers; and in the end, Jesus seeming abandonment by God in his greatest hour of need, all of these are before us with little to alleviate their impact. Through it all Mark has Jesus remain silent.

Each of the Evangelists offers a special focus for reflection in depicting the death of Jesus. Mark's emphasis speaks poignantly to the human experience of shame and humiliation. Jesus knew it to the extreme, but for all of us it is a familiar experience. We know the shame of moral failures, of human inadequacies, of the exposure and helplessness that sickness can occasion, dry and dark times in the spiritual quest. Persons who have been sexually abused are most often left with a profound sense of shame, often through life.

Blessed Elizabeth speaks from personal experience when she writes with such intensity of her hour of humiliation, annihilation and even of abandonment, desertion and anguish. This is not poetic language but the depiction of someone in the midst of great suffering. And yet through this tapestry of suffering are woven words of encouragement. Her many years of attentiveness to God's indwelling presence are like golden threads that focuses the mind to see deeper realities—that quiet place within where her union with Christ in his suffering releases a flow of "divine sweetness" that intermingles with the bitterness of the moment. We find here no words of self-pity but rather the reflections of someone who has found meaning even in her times of most intense suffering.

Today's Passion Narrative stirs the heart to compassion for Christ in his suffering. It also encourages us to reflect on our own attitude toward suffering and toward the inevitable experience of being humiliated, shamed, or feeling abandoned. How do I respond? Is my first reaction to lose all perspective and immediately sink into the morass of self-pity? Christ was Elizabeth's guide in her own dark times. Do I turn to Christ asking help to find the golden threads, the hidden blessings woven into every human experience? In union with Christ am I open to receive with a willing heart the divine sweetness even in bitter moments?

PRAYER

God of Compassion, I can only marvel at the profound mystery of love by which Divine Wisdom becomes one of us in the person of Jesus Christ; that with us he willingly experiences the depth of human pain and humiliation. Having passed through Christ in his earthly life, all suffering is now energized with power for generating new life within the depth of our being. Open my heart to receive this inflow of divine life when sorrow would weigh me down in self-absorption. With Blessed Elizabeth my I experience divine sweetness even in life's bitterest moments. I offer this prayer in the name of your beloved Son who suffered for love of me. Amen.

Palm Sunday – Year C

Gospel

Procession with Palms

Jesus proceeded on his journey up to Jerusalem. As he drew near to Bethpage and Bethany at the place called the Mount of Olives, he sent two of his disciples. He said, "Go into the village opposite you, and as you enter it you will find a colt tethered on which no one has ever sat. Untie it and bring it here. And if anyone should ask you, 'Why are you untying it?' you will answer, 'The Master has need of it.'" So those who had been sent went off and found everything just as he had told them. And as they were untying the colt, its owners said to them, "Why are you untying this colt?" They answered, "The Master has need of it." So they brought it to Jesus, threw their cloaks over the colt, and helped Jesus to mount. As he rode along, the people were spreading their cloaks on the road; and now as he was approaching the slope of the Mount of Olives, the whole multitude of his disciples began to praise God aloud with joy for all the mighty deeds they had seen. They proclaimed: / "Blessed is the king who comes in the name of the Lord. / Peace in heaven and glory in the highest." / Some of the Pharisees in the crowd said to him, "Teacher, rebuke your disciples." He said in reply, "I tell you, if they keep silent, the stones will cry out!"

Luke 19: 28-40

Gospel

Mass

When the hour came, Jesus took his place at table with the apostles. He said to them, "I have eagerly desired to eat this Passover with you before I suffer, for, I tell you, I shall not eat it again until there is fulfillment in the kingdom of God." Then he took a cup, gave thanks, and said, "Take this and share it among yourselves; for I tell you that from this time on I shall not drink of the fruit of the vine until the kingdom of God comes." Then he took the bread, said the blessing, broke it, and gave it to them, saying, "This is my body, which will be given for you; do this in memory of me." And likewise the cup after they had eaten, saying, "This cup is the new covenant in my blood, which will be shed for you.

"And yet behold, the hand of the one who is to betray me is with me on the table; for the Son of Man indeed goes as it has been determined; but woe to that man by whom he is betrayed." And they began to debate among themselves who among them would do such a deed.

Then an argument broke out among them about which of them should be regarded as the greatest. He said to them, "The kings of the Gentiles lord it over them and those in authority over them are addressed as 'Benefactors'; but among you it shall not be so. Rather, let the greatest among you be as the youngest, and the leader as the servant. For who is greater: the one seated at table or the one who serves? Is it not the one seated at table? I am among you as the one who serves. It is you who have stood by me in my trials; and I confer a kingdom on you, just as my Father has conferred one on me, that you may eat and drink at my table in my kingdom; and you will sit on thrones judging the twelve tribes of Israel.

"Simon, Simon, behold Satan has demanded to sift all of you like wheat, but I have prayed that your own faith may not fail; and once you have turned back, you must strengthen your brothers." He said to him, "Lord, I am prepared to go to prison and to die with you." But he replied, "I tell you, Peter, before the cock crows this day, you will deny three times that you know me."

He said to them, "When I sent you forth without a money bag or a sack or sandals, were you in need of anything?" "No, nothing," they replied. He said to them, "But now one who has a money bag should take it, and likewise a sack, and one who does not have a sword should sell his cloak and buy one. For I tell you that this Scripture must be fulfilled in me, namely, *He was counted among the wicked;* and indeed what is written about me is coming to fulfillment." Then they said, "Lord, look, there are two swords here." But he replied, "It is enough!"

Then going out, he went, as was his custom, to the Mount of Olives, and the disciples followed him. When he arrived at the place he said to them, "Pray that you may not undergo the test." After withdrawing about a stone's throw from them and kneeling, he prayed, saying, "Father, if you are willing, take this cup away from me; still, not my will but yours be done." And to strengthen him an angel from heaven appeared to him. He was in such agony and he prayed so fervently that his sweat became like drops of blood falling on the ground. When he rose from prayer and returned to his disciples, he found them sleeping from grief. He said to them, "Why are you sleeping? Get up and pray that you may not undergo the test."

While he was still speaking, a crowd approached and in front was one of the Twelve, a man named Judas. He went up to Jesus to kiss him. Jesus said to him, "Judas, are you betraying the Son of Man with a kiss?" His disciples realized what was about to happen, and they asked, "Lord, shall we strike with a sword?" And one of them struck the high priest's servant and cut off his right ear. But Jesus said in reply, "Stop, no more of this!" Then he touched the servant's ear and healed him. And Jesus said to the chief priests and temple guards and elders who had come for him, "Have you come out as against a robber, with swords and clubs? Day after day I was with you in the temple area, and you did not seize me; but this is your hour, the time for the power of darkness."

After arresting him they led him away and took him into the house of the high priest; Peter was following at a distance. They lit a fire in the middle of the courtyard and sat around it, and Peter sat down with them. When a maid saw him seated in the light, she looked intently at him and said, "This man too was with him." But he denied it saying, "Woman, I do not know him." A short while later someone else saw him and said, "You too are one of them"; but Peter answered, "My friend, I am not." About an hour later, still another insisted, "Assuredly, this man too was with him, for he also is a Galilean." But Peter said, "My friend, I do not know what you are talking about." Just as he was saying this, the cock crowed, and the Lord turned and looked at Peter; and Peter remembered the word of the Lord, how he had said to him, "Before the cock crows today, you will deny me three times." He went out and began to weep bitterly. The men who held Jesus in custody were ridiculing and beating him. They blindfolded him and questioned him, saying, "Prophesy! Who is it that struck you?" And they reviled him in saying many other things against him.

When day came the council of elders of the people met, both chief priests and scribes, and they brought him before their Sanhedrin. They said, "If you are the Christ, tell us," but he replied to them, "If I tell you, you will not believe, and if I question, you will not respond. But from this time on the Son of Man will be seated at the right hand of the power of God." They all asked, "Are you then the Son of God?" He replied to them, "You say that I am." Then they said, "What further need have we for testimony? We have heard it from his own mouth."

Then the whole assembly of them arose and brought him before Pilate. They brought charges against him, saying, "We found this man misleading our people; he opposes the payment of taxes to Caesar and maintains that he is the Christ, a king." Pilate asked him, "Are you the king of the Jews?" He said to him in reply, "You say so." Pilate then addressed the chief priests and the crowds, "I find this man not guilty." But they were adamant and said, "He is inciting the people with his teaching throughout all Judea, from Galilee where he began even to here."

On hearing this Pilate asked if the man was a Galilean; and upon learning that he was under Herod's jurisdiction, he sent him to Herod, who was in Jerusalem at that time. Herod was very glad to see Jesus; he had been wanting to see him for a long time, for he had heard about him and had been hoping to see him perform some sign. He questioned him at length, but he gave him no answer. The chief priests and scribes, meanwhile, stood by accusing him harshly. Herod and his soldiers treated him contemptuously and mocked him, and after clothing him in resplendent garb, he sent him back to Pilate. Herod and Pilate became friends that very day, even though they had been enemies formerly. Pilate then summoned the chief priests, the rulers, and the people and said to them, "You brought this man to me and accused him of inciting the people to revolt. I have conducted my investigation in your presence and have not found this man guilty of the charges you have brought against him, nor did Herod, for he sent him back to us. So no capital crime has been committed by him. Therefore I shall have him flogged and then release him."

But all together they shouted out, "Away with this man! Release Barabbas to us." —Now Barabbas had been imprisoned for a rebellion that had taken place in the city and for murder.— Again Pilate addressed them, still wishing to release Jesus, but they continued their shouting, "Crucify him! Crucify him!" Pilate addressed them a third time, "What evil has this man done? I found him guilty of no capital crime. Therefore I shall have him flogged and then release him." With loud shouts, however, they persisted in calling for his crucifixion, and their voices prevailed. The verdict of Pilate was that their demand should be granted. So he released the man who had been imprisoned for rebellion and murder, for whom they asked, and he handed Jesus over to them to deal with as they wished.

As they led him away they took hold of a certain Simon, a Cyrenian, who was coming in from the country; and after laying the cross on him, they made him carry it behind Jesus. A large crowd of people followed Jesus, including many women who mourned and lamented him. Jesus turned to them and said, "Daughters of Jerusalem, do not weep for me; weep instead for yourselves and for your children for indeed, the days are coming when people will say, 'Blessed are the barren, the wombs that never bore and the breasts that never nursed.' At that time people will say to the mountains, 'Fall upon us!' and to the hills, 'Cover us!' for if these things are done when the wood is green, what will happen when it is dry?" Now two others, both criminals, were led away with him to be executed.

When they came to the place called the Skull, they crucified him and the criminals there, one on his right, the other on his left. Then Jesus said, "Father, forgive them, they know not what they do." They divided his garments by casting lots. The people stood by and watched; the rulers, meanwhile, sneered at him and said, "He saved others, let him save himself if he is the chosen one, the Christ of God." Even the soldiers jeered at him. As they approached to offer him wine they called out, "If you are King of the Jews, save yourself." Above him there was an inscription that read, "This is the King of the Jews."

Now one of the criminals hanging there reviled Jesus, saying, "Are you not the Christ? Save yourself and us." The other, however, rebuking him, said in reply, "Have you no fear of God, for you are subject to the same condemnation? And indeed, we have been condemned justly, for the sentence we received corresponds to our crimes, but this man has done nothing criminal." Then he said, "Jesus, remember me when you come into your kingdom." He replied to him, "Amen, I say to you, today you will be with me in Paradise."

It was now about noon and darkness came over the whole land until three in the afternoon because of an eclipse of the sun. Then the veil of the temple was torn down the middle. Jesus cried out in a loud voice, "Father, into your hands I commend my spirit"; and when he had said this he breathed his last.

Here all kneel and pause for a short time.

The centurion who witnessed what had happened glorified God and said, "This man was innocent beyond doubt." When all the people who had gathered for this spectacle saw what had happened, they returned home beating their breasts; but all his acquaintances stood at a distance, including the women who had followed him from Galilee and saw these events.

Now there was a virtuous and righteous man named Joseph, who, though he was a member of the council, had not consented to their plan of action. He came from the Jewish town of Arimathea and was awaiting the kingdom of God. He went to Pilate and asked for the body of Jesus.

> After he had taken the body down, he wrapped it in a linen cloth and laid him in a rock-hewn tomb in which no one had yet been buried. It was the day of preparation, and the sabbath was about to begin. The women who had come from Galilee with him followed behind, and when they had seen the tomb and the way in which his body was laid in it, they returned and prepared spices and perfumed oils. Then they rested on the sabbath according to the commandment.
>
> Luke 22: 14-71 & 23: 1-56
>
> Shorter form: Luke 23:1-49

BLESSED ELIZABETH OF THE TRINITY

The following is an excerpt from a letter written to Abbe Chevignard shortly before his ordination to the priesthood.

"Let us be for Him, in a way, another humanity in which He may renew His whole Mystery. I have asked Him to make His home in me as Adorer, as Healer, and as Savior, and I cannot tell you what peace it gives my soul to think that He makes up for my weaknesses and, if I fall at every passing moment, He is there to help me up again and carry me farther into Himself, into the depths of that divine essence where we already live by grace and where I would like to bury myself so deeply that nothing could make me leave."

Complete Works, vol. 2: Letter 214

REFLECTION

A prayerful reading of Luke's Passion Narrative yields much to enrich our lives but what particularly stands out is Jesus' willingness to forgive, along with his unwillingness to counteract violence with more violence. In the garden of his betrayal by Judas, when one of his disciples cuts off the ear of the high priest's servant, Jesus sharply demands: "Stop, no more of this!"

Peter is not rejected, but forgiven after his threefold denial. Jesus gives comfort to the women over the impending fall of Jerusalem even in the midst of his own extreme pain from the weight of the cross and from having been flogged. On the cross, Jesus offers forgiveness to the repentant thief and seeming with inner peace—in spite of intense pain and verbal abuse—cries out with a loud voice, "Father, into your hands I commend my spirit." Jesus speaks no words of condemnation but passes through death to be on hand to welcome the repentant thief into Paradise. Having been violently done away with, through his resurrection, Jesus triumphs over death, and without accusation, welcomes back his frightened disciples. Having ascended to his Father, Jesus sends his own Spirit to strengthen and inflame his fragile followers. Through the ages, the gift of his Spirit has been available to all willing to receive the gift.

Blessed Elizabeth has penetrated deeply into the forgiving heart of Christ. Her weakness, even if she were "to fall at every passing moment," still leaves her with the confidence that he would be there to help her up again and carry her farther into himself, into the depths of the divine essence where she already lives by grace.

Does this not stir wonder? "Who are we God, that you are so mindful of us?" Who are we that you are there to help us again after our failures, and would carry us farther into yourself, into the depth of that divine essence where we already live by grace? Who am I? How does this question answer itself deep within? What do I hear? But the question also asks itself; who is God? How does my heart respond? Does my self-understanding and my perception of God leave me willing to bury myself so deeply in God that nothing could make me leave?

PRAYER

God of Mystery, dare I believe that your love for me is what stirs the desire within me that you come into my heart as Adorer, as Healer as Savior? That I be for you another humanity in which you renew your mysteries? Through the passion and death of Jesus and the help of blessed Elizabeth, renew in me the faith that I need to allow you to carry me ever further into yourself. I offer this prayer in your name Jesus, in gratitude for the gift of your forgiving love. Amen.

MONDAY OF HOLY WEEK

GOSPEL

Six days before Passover Jesus came to Bethany, where Lazarus was, whom Jesus had raised from the dead. They gave a dinner for him there, and Martha served, while Lazarus was one of those reclining at table with him. Mary took a liter of costly perfumed oil made from genuine aromatic nard and anointed the feet of Jesus and dried them with her hair; the house was filled with the fragrance of the oil. Then Judas the Iscariot, one of his disciples, and the one who would betray him, said, "Why was this oil not sold for three hundred days' wages and given to the poor?" He said this not because he cared about the poor but because he was a thief and held the money bag and used to steal the contributions. So Jesus said, "Leave her alone. Let her keep this for the day of my burial. You always have the poor with you, but you do not always have me."

The large crowd of the Jews found out that he was there and came, not only because of him, but also to see Lazarus, whom he had raised from the dead. And the chief priests plotted to kill Lazarus too, because many of the Jews were turning away and believing in Jesus because of him.

JOHN 12: 1-11

BLESSED ELIZABETH OF THE TRINITY

In a chapter entitled, The Greatness of Our Vocation, Blessed Elizabeth writes:

"It seems to me that the soul that is aware of its greatness enters into that 'holy freedom of the children of God' of which the Apostle speaks, that is it transcends all things, including self. The freest soul, I think, is the one most forgetful of self. If anyone were to ask me the secret of happiness, I would say it is to no longer think of self, to deny oneself always. That is a good way to kill pride: let it starve to death! You see, pride is love of ourselves; well, love of God must be so strong that it extinguishes

all our self-love. St. Augustine says we have two cities within us, the city of God and the city of SELF. To the extent that the first increases, the second will be destroyed."

Complete Works, vol. 1: 125

REFLECTION

In this selection, the words of Blessed Elizabeth can best be heard like the notes of accompanying instruments that enrich the melody of a serious piece of music. The Gospel pictures Jesus at dinner at the home of Martha and Mary. Lazarus, raised from the dead, reclines at table with them. As Martha serves, Mary is seen rising from table, and to the astonishment of everyone, begins to anoint the feet of Jesus with fragrant oil; and more astonishing still, she dries his feet with her hair.

But suddenly a discordant note is heard which disrupts the sacred harmony of the moment. Judas objects: Why is this oil not sold and given to the poor? Jesus adds a note of his own: Leave her alone. The poor you have always, you do not always have me. The crowd arrives with obvious mixed motives. Not only to be with Jesus, but they were also curious to see Lazarus. The chief priests add their own rhythmic beat as in their heart they plot not only to kill Jesus, but also Lazarus.

Blessed Elizabeth invites us to self-transcendence through forgetfulness of self. For this to be realized the soul must first be aware of its greatness before God. Pride is love of self without reference to God. Love for God is what extinguishes pride's distorted love of self.

These insight into the nature of the self with its true identity to be found only in relationship with God, attunes our ears to the underlying rhythm of today's Gospel: the conflict between distorted self-love and its opposite, self-giving love through forgetfulness of self. In different ways, Martha and Mary both exemplify forgetfulness of self. Forgetful of self, with generosity of spirit, Martha graciously serves at table, her eyes lovingly fixed on Jesus, her honored guest. In the same spirit, her sister Mary, moved by a sudden outpouring of love, reaches for her flask of fragrant oil and begins to anoint the feet of her beloved Master.

Suddenly the mood of the harmony changes with tones of condemnation and disapproval. Judas, in distorted self-love, sees gain squandered before his eyes. The city of self was stronger than the city of God so he rationalizes with words about helping the poor. Jesus restores the harmony to the discord by his defense of Mary and by words of praise for her prophetic act. From the chief priests come sounds like distant rumbling thunder moving ever closer. Others hear the beauty of the music and believe in Jesus because of Lazarus, Jesus' saving deed of love for Martha and Mary in restoring him to life.

What do I hear within myself as I listen to the sounds of this Gospel? Do I hear myself having played false notes of pride and distorted self-love as dishonesty in business dealings come to mind? Does desire for gain in the city of self, play notes of rationalization to alleviate feelings of guilt for treating others unjustly, in ways small or great? Do I create harmony within the music of family life?

PRAYER

Jesus, I pray that you allow the music of your forgiving love to open my heart to the greatness within the gift of your indwelling presence. Free me from distorted self-love, so that forgetful of self, like Martha and Mary I can serve you with inner freedom in whatever capacity each moment calls forth from me. In your name I pray. Amen.

Tuesday of Holy Week

Gospel

Reclining at table with his disciples, Jesus was deeply troubled and testified, "Amen, amen, I say to you, one of you will betray me." The disciples looked at one another, at a loss as to whom he meant. One of his disciples, the one whom Jesus loved, was reclining at Jesus' side. So Simon Peter nodded to him to find out whom he meant. He leaned back against Jesus' chest and said to him, "Master, who is it?" Jesus answered, "It is the one to whom I hand the morsel after I have dipped it." So he dipped the morsel and took it and handed it to Judas, son of Simon the Iscariot. After Judas took the morsel, Satan entered him. So Jesus said to him, "What you are going to do, do quickly." Now none of those reclining at table realized why he said this to him. Some thought that since Judas kept the money bag, Jesus had told him, "Buy what we need for the feast," or to give something to the poor. So Judas took the morsel and left at once. And it was night.

When he had left, Jesus said, "Now is the Son of Man glorified, and God is glorified in him. If God is glorified in him, God will also glorify him in himself, and he will glorify him at once. My children, I will be with you only a little while longer. You will look for me, and as I told the Jews, 'Where I go you cannot come,' so now I say it to you."

Simon Peter said to him, "Master, where are you going?" Jesus answered him, "Where I am going, you cannot follow me now, though you will follow later." Peter said to him, "Master, why can I not follow you now? I will lay down my life for you." Jesus answered, "Will you lay down your life for me? Amen, amen, I say to you, the cock will not crow before you deny me three times."

John 13: 21-33, 36-38

BLESSED ELIZABETH OF THE TRINITY

In 1902, the antireligious government in France was closing all private schools and many Congregations of Religious women and men were forced to flee the country. In this context, Blessed Elizabeth writes to her friend, Madame de Bobet:

"Yes, the future is very dark, and don't you feel the need to love much in order to make reparation . . . in order to console this adored Master. . . . Let us make a solitary place for Him in the inner-most part of our soul and remain there with Him; let us never leave Him, for it is His commandment: 'Remain in me, and I in you.' Nothing will be able to rob us of this interior cell, no matter what trials we undergo: I carry my One Treasure 'inside me,' and all the rest is nothing."

Complete Works, vol. 2: Letter 160

REFLECTION

The future is also very dark for Jesus as it was for France at that time. Jesus, "deeply troubled," reclines at table with his disciples. He knows his hour had come. In John's Gospel, Jesus is always in command of his life so he says to Judas, "what you are going to do, do quickly." Was the morsel Jesus then offered Judas a morsel of loving compassion inviting conversion of heart? Judas takes the morsel and instead, goes out into the "night" of his soul's inner darkness.

With Judas gone, Jesus speaks words puzzling to his hearers. "Now is the Son of Man glorified, and God is glorified in Him." "I will be with you only a little while longer . . . where I go you cannot come." There are moments in the lives of each that can only be traveled alone without human accompaniment. These are often painful moments in which we need to recall the words of Blessed Elizabeth: "Let us make a solitary place for him in the inner-most part of our soul and remain there with him; let us never leave him, for it is his commandment: "Remain in me, and I in you." When we are mindful of the one Treasure inside ourselves, we find perspective and can say with Elizabeth, "and all the rest is nothing." Perhaps in this light could Jesus say: Now is the Son of Man glorified, and God is glorified in him. In spite of the ordeal before him, Jesus knew that death's seeming finality had no hold on him.

Peter has yet much to learn. Impetuous in his love for Jesus, he promises to lay down his life for him only to hear warnings that the cock would not crow before Peter would deny Jesus three times. We know that Peter wept bitterly over his threefold denial and that, in the end, he did lay down his life for Jesus. We can only hope that Judas also discovered the solitary place of Christ's indwelling presence within and also came to repentance.

In dark times, when I am deeply troubled, where do I look to find help and strength? Have I discovered the solitary place in the innermost part of my soul where I can "remain there with him?" Or instead, do I in desperation turn to alcohol, to over-eating, or to other forms of escape to assuage my pain?

PRAYER

Ever-loving Lord Jesus, lead me to that solitary place within, to the innermost center of myself where you abide in me and where you invite me to also abide in You. Be my inner strength. In troubled times, or when my own darkness tempts me to deny you, may I have the courage to be faithful to you. Instead of denying you by my actions, may you be glorified in me through all the events of every day. With confidence in your love, I offer my prayer to you with deep gratitude in my heart. Amen.

WEDNESDAY OF HOLY WEEK

GOSPEL

One of the Twelve, who was called Judas Iscariot, went to the chief priests and said, "What are you willing to give me if I hand him over to you?" They paid him thirty pieces of silver, and from that time on he looked for an opportunity to hand him over.

On the first day of the Feast of Unleavened Bread, the disciples approached Jesus and said, "Where do you want us to prepare for you to eat the Passover?" He said, "Go into the city to a certain man and tell him, 'The teacher says, "My appointed time draws near; in your house I shall celebrate the Passover with my disciples."'" The disciples then did as Jesus had ordered, and prepared the Passover.

When it was evening, he reclined at table with the Twelve. And while they were eating, he said, "Amen, I say to you, one of you will betray me." Deeply distressed at this, they began to say to him one after another, "Surely it is not I, Lord?" He said in reply, "He who has dipped his hand into the dish with me is the one who will betray me. The Son of Man indeed goes, as it is written of him, but woe to that man by whom the Son of Man is betrayed. It would be better for that man if he had never been born." Then Judas, his betrayer, said in reply, "Surely it is not I, Rabbi?" He answered, "You have said so."

MATTHEW 26: 14-25

BLESSED ELIZABETH OF THE TRINITY

In the second day of her last retreat Blessed Elizabeth writes:

"A soul that debates with its self, that is taken up with its feelings, and pursues useless thoughts and desires, scatters its forces, for it is not wholly directed toward God. Its lyre does not vibrate in unison and when the Master plays it, He cannot draw from it divine harmonies, for it is still too human and discordant."

Complete Works, vol. 1: 142

REFLECTION

Today we read Matthew's account of the betrayal of Judas. As we reflect on Judas betrayal, we might wonder, how could this happen? Jesus had chosen Judas as one of the twelve. Judas had been with Jesus many months; he had heard his profound message of God's love and compassion for sinners and had seen the many miracles Jesus performed. How could he turn traitor? Even more puzzling, how could he face Jesus and attempt to hide his guilt: "Surely it is not I, Rabbi?" Knowing that Jesus had read his heart, and undeterred by Jesus' words of woe to the one by whom the Son of Man is betrayed, Judas does not repent but leaves to pursue his course of action. Indeed, how could this happen!

Perhaps Blessed Elizabeth has something to offer us. Is it possible that Judas began to be taken up with particular thoughts and desires that left him increasingly scattered and less committed in following Jesus? Did he notice the Jewish authorities growing antipathy toward Jesus? With his forces scattered and not wholly directed toward God, did Judas allow unconscious desires, perhaps a need to be on the winning team, create increasingly discordant harmonies between himself, Jesus and the other disciples?

Did Judas then debate within himself that surely he had a responsibility to provide for his own future so he began to steal from the purse intended for the poor? Then the moment came when his lyre ceased to vibrate with his once beloved Master whom Judas now suspected would soon be done away with. The next step seemed to take on a life of its own. His self-serving interests seemed to flow like a powerful current to betrayal.

Today's Gospel, with its focus on Judas' betrayal, is like a sad musical prelude to the events soon to follow as we enter more deeply into the mystery of this holiest of weeks. As we recognize in our own lives the disharmony within, feelings of compassion for Judas and trust in God's compassionate love prepares us for the days ahead.

Ours has rightly been called an age of narcissism. This causes me to reflect: Do I try to be alert for to the self-serving thoughts that keep me centered on myself and inattentive toward others? Do "useless thoughts and feelings" keep me inattentive to the needs of the present moment? Do the weaknesses of others so scandalize me that I lose sight of my own inadequacies?

PRAYER

Jesus, my heart fills with desire to be faithful to you as I see Judas intent on his purpose of betrayal. At the same time, reflecting on this Gospel helps me to recognize the "Judas" within and the many ways, small and great, that I too betray you: injustice towards others because of financial greed, my excuses for not attending Mass or spending time in prayer are just a few of my betrayals of you who are ever present desiring to draw me to yourself. Tune the lyre of my heart to play in harmony with you in all the circumstances of my life. O compassionate One, in your name I pray. Amen.

Holy Thursday – Chrism Mass[†]

GOSPEL

Jesus came to Nazareth, where he had grown up, and went according to his custom into the synagogue on the sabbath day. He stood up to read and was handed a scroll of the prophet Isaiah. He unrolled the scroll and found the passage where it was written:

The Spirit of the Lord is upon me,
because he has anointed me
>*to bring glad tidings to the poor.*
He has sent me to proclaim liberty to captives
>*and recovery of sight to the blind,*
>*to let the oppressed go free,*
and to proclaim a year acceptable to the Lord.

Rolling up the scroll, he handed it back to the attendant and sat down, and the eyes of all in the synagogue looked intently at him. He said to them, "Today this Scripture passage is fulfilled in your hearing."

LUKE 4: 16-21

BLESSED ELIZABETH OF THE TRINITY

Following the community retreat during which "Pere Vallee spoke to us the whole time on Jesus Christ," Blessed Elizabeth writes to her friend, Madame Angles:

"On the eve of His Passion, He said to His Father in speaking of those who were His own: 'The words which you gave me, I have given to them; the brightness that I had in you before the world began, I have given to them.' He is always living, always at work in our souls; let us allow ourselves to be formed by Him; may he be the Soul of our soul, the Life of our

---

† The Chrism Mass is the annual Mass when the bishop blesses the oils that will be used for the sacraments throughout the year in the diocese.

life, so that we may say with Saint Paul: 'For me to live is Christ.'"
Complete Works, vol. 2: Letter 145

REFLECTION

The Chrism Mass of Holy Thursday takes us back to what we might call Jesus' inaugural address. Using the words of the prophet Isaiah, Jesus declares his mission to be a mission of mercy. He proclaims, not condemnation but glad tiding to the poor, liberty to captives, recovery of sight to the blind and freedom for the oppressed. Do Jesus' words not describe each one of us? We are poor in our absolute dependence on God; sin, along with our attachments and addictions, holds us in bondage; all of these oppress us and leave us lacking in inner freedom

The blessing of the Holy Oils on Holy Thursday, at what is called the Chrism Mass, is most often a gathering of priests celebrating their priestly anointing. However, in itself, it is about the People of God, the entire church. We have all been anointed with the holy oils at our Baptism and can claim Christ's name as our own. We are "Christians." Christ is our true identity and our life journey is increasingly to grow in His likeness.

The anointing of the sick is Christ's gift to strengthen us in our suffering as Christ continues his suffering in us. This sacrament imparts energy for healing and when our time comes it prepares us, through an ever-deeper incorporation in Christ, for eternal blessedness in the heart of God.

Blessed Elizabeth reminds us that "he is always living, always at work in our souls." Today's Gospel also reminds us in the words of Elizabeth, to allow ourselves to be formed by Him that He may be the Soul of our soul, the Life of our life, so that we may say with Saint Paul: "For me to live is Christ." His mission of mercy, of bringing glad tidings to the poor is our mission regardless of our way of life. We are "priestly people" called to serve one another.

Each year we celebrate a birthday. Do you also celebrate the anniversary of your baptism, the birthday of your new life in Christ? Do you ever reflect that like Christ, the Spirit of the Lord is upon you—that you are Christ's presence in our world today?

PRAYER

Spirit of Jesus, enlighten the darkness of my mind. Help me to penetrate the mystery of my life in Christ. Enlarge my heart to love with your own Love so that with Blessed Elizabeth, I can say in truth: for me to live is Christ. I make this prayer in your name, Lord Jesus, thanking you for your indwelling Spirit who frees me from the bondage of sin. Amen.

PASCHAL TRIDUUM

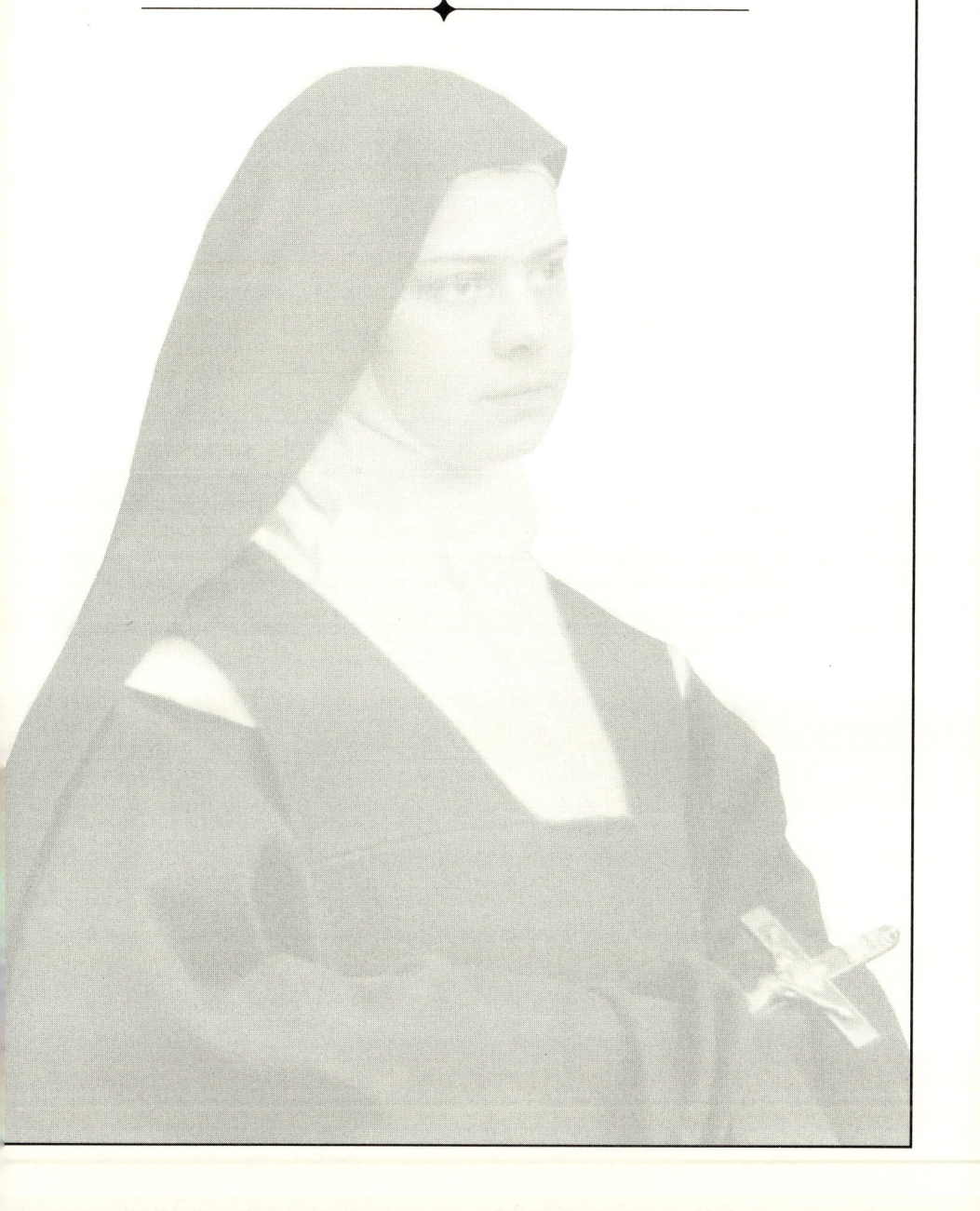

Holy Thursday – Evening Mass of the Lord's Supper

Gospel

Before the feast of Passover, Jesus knew that his hour had come to pass from this world to the Father. He loved his own in the world and he loved them to the end. The devil had already induced Judas, son of Simon the Iscariot, to hand him over. So, during supper, fully aware that the Father had put everything into his power and that he had come from God and was returning to God, he rose from supper and took off his outer garments. He took a towel and tied it around his waist. Then he poured water into a basin and began to wash the disciples' feet and dry them with the towel around his waist. He came to Simon Peter, who said to him, "Master, are you going to wash my feet?" Jesus answered and said to him, "What I am doing, you do not understand now, but you will understand later." Peter said to him, "You will never wash my feet." Jesus answered him, "Unless I wash you, you will have no inheritance with me." Simon Peter said to him, "Master, then not only my feet, but my hands and head as well." Jesus said to him, "Whoever has bathed has no need except to have his feet washed, for he is clean all over; so you are clean, but not all." For he knew who would betray him; for this reason, he said, "Not all of you are clean."

So when he had washed their feet and put his garments back on and reclined at table again, he said to them, "Do you realize what I have done for you? You call me 'teacher' and 'master,' and rightly so, for indeed I am. If I, therefore, the master and teacher, have washed your feet, you ought to wash one another's feet. I have given you a model to follow, so that as I have done for you, you should also do."

John 13: 1-15

BLESSED ELIZABETH OF THE TRINITY

In her reflections entitled, *The Greatness of Our Vocation*, Blessed Elisabeth writes:

"Framboise, this doctrine of dying to self is the law for every Christian, for Christ said: 'If anyone wants to follow Me, let him take up his cross and deny himself.' But this doctrine which seems so austere, takes on a delightful sweetness when we consider the outcome of this death—life in God in place of our life of sin and misery. That is what St. Paul meant when he wrote: 'strip off the old man and clothe yourselves anew in the image of Him who created you.' This image is God Himself. Do you recall His wish which He so clearly expressed on the day of creation: 'Let us make man in our image and likeness?'"

Complete Works, vol. 1: 125

REFLECTION

In today's Gospel to the amazement of the disciples, Jesus kneels to wash their feet, a task assigned to slaves. To Peter's protestations Jesus insists that this act is integral to having inheritance with him. Jesus is giving Peter a model to follow if he would strip off the old self and clothe himself anew in the image—the divine image and likeness of the One who created him.

Jesus' entire life has been a gradual unfolding of the inner life of God—the infinite One whom Jesus calls Father and whose Spirit rests upon Jesus as manifest in his baptism. By his actions during his public ministry, Jesus reveals a God who forgives sins, who heals our illnesses, and who reaches out in love as Jesus does to those around him. In doing so Jesus models for us the depth of our own inner self and the life we are to live if we are to be his followers.

By washing the disciples feet, at what Jesus knew to be his last supper with them before his death, Jesus continues his ministry of divine unfolding into the mystery of God as a trinity of self-giving love. The humble service of foot washing provides a ray of light into the heart's understanding of God's eternal Word accepting to be emptied of the divine state, 'to assume the condition of a slave.' The eternity of God humbly enters into the limitations of time of which the foot washing can be seen as a symbolic action manifesting God's incredible Self-gift to the human family by becoming one of us.

God's mutuality in outgoing love within the Trinity, one toward the other, must find human expression in our lives if with the disciples we are to have inheritance with Jesus. Blessed Elizabeth invites us to clothe ourselves anew in the image of Him who created us. If we are to live our human reality as created in the divine image and likeness, we need to live in a God-like manner and be willing to humble ourselves in loving service graciously extended to those in need.

Today's Gospel focuses our attention on the washing of the feet but our thoughts also bring us to the gift of the Eucharist as integral to God's Self-gift in Jesus. God, like a nursing mother, personally bends over as it were, to feed us with God's very own substance through the Eucharistic—the Body and Blood of Christ—so that we might be empowered to live, in and through Christ in a God-like manner. Each of our Lenten reflections has taken us deeper into the reality of God's Self-gift in Christ and into our share in this mystery. To be created in the divine image and likeness has very practical implications for daily living.

What in my life needs to change if my actions are to be a true reflection of God as self-giving love? Am I willing to "wash the feet" of persons who need my help, even of those I might dislike? In my own times of need am I able graciously to accept the help others might offer? Do I receive the Eucharist with reverent awe in the realization that our creating God would transform me into the gift I have received?

PRAYER

Draw me, O Blessed Trinity, into the flow of your Trinitarian Love that in Jesus, my life may be but a radiance of your divine life ever present within the depth of my being. Grace me with love for humble service. Help me to die to all that does not reflect Christ's life within so that I may be completely transformed in His divine Image. I make this prayer in your name Lord Jesus, as I trust you to clothe me anew in your divine image. Amen.

Good Friday of the Lord's Passion

Gospel

Jesus went out with his disciples across the Kidron valley to where there was a garden, into which he and his disciples entered. Judas his betrayer also knew the place, because Jesus had often met there with his disciples. So Judas got a band of soldiers and guards from the chief priests and the Pharisees and went there with lanterns, torches, and weapons. Jesus, knowing everything that was going to happen to him, went out and said to them, "Whom are you looking for?" They answered him, "Jesus the Nazorean." He said to them, "I AM." Judas his betrayer was also with them. When he said to them, "I AM," they turned away and fell to the ground. So he again asked them, "Whom are you looking for?" They said, "Jesus the Nazorean." Jesus answered, "I told you that I AM. So if you are looking for me, let these men go." This was to fulfill what he had said, "I have not lost any of those you gave me." Then Simon Peter, who had a sword, drew it, struck the high priest's slave, and cut off his right ear. The slave's name was Malchus. Jesus said to Peter, "Put your sword into its scabbard. Shall I not drink the cup that the Father gave me?"

So the band of soldiers, the tribune, and the Jewish guards seized Jesus, bound him, and brought him to Annas first. He was the father-in-law of Caiaphas, who was high priest that year. It was Caiaphas who had counseled the Jews that it was better that one man should die rather than the people.

Simon Peter and another disciple followed Jesus. Now the other disciple was known to the high priest, and he entered the courtyard of the high priest with Jesus. But Peter stood at the gate outside. So the other disciple, the acquaintance of the high priest, went out and spoke to the gatekeeper and brought Peter in. Then the maid who was the gatekeeper said to Peter, "You are not one of this man's disciples, are you?" He said, "I am not." Now the slaves and the guards were standing around a charcoal fire that they had made, because it was cold, and were warming themselves. Peter was also standing there keeping warm.

The high priest questioned Jesus about his disciples and about his doctrine. Jesus answered him, "I have spoken publicly to the world. I have always taught in a synagogue or in the temple area where all the Jews gather, and in secret I have said nothing. Why ask me? Ask those who heard me what I said to them. They know what I said." When he had said this, one of the temple guards standing there struck Jesus and said, "Is this the way you answer the high priest?" Jesus answered him, "If I have spoken wrongly, testify to the wrong; but if I have spoken rightly, why do you strike me?" Then Annas sent him bound to Caiaphas the high priest.

Now Simon Peter was standing there keeping warm. And they said to him, "You are not one of his disciples, are you?" He denied it and said, "I am not." One of the slaves of the high priest, a relative of the one whose ear Peter had cut off, said, "Didn't I see you in the garden with him?" Again Peter denied it. And immediately the cock crowed.

Then they brought Jesus from Caiaphas to the praetorium. It was morning. And they themselves did not enter the praetorium, in order not to be defiled so that they could eat the Passover. So Pilate came out to them and said, "What charge do you bring against this man?" They answered and said to him, "If he were not a criminal, we would not have handed him over to you." At this, Pilate said to them, "Take him yourselves, and judge him according to your law." The Jews answered him, "We do not have the right to execute anyone," in order that the word of Jesus might be fulfilled that he said indicating the kind of death he would die. So Pilate went back into the praetorium and summoned Jesus and said to him, "Are you the King of the Jews?" Jesus answered, "Do you say this on your own or have others told you about me?" Pilate answered, "I am not a Jew, am I? Your own nation and the chief priests handed you over to me. What have you done?" Jesus answered, "My kingdom does not belong to this world. If my kingdom did belong to this world, my attendants would be fighting to keep me from being handed over to the Jews. But as it is, my kingdom is not here." So Pilate said to him, "Then you are a king?" Jesus answered, "You say I am a king. For this I was born and for this I came into the world, to testify to the truth. Everyone who belongs to the truth listens to my voice." Pilate said to him, "What is truth?"

When he had said this, he again went out to the Jews and said to them, "I find no guilt in him. But you have a custom that I release one prisoner to you at Passover. Do you want me to release to you the King of the Jews?" They cried out again, "Not this one but Barabbas!" Now Barabbas was a revolutionary.

Then Pilate took Jesus and had him scourged. And the soldiers wove a crown out of thorns and placed it on his head, and clothed him in a purple cloak, and they came to him and said, "Hail, King of the Jews!" And they struck him repeatedly. Once more Pilate went out and said to them, "Look, I am bringing him out to you, so that you may know that I find no guilt in him." So Jesus came out, wearing the crown of thorns and the purple cloak. And he said to them, "Behold, the man!" When the chief priests and the guards saw him they cried out, "Crucify him, crucify him!" Pilate said to them, "Take him yourselves and crucify him. I find no guilt in him." The Jews answered, "We have a law, and according to that law he ought to die, because he made himself the Son of God." Now when Pilate heard this statement, he became even more afraid, and went back into the praetorium and said to Jesus, "Where are you from?" Jesus did not answer him. So Pilate said to him, "Do you not speak to me? Do you not know that I have power to release you and I have power to crucify you?" Jesus answered him, "You would have no power over me if it had not been given to you from above. For this reason the one who handed me over to you has the greater sin." Consequently, Pilate tried to release him; but the Jews cried out, "If you release him, you are not a Friend of Caesar. Everyone who makes himself a king opposes Caesar."

When Pilate heard these words he brought Jesus out and seated him on the judge's bench in the place called Stone Pavement, in Hebrew, Gabbatha. It was preparation day for Passover, and it was about noon. And he said to the Jews, "Behold, your king!" They cried out, "Take him away, take him away! Crucify him!" Pilate said to them, "Shall I crucify your king?" The chief priests answered, "We have no king but

Caesar." Then he handed him over to them to be crucified.

So they took Jesus, and, carrying the cross himself, he went out to what is called the Place of the Skull, in Hebrew, Golgotha. There they crucified him, and with him two others, one on either side, with Jesus in the middle. Pilate also had an inscription written and put on the cross. It read, "Jesus the Nazorean, the King of the Jews." Now many of the Jews read this inscription, because the place where Jesus was crucified was near the city; and it was written in Hebrew, Latin, and Greek. So the chief priests of the Jews said to Pilate, "Do not write 'The King of the Jews,' but that he said, 'I am the King of the Jews'." Pilate answered, "What I have written, I have written."

When the soldiers had crucified Jesus, they took his clothes and divided them into four shares, a share for each soldier. They also took his tunic, but the tunic was seamless, woven in one piece from the top down. So they said to one another, "Let's not tear it, but cast lots for it to see whose it will be," in order that the passage of Scripture might be fulfilled that says:

*They divided my garments among them,
    and for my vesture they cast lots.*

This is what the soldiers did. Standing by the cross of Jesus were his mother and his mother's sister, Mary the wife of Clopas, and Mary of Magdala. When Jesus saw his mother and the disciple there whom he loved he said to his mother, "Woman, behold, your son." Then he said to the disciple, "Behold, your mother." And from that hour the disciple took her into his home.

After this, aware that everything was now finished, in order that the Scripture might be fulfilled, Jesus said, "I thirst." There was a vessel filled with common wine. So they put a sponge soaked in wine on a sprig of hyssop and put it up to his mouth. When Jesus had taken the wine, he said, "It is finished." And bowing his head, he handed over the spirit.

Here all kneel and pause for a short time.

Now since it was preparation day, in order that the bodies might not remain on the cross on the sabbath, for the sabbath day of that week was a solemn one, the Jews asked Pilate that their legs be broken and that they be taken down. So the soldiers came and broke the legs of the first and then of the other one who was crucified with Jesus. But when they came to Jesus and saw that he was already dead, they did not break his legs, but one soldier thrust his lance into his side, and immediately blood and water flowed out. An eyewitness has testified, and his testimony is true; he knows that he is speaking the truth, so that you also may come to believe. For this happened so that the Scripture passage might be fulfilled: *Not a bone of it will be broken.* And again another passage says: *They will look upon him whom they have pierced.*

After this, Joseph of Arimathea, secretly a disciple of Jesus for fear of the Jews, asked Pilate if he could remove the body of Jesus. And Pilate permitted it. So he came and took his body. Nicodemus, the one who had first come to him at night, also came bringing a mixture of myrrh and aloes weighing about one hundred pounds. They took the body of Jesus and bound it with burial cloths along with the spices, according to the Jewish burial custom. Now in the place where he had been crucified there was a garden, and in the garden a new tomb, in which no one had yet been buried. So they laid Jesus there because of the Jewish preparation day; for the tomb was close by.

JOHN 18: 1-40 & 19: 1-42

BLESSED ELIZABETH OF THE TRINITY

On the eighth day of her retreat in her text entitled Heaven in Faith, Blessed Elizabeth writes:

"Let us lovingly eat this bread of the will of God. If sometimes His will is more crucifying, we can doubtless say with our adored Master: 'Father, if it is possible, let this cup pass me by,' but we will add immediately: 'Yet not as I will, but as You will,' and in strength and serenity, with the divine Crucified, we will also climb our calvary singing in the depths of our hearts and raising a hymn of thanksgiving to the father. For those who march on this way of sorrows are those 'whom He foreknew and predestined to be confirmed to the image of his divine Son,' the One crucified by love!"

Complete Works, vol. 1: 106–7

REFLECTION

In the Gospel of John, after the Last Supper discourse, Jesus and his disciples leave the upper room and cross the Kidron Valley to a garden. Judas his betrayer also knows the place. Jesus had often met there with his disciples. Upon their arrival, Judas appears with a band of soldiers intent on arresting Jesus.

The majestic Christ of John's Gospel does not allow for the Synoptic portrayal of Jesus' struggle in the Garden of Gethsemane. However, shortly before the Passover, and following Jesus triumphant entry into Jerusalem, John records Philip approaching Jesus with the request of the Greeks to see Jesus. Jesus replies with a prediction of his passion: his hour has come—the grain of wheat must fall into the ground and die to bear much fruit. He concludes his words about willingness to lose one's life in this world to keep it for eternal life by saying:

"Now is my soul troubled. What shall I say:
Father, save me from this hour?
But for this very reason I have come to this hour
Father, glorify your name!" (John 12:23–28)

In the Synoptic accounts and in John's version, the reality of suffering, along with the invitation to surrender to God's will, confronts us. Jesus came as a divine healer and cured all who approached him so it appears that *God's will is not that humans suffer*. Instead, as Jesus also demonstrates by his passion and death, *God's will is that we surrender to the reality of being human* and accept the hardships and sufferings inevitable to human, sinful fragility. Love is the key to understanding the meaning of suffering.

Knowing that suffering is inevitable to being human, Blessed Elizabeth invites us to eat lovingly the bread of the will of God. If sometimes His will is more crucifying, we can say with Jesus, "Now is my soul troubled." But we will add immediately: "But for this reason I have come to this hour" knowing that suffering, accepted with love for the crucified Christ, conforms us in his image.

With Mary we stand at the foot of his Cross. We might not be called to suffer the extremes of physical pain and thirst from which Christ suffered but we will be drawn into the divine thirst that all persons be drawn to God. With Mary, our hearts are opened to become like a welcoming abyss eager to receive the saving blood that flows from the Heart of God. The overflow of God's love in the heart of Christ here receives a welcome within his human heart. From this mystical moment of cosmic proportions, the Church, as the People of God, issues forth from Christ's opened side. The heart of the Church's life therefore is both our participation in the life, passion and death of Christ through the Eucharist and through the everydayness of life in Christ. "Eternal Life" is already ours as increasingly we come "to know the one true God and Jesus Christ whom God has sent."

What is my attitude toward suffering? Do I meditate on the sufferings of Christ? With Christ, do I do all that I can to alleviate suffering in others? What would enable me to experience strength and serenity when personally confronted with suffering? Blessed Elizabeth repeatedly reminded me that my Christian calling is to be identified with Christ. What does membership in the Church mean to me? Have I been opened through these Lenten reflections to see more deeply into its reality, beyond the sins and limitations of its members, bishops, priests, and laity?

PRAYER

Christ Jesus, crucified by love, grant me the grace with Blessed Elizabeth to lovingly eat the bread of Your will, whatever this might mean in my life. Should intense suffering come my way, grace me with strength and serenity to climb my Calvary in union with Mary who so courageously stood at the foot of your cross. Teach me what it means to be faithful to your Church and enlighten me in my efforts to live your Gospel of love. I offer my prayer to you with love and gratitude. Amen.

Saturday – Easter Vigil in the Holy Night of Easter – Year A

GOSPEL

After the sabbath, as the first day of the week was dawning, Mary Magdalene and the other Mary came to see the tomb. And behold, there was a great earthquake; for an angel of the Lord descended from heaven, approached, rolled back the stone, and sat upon it. His appearance was like lightning and his clothing was white as snow. The guards were shaken with fear of him and became like dead men. Then the angel said to the women in reply, "Do not be afraid! I know that you are seeking Jesus the crucified. He is not here, for he has been raised just as he said. Come and see the place where he lay. Then go quickly and tell his disciples, 'He has been raised from the dead, and he is going before you to Galilee; there you will see him.' Behold, I have told you." Then they went away quickly from the tomb, fearful yet overjoyed, and ran to announce this to his disciples. And behold, Jesus met them on their way and greeted them. They approached, embraced his feet, and did him homage. Then Jesus said to them, "Do not be afraid. Go tell my brothers to go to Galilee, and there they will see me."

MATTHEW 28: 1-10

BLESSED ELIZABETH OF THE TRINITY

The following reflection from Let Yourself Be Loved, written for her prioress shortly before Blessed Elizabeth's death, could easily be the hope of the Risen Christ for his disciples:

"Mother, the fidelity that the Master asks of you is to remain in communion with Love, flow into, be rooted in this Love who wants to mark your soul with the seal of His power and His grandeur. You will never be common place if you are vigilant in love! But in the hours when you feel only oppression and lassitude, you will please Him even more if you faithfully believe that He is still working, that He is loving you just the same, and even more: because His love is free and that is how He wants to be magnified in you."

Complete Works, vol. 1: 180

REFLECTION

Mary Magdalene and the other Mary, after the Sabbath as the day was dawning, *having remained in communion with Love,* immediately returned to the tomb where their Beloved had been buried. The oppression and lassitude they felt after witnessing the horrors of the crucifixion did not deter them, so great was their faith.

Because of their unwavering love for Jesus, they had the privilege of being the first of His followers to see their Risen Lord. It was to them that Jesus entrusted the mission of announcing His Resurrection to the apostles. They became the first to proclaim the good news upon which our faith is founded: that he who died is risen from the dead. Commissioned by Jesus, they become apostles to the apostles and Jesus was magnified through them.

Jesus also wishes to be magnified in us. Blessed Elizabeth expresses the confidence that we will never be commonplace if we are vigilant in love. Instinctive within us is a desire to be special, not commonplace. This deep desire is rooted in the reality that God <u>uncommonly</u> loves each one of us. We need only reflect on the events of Holy Week to realize the depths of God's love with its ultimate manifestation in Christ's passion and death.

Notice that Jesus does not reject those who fled in His hour of need. Instead, with tenderness in his voice, he calls them "his brothers." In our own times of oppression and lassitude, if we but faithfully believe that *Jesus is loving us just the same and even more,* the seal of His power and His grandeur, the grandeur of His Risen Life, will flow through us.

Do I truly believe that God uncommonly loves me? Can I dare to believe that in spite of my sinful actions the Risen Christ never stops loving me? Reflect that it is His love in the depths of your heart that stirs your heart to conversion and renews you in love. Let these realities well up within you and give voice to expressions of deep gratitude for His power and grandeur working within you as you sing Easter's joyous *Alleluia*.

PRAYER

Risen Christ, ever faithful in your love, help me to believe when my sinfulness stares me in the face, that in such times of oppression, you are still working and loving in me. Inflame my heart with the love of the two Marys that I too may spread the good news of your desire to be magnified in each person. May your faithfulness and love fill my heart with Easter joy. With grateful love I offer this prayer in the name of our glorious Risen Savior. Amen.

SATURDAY – EASTER VIGIL IN THE HOLY NIGHT OF EASTER – YEAR B

GOSPEL

When the sabbath was over, Mary Magdalene, Mary, the mother of James, and Salome bought spices so that they might go and anoint him. Very early when the sun had risen, on the first day of the week, they came to the tomb. They were saying to one another, "Who will roll back the stone for us from the entrance to the tomb?" When they looked up, they saw that the stone had been rolled back; it was very large. On entering the tomb they saw a young man sitting on the right side, clothed in a white robe, and they were utterly amazed. He said to them, "Do not be amazed! You seek Jesus of Nazareth, the crucified. He has been raised; he is not here. Behold the place where they laid him. "But go and tell his disciples and Peter, 'He is going before you to Galilee; there you will see him, as he told you.'"

Mark 16: 1-7

BLESSED ELIZABETH OF THE TRINITY

The following are words from the very last letter written by Blessed Elizabeth before her death. They are addressed to Charles Hallo:

"My little brother,

Before going to Heaven your Elizabeth wants to tell you once more of her deep affection for you and her plan to help you, day by day until you join her in Heaven. My darling Charles, I want you to walk in the footsteps of your father, in the valiant faith that keeps the will always faithful. You will have battles to fight, my little brother, you will encounter obstacles on the path of life, but do not be discouraged, call me. Yes call your little sister; in this way you will increase her happiness in Heaven; she will be so glad to help you triumph, to remain worthy of God, of your venerable father, of your mother whose joy you must be."

Complete Works, vol. 2: Letter 342

REFLECTION

In Mark's account of the resurrection, three women come to the tomb when the Sabbath is over. Mary Magdalene, Mary the mother of James, and Salome who brings spices to anoint the body of Jesus. Upon seeing that the stone is rolled back, they enter the tomb and see a young man clothed in a white robe. This young man, presumably an angel, sends them to announce to Peter and the disciples the good news of Jesus resurrection. "He is going before you to Galilee; there you will see him, *as he told you.*"

Here, it is a young man, not Jesus himself, who sends the women to the disciples. Can we detect a hint of tender rebuke in the reminder, "as he told you?" Should they have remembered Jesus words that after three days he would rise again? And yet we know that in spite of their forgetfulness, Jesus welcomed them without reproach.

Blessed Elizabeth's parting words to Charles Hallo so reflect the heart of the Risen One that they could be Jesus own words as he prepared his followers for his physical departure. Like Blessed Elizabeth, Jesus would certainly express deep affection. Jesus would remind them that there would be obstacles on the path of life with many battles to fight. Jesus knew this from his own experience. But they were not to be discouraged; they should call on him for help. He would always be there to help them triumph and to remain worthy of being his followers. Jesus would then rejoice in their valiant faith as they walked in his footsteps toward eternal life with him in heaven.

Each time we receive our Risen Lord in the Eucharist, the sentiments of his heart, expressed through the words of Elizabeth, and in the Gospels, might be heard in the depth of our own heart. Jesus not only goes before us, but as he promised his disciples, he is with us always. We may leave him, but he never leaves us. And when we return in repentance of heart, it is because he has remained with us, enticing us back to him. Our Easter joy is rooted in the reality that the Risen Christ has identified himself with our innermost being. Through the gift of His indwelling Spirit, Christ and ourselves increasingly become what we already are—united as one!

Do I truly believe that the Risen Christ *has deep affection for me?*

Do past hurts, experiences of rejection and the like, block my capacity to believe in such an awesome truth? What in my life needs to change so that I might better hear the echo of Jesus words to the disciples as spoken to me? What grace do I need to pray for that my heart be opened to become for Christ a welcoming presence?

PRAYER

Gloriously Risen One, your victory over such painful suffering and degrading death encourages me not to lose hope in life's dark times. Help me to remember that you are always with me. Give me the grace never to lose sight of your abiding, loving, and encouraging presence. I offer my prayer to you with deep trust in your forgiving and transforming love. Amen.

SATURDAY – EASTER VIGIL IN THE
HOLY NIGHT OF EASTER – YEAR C

GOSPEL

At daybreak on the first day of the week the women who had come from Galilee with Jesus took the spices they had prepared and went to the tomb. They found the stone rolled away from the tomb; but when they entered, they did not find the body of the Lord Jesus. While they were puzzling over this, behold, two men in dazzling garments appeared to them. They were terrified and bowed their faces to the ground. They said to them, "Why do you seek the living one among the dead? He is not here, but he has been raised. Remember what he said to you while he was still in Galilee, that the Son of Man must be handed over to sinners and be crucified, and rise on the third day." And they remembered his words. Then they returned from the tomb and announced all these things to the eleven and to all others. The women were Mary Magdalene, Joanna, and Mary the mother of James; the others who accompanied them also told this to the apostles, but their story seemed like nonsense and they did not believe them. But Peter got up and ran to the tomb, bent down, and saw the burial cloths alone; then he went home amazed at what had happened.

LUKE 24: 1-12

BLESSED ELIZABETH OF THE TRINITY

In her retreat reflections, entitled *Heaven in Faith,* written shortly before her death, with some changes, Blessed Elizabeth again makes the words of Ruysbroeck her own:

"*Christ 'comes with His treasures, but such is the mystery of the divine swiftness that His is continually coming, always for the first time as if He had never come; for His coming, independent of time, consists in an eternal 'now' and an eternal desire eternally renews the joys of the coming. The delights that He brings are infinite, since they are Himself.' 'The capacity of the soul, enlarged by the coming of the Master, seems to go out of itself in order to pass through the walls into the immensity of Him who comes; and a phenomenon occurs: God, who is in our depths, receives God coming to us, and God contemplates God! God in whom beatitude consists.'"*

Complete Works, vol. 1: 100

REFLECTION

As is true of the other Evangelists, Luke offers his own account of the great day of Jesus resurrection. Here *"women who had come from Galilee"* are the ones who find the stone rolled away. Among these women, three are identified: Mary Magdalene, Joanna, and Mary the mother of James. They enter and behold two men in dazzling garments. Terrified, they fall to the ground. The women remember the words of which the angel reminds them; that Jesus would rise on the third day. Together this group of women proclaims the Good News to the eleven, who with the others present, refuse to believe and remain locked in their fears and dead hopes. Peter alone runs to the tomb. No angels address him, but he sees the burial cloths and returns home amazed at what has happened.

Perhaps Peter's *amazement* helps express the wonders of the Easter Night Vigil. We too are amazed as we listen to the glories of salvation history triumphantly sung in the Exultant. The church's darkness, at first lit only by our flickering Easter candles, suddenly breaks into light, as the Gloria is solemnly intoned. Before the Gospel, the solemn proclamation of the Alleluias resounds to break its Lenten silence. Does not all of this leave us amazed as we celebrate this sacred night of the Lord's Resurrection?

This night that we celebrate, this mystery of Christ's Resurrection, is a mystery that shapes our very being as Christians. It is not just a yearly celebration. Today's reflections from Blessed Elizabeth draw the mystery into our everyday lives. The Risen Christ continually comes to us with such newness that it is always as if for the first time. Our Risen Lord, who now lives independent of time, comes to us in the *Eternal*

Now. His abiding Presence enlarges the capacity of our soul so that, as Elizabeth writes, "God, who is in our depths, receives God coming to us, and God contemplates God!" Is not this an amazing reality? That we have entered into these Lenten reflections with Christ and Blessed Elizabeth is an example of the Risen Christ present within, enlarging our capacity to desire and love God in Christ with an ever-deeper intensity. Like the women in the Gospel, we are now to share the good news of our own rising to new life in Christ by our Christ-like behavior.

What differences do you notice in yourself as the fruit of your Lenten reflection with Jesus Christ and Blessed Elizabeth? Has your self-understanding changed by Blessed Elizabeth's repeated allusions to God's Trinitarian indwelling Presence? What are some concrete ways that you might share Christ's compassion and care for you with those whom God has placed in your life?

PRAYER

Risen Christ, as the marvel of your love increasingly penetrates my heart, I desire to live in such a way that everything I say or do is done for you. With your indwelling Spirit inspire my words and actions. In my own dark times grant me patient endurance with a deepened faith to enable me to also share in the glories of your Resurrection. I offer this prayer to you with deep gratitude for the gift of your Risen Life. Amen.

EASTER SUNDAY

Easter Sunday

GOSPEL

On the first day of the week, Mary of Magdala came to the tomb early in the morning, while it was still dark, and saw the stone removed from the tomb. So she ran and went to Simon Peter and to the other disciple whom Jesus loved, and told them, "They have taken the Lord from the tomb, and we don't know where they put him." So Peter and the other disciple went out and came to the tomb. They both ran, but the other disciple ran faster than Peter and arrived at the tomb first; he bent down and saw the burial cloths there, but did not go in. When Simon Peter arrived after him, he went into the tomb and saw the burial cloths there, and the cloth that had covered his head, not with the burial cloths but rolled up in a separate place. Then the other disciple also went in, the one who had arrived at the tomb first, and he saw and believed. For they did not yet understand the Scripture that he had to rise from the dead.

JOHN 20: 1-9

Alternative readings from Easter Vigil or LUKE 24:13-35 at an afternoon or evening Mass.

BLESSED ELIZABETH OF THE TRINITY

Blessed Elizabeth wrote the following to Doctor Barbier a few days before her death. She begins by expressing her gratitude for the good care he had lavished on her during her final months of suffering and then continues:

"I also want to tell you that it is my turn now; I feel my mission is beginning on your behalf. Yes, God is entrusting you to your little patient, and she is to be the invisible angel, close to Him, who will lead you, by the path of duty, to the goal of every creature born of God. In this last hour of my exile, in this beautiful evening of life, how solemn everything looks to me in the light coming to me from eternity. . . . I wish I could make souls *understand, tell them the vanity, the emptiness of anything not done for God. At least I am sure you understand me, dear Doctor, for you have always understood me; I felt it very much and it made me so happy in the depths of my heart. Oh! frequently go back over the things we've talked about together, and let your soul resonate under the action of the grace they will bring to it; but do that to conform your will faithfully to what God asks, through His law and through His Holy Church."*

Complete Works, vol. 2: Letter 340

REFLECTION

In John's resurrection account, early in the morning while it was still dark, Mary Magdalene comes alone to the tomb. Seeing the stone removed, she *runs* to Simon Peter and to the other disciple *whom Jesus loved* and breathlessly announces, "they have taken the Lord from the tomb, and we don't know where they put him." Peter and the other disciple both *run* to the tomb, the disciple outruns Peter and looking into the tomb, sees the burial cloths. Peter arrives next; he goes in and also sees the burial cloths. The other disciple who came to the tomb with Peter *saw and believed.* What he came to believe is unclear since the Gospel ends with the words: For they did not yet understand the Scripture that he had to rise from the dead.

Peter, the disciple whom Jesus loved, and the other disciples did eventually come to Easter faith after Jesus appeared to them, showed them the wounds in his hands and side, and ate with them. The strength of their faith became such that they willingly suffered martyrdom for their belief. Their faith in Christ has been handed down through the ages, so that we who now believe are blessed to be able to greet this day with the glorious cry: *Christ is truly Risen!*

As we sing our alleluias throughout this joyous Paschal Season, having experienced the benefits of reflection on the daily scriptures, we can take to heart the words of Blessed Elizabeth and hear them as Christ's parting words to us. After his ascension into heaven, Christ's mission on our behalf also begins anew as "always interceding for us before the Father." He remains so close to us as to "make his home in us" and is *the one who always understands us.* He becomes our food and drink when we receive Him in the Eucharist. Our body becomes His body.

Just as Blessed Elizabeth encouraged the doctor to continue to remember and reflect upon the beneficial conversations they had as he cared for her during her last illness, so Christ promised His followers that He would send His Holy Spirit to remind them of all He has said to them.

Christ's indwelling Spirit will also remind us of the many things in our Lenten reflections that both inspired us and challenged us to be more faithful to our Christian calling as members of Christ's Body, the Church. Blessed Elizabeth will also continue to grace us with awareness of God's indwelling, Trinitarian Presence, that with her, we too may be a *Praise of Glory.*

What in particular remains with you as you conclude your Lenten Journey with Jesus Christ and with Blessed Elizabeth of the Trinity? The Risen Christ rises anew in the heart of each one of us. Can you identify areas in your life that are now more alive as the fruit of your Lenten reflections?

PRAYER

Risen Christ, with deepest gratitude, I offer You praise and thanksgiving for the many graces of this Lenten Season. Thank you for the life and writings of Blessed Elizabeth. Give me the grace to be faithful to daily Scripture reflection and to living with greater mindfulness of Your indwelling Presence. With Mary of Magdala may I seek and find you, not only in prayer, but also in all the events and persons that gift each new day of this Paschal season and always. I offer my prayer to you, Lord Jesus in whom I place my trust. Amen.

EPILOGUE

Blessed Elizabeth has a special mission for our world today. As she expressed it:

"I think that in heaven my mission will be to draw souls by helping them go out of themselves to cling to God by a wholly simple and loving movement, and to keep them in this great silence within that will allow God to communicate Himself to them and transform them into Himself" (Letter 335).

Our Lenten journey with Jesus Christ and Blessed Elizabeth invited us into a closer relationship with God in Christ. This relationship will sustain us as each new day unfolds. Blessed Elizabeth promises to be with us as we pray to deepen in this relationship. She reminds us to take moments of silent stillness even in the midst of our busy lives—to enter within "the heaven of our soul" to reconnect with Christ whose abiding Presence sustains and invites us into ever greater depth of divine intimacy. She teaches us how to live the sacred art of mindfulness.

The first step in the sacred art of mindfulness is what Carmelites call, "The practice of the presence of God." This practice leads to an increasing awareness of God's indwelling Presence in the center of the soul.

To help realize this within the complexity of daily living I offer the following:

1. Pray for the grace to become more aware of God's abiding Presence. This is a gift already given, but our challenge is to access it through faith and make it part of our conscious life.

2. When time permits, seek a quiet moment to reflect on

your earliest remembered awakening to God. For some this happens early in life, for others much later.

3. Before retiring at night, or at some other convenient time, slowly read and re-read Jesus' Last Supper discourse in the Gospel of John. Ponder Jesus words: "If anyone loves me my Father will love them and we will come to them and make our home in them." To love Christ is to realize ourselves as temples of the Triune God who in inadequate human language we know as Father, Son and Holy Spirit. Jesus' parting words on the Mount of the Ascension reassures us: "Behold I am with you always even until the end of time." God is mysteriously present even in the depth of our sin inviting us to conversion.

4. Pray for the gift of a listening heart that like Blessed Elizabeth "we may hear everything that is being sung in the soul" (Letter 164).

5. Schedule at least fifteen minutes of time to simply be still and listen to your breath, God breathing in and through you. As thoughts occur, look at them with the mind's eye and let them go without judging or blaming yourself for having them.

Simply do little by little what is possible to you and trust God to do the rest.

APPENDIX A:
CALENDAR OF LENT 2012–2021 & LECTIONARY CYCLE

Ash Wednesday–Easter

Year	Sunday Year	Lent	Date
2012	B	Ash Wednesday	February 22
		1st Sunday of Lent	February 26
		2nd Sunday of Lent	March 4
		3rd Sunday of Lent	March 11
		4th Sunday of Lent	March 18
		5th Sunday of Lent	March 25
		Palm Sunday	April 1
		Easter Triduum	April 5
		Easter Sunday	April 8
2013	C	Ash Wednesday	February 13
		1st Sunday of Lent	February 17
		2nd Sunday of Lent	February 24
		3rd Sunday of Lent	March 3
		4th Sunday of Lent	March 10
		5th Sunday of Lent	March 17
		Palm Sunday	March 24
		Easter Triduum	March 28
		Easter Sunday	March 31

Year	Sunday Year	Lent	Date
2014	A	Ash Wednesday	March 5
		1st Sunday of Lent	March 9
		2nd Sunday of Lent	March 16
		3rd Sunday of Lent	March 23
		4th Sunday of Lent	March 30
		5th Sunday of Lent	April 6
		Palm Sunday	April 13
		Easter Triduum	April 17
		Easter Sunday	April 20
2015	B	Ash Wednesday	February 18
		1st Sunday of Lent	February 22
		2nd Sunday of Lent	March 1
		3rd Sunday of Lent	March 8
		4th Sunday of Lent	March 15
		5th Sunday of Lent	March 22
		Palm Sunday	March 29
		Easter Triduum	April 2
		Easter Sunday	April 5

Year	Sunday Year	Lent	Date
2016	C	Ash Wednesday	February 10
		1st Sunday of Lent	February 14
		2nd Sunday of Lent	February 21
		3rd Sunday of Lent	February 28
		4th Sunday of Lent	March 6
		5th Sunday of Lent	March 13
		Palm Sunday	March 20
		Easter Triduum	March 24
		Easter Sunday	March 27
2017	A	Ash Wednesday	March 1
		1st Sunday of Lent	March 5
		2nd Sunday of Lent	March 12
		3rd Sunday of Lent	March 19
		4th Sunday of Lent	March 26
		5th Sunday of Lent	April 2
		Palm Sunday	April 9
		Easter Triduum	April 13
		Easter Sunday	April 16

Year	Sunday Year	Lent	Date
2018	B	Ash Wednesday	February 14
		1st Sunday of Lent	February 18
		2nd Sunday of Lent	February 25
		3rd Sunday of Lent	March 4
		4th Sunday of Lent	March 11
		5th Sunday of Lent	March 18
		Palm Sunday	March 25
		Easter Triduum	March 29
		Easter Sunday	April 1
2019	C	Ash Wednesday	March 6
		1st Sunday of Lent	March 10
		2nd Sunday of Lent	March 17
		3rd Sunday of Lent	March 24
		4th Sunday of Lent	March 31
		5th Sunday of Lent	April 7
		Palm Sunday	April 14
		Easter Triduum	April 18
		Easter Sunday	April 16

Year	Sunday Year	Lent	Date
2020	A	Ash Wednesday	February 26
		1st Sunday of Lent	March 1
		2nd Sunday of Lent	March 8
		3rd Sunday of Lent	March 15
		4th Sunday of Lent	March 22
		5th Sunday of Lent	March 29
		Palm Sunday	April 5
		Easter Triduum	April 9
		Easter Sunday	April 12
2021	A	Ash Wednesday	February 17
		1st Sunday of Lent	February 21
		2nd Sunday of Lent	February 28
		3rd Sunday of Lent	March 7
		4th Sunday of Lent	March 14
		5th Sunday of Lent	March 21
		Palm Sunday	March 28
		Easter Triduum	April 1
		Easter Sunday	April 4

APPENDIX B:
SELECTIONS FROM THE WRITINGS OF BLESSED ELIZABETH OF THE TRINITY

Day	Quote
Ash Wednesday	*Complete Works*, vol. 2: Letter 225
Thursday	*The Praise of Glory*, 47
Friday	*The Praise of Glory*, 197
Saturday	*The Praise of Glory*, 19
1st Sunday A	*The Praise of Glory*, 95
1st Sunday B	*Complete Works*, vol. 1: 142
1st Sunday C	*The Praise of Glory*, 251
Monday 1	*The Praise of Glory*, 135
Tuesday 1	*The Praise of Glory*, 299–300
Wednesday 1	*The Praise of Glory*, 95–96
Thursday 1	*Complete Works*, vol. 2: Letter 291
Friday 1	*The Praise of Glory*, 189
Saturday 1	*Complete Works*, vol. 1: 152–53
2nd Sunday A	*Complete Works*, vol. 1: 97
2nd Sunday B	*Complete Works*, vol. 1: 183
2nd Sunday C	*Complete Works*, vol. 2: 127
Monday 2	*Complete Works*, vol. 1: 109
Tuesday 2	*Complete Works*, vol. 1: 109–10
Wednesday 2	*Complete Works*, vol. 1: 146
Thursday 2	*Complete Works*, vol. 1: 104
Friday 2	*Complete Works*, vol. 1: 103
Saturday 2	*Complete Works*, vol. 2: Letter 256
3rd Sunday A	*Complete Works*, vol. 1: 108
3rd Sunday B	*Complete Works*, vol. 1: 146
3rd Sunday C	*Complete Works*, vol. 2: Letter 249
Monday 3	*Complete Works*, vol. 2: Letter 278
Tuesday 3	*Complete Works*, vol. 2: Letter 256
Wednesday 3	*Complete Works*, vol. 2: Letter 333
Thursday 3	*Complete Works*, vol. 2: Letter 333
Friday 3	*Complete Works*, vol. 1: 112
Saturday 3	*Complete Works*, vol. 1: 125–26
4th Sunday A	*Complete Works*, vol. 1: 102
4th Sunday B	*Complete Works*, vol. 1: 128
4th Sunday C	*Complete Works*, vol. 2: 230
Monday 4	*Complete Works*, vol. 2: 246
Tuesday 4	*Complete Works*, vol. 2: 313

Day	Quote
Wednesday 4	*The Praise of Glory*, 84
Thursday 4	*Complete Works*, vol. 1: 145
Friday 4	*Complete Works*, vol. 1: 110
Saturday 4	*Complete Works*, vol. 1: 99
5th Sunday A	*Complete Works*, vol. 2: Letter 200
5th Sunday B	*Complete Works*, vol. 1: 126
5th Sunday C	*Complete Works*, vol. 1: 156
Monday 5 Years A and B	*Complete Works*, vol. 1: 179
Monday Year C	*Complete Works*, vol. 2: Letter 331
Tuesday 5	*Complete Works*, vol. 1: 156
Wednesday 5	*Complete Works*, vol. 1: 145
Thursday 5	*Complete Works*, vol. 1: 105–6
Friday 5	*Complete Works*, vol. 1: 99
Saturday 5	*Complete Works*, vol. 1: 148
Palm Sunday A	*Complete Works*, vol. 2: Letter 278
Palm Sunday B	*Complete Works*, vol. 1: 159
Palm Sunday C	*Complete Works*, vol. 2: Letter 214
Monday of Holy Week	*Complete Works*, vol. 1: 125
Tuesday of Holy Week	*Complete Works*, vol. 2: Letter 160
Wednesday of Holy Week	*Complete Works*, vol. 1: 142
Chrism Mass	*Complete Works*, vol. 2: Letter 145
Holy Thursday	*Complete Works*, vol. 1: 125
Good Friday	*Complete Works*, vol. 1: 106–7
Holy Saturday-Vigil Mass A	*Complete Works*, vol. 1: 180
Holy Saturday-Vigil Mass B	*Complete Works*, vol. 2: Letter 342
Holy Saturday-Vigil Mass C	*Complete Works*, vol. 1: 100
Easter Sunday	*Complete Works*, vol. 2: Letter 340

SUGGESTIONS FOR FURTHER READING

ELIZABETH OF THE TRINITY

Amabel du Couer de Jésus, Mother Mary, O.D.C. *The Doctrine of the Divine Indwelling: A Commentary on the Prayer of Elizabeth of the Trinity*. Westminster, MD: Newman Press, 1950.

———. *A Soul of Silence: Elizabeth of the Trinity*. Cork, Ireland: Mercier Press, 1955.

Borriello, Lugi, O.C.D. *Spiritual Doctrine of Blessed Elizabeth of the Trinity*. Staten Island, NY: Alba House, c1986.

Elizabeth of the Trinity. *The Complete Works of Elizabeth of the Trinity*. Vol. 1. Washington, DC: ICS Publications 1984. The quotations for the reflections herein are from this work.

———. *The Complete Works of Elizabeth of the Trinity*. Vol. 2. Washington, DC: 1995. The quotations for the reflections herein are from this work.

———. *Light Love Life: A Look at a Face and A Heart*. Washington, DC: ICS Publications, 1987.

———. *The Praise of Glory*. London: Burns, Oates & Washbourne, 1913. Reprint, Westminster, MD: Newman Press, 1962. The quotations for the reflections herein are from the 1913 edition of this work. Available at the Web site of the University of Toronto Internet Archives at http://www.archive.org/details/thepraiseofglory00elizuoft.

———. *Trinity Whom I Adore: Prayer of Sr. Elizabeth of the Trinity.* New York: Frederick Pustet, 1953.

Meester, Conrad de. *Your Presence is My Joy.* England: Darlington Carmel, n.d.

Moorcroft, Jennifer. *He Is My Heaven: The Life of Elizabeth of the Trinity.* Washington, DC: ICS Publications, 2001.

Philipon, M. M. *The Spiritual Doctrine of Sister Elizabeth of the Trinity.* Westminster, MD: Newman Bookshop, 1947. Reprint, 1961.

INTERNET RESOURCES

Barrington Carmelite Monastery Web site available at
http://www.barringtoncarmel.com/home.htm

Carmelite Communities Associated Web site available at
http://www.ccacarmels.org/

ICS Publications Web site available at
http://www.icspublications.org

Order of Discalced Carmelite Web site available at
http://www.discalcedcarmel.com/

Christus Publishing, LLC Web site available at
http://www.christuspublishing.com

ABOUT THE AUTHOR

Vilma Seelaus, O.C.D., is a nun of the Carmelite Monastery in Barrington, Rhode Island, where she has served as prioress and formation directress. A member of the Carmelite Forum, she is known for her insightful lectures at their annual meetings. As an author, her interest is to offer a contemporary understanding of the presence of God in human life with a focus on the interface between psychological, ecological, and spiritual realities. Audio tapes and CDs on spirituality have been published by Alba House and she has contributed articles to spiritual journals such as *Spiritual Life, Carmelite Digest, The Way, Review for Religious* and others. Her book, *Distractions in Prayer: Blessing or Curse, Teresa of Avila's Teaching in the Interior Castle* has been translated into Korean.

green press
INITIATIVE

Christus Publishing, LLC is committed to preserving ancient forests and natural resources. We elected to print this title on 30% postconsumer recycled paper, processed chlorine-free. As a result, we have saved:

7 Trees (40' tall and 6-8" diameter)
3 Million BTUs of Total Energy
630 Pounds of Greenhouse Gases
2,840 Gallons of Wastewater
180 Pounds of Solid Waste

Christus Publishing, LLC made this paper choice because our printer, Thomson-Shore, Inc., is a member of Green Press Initiative, a nonprofit program dedicated to supporting authors, publishers, and suppliers in their efforts to reduce their use of fiber obtained from endangered forests.

For more information, visit www.greenpressinitiative.org

Environmental impact estimates were made using the Environmental Defense Paper Calculator. For more information visit: www.edf.org/papercalculator